ALSO BY MIKE BYNUM

High Tide, A Story of Class and Courage
Bryant—The Man, The Myth
Never Say Quit
Aggie Pride
We Believe
Bound for Glory
Bear Bryant's Boys of Autumn
Knute Rockne: His Life and Legend
Many Autumns Ago: The Frank Leahy Era
   at Boston College and Notre Dame
Vince Lombardi: Memories of a Special Time

WOODY HAYES
THE MAN & HIS DYNASTY

WOODY HAYES
THE MAN & HIS DYNASTY

Edited
by
MIKE BYNUM

GRIDIRON
FOOTBALL
PROPERTIES

Portions of this book have been previously published. Listed below is their original source of publication:

Chapter 1 first appeared in the February 20, 1951 edition of *The Columbus Citizen*.

Chapters 2, 5, 6, 7, 8, 9, 11, 12, 13, 14, 15, 16 and 17 first appeared in *Sports Illustrated*. Reprinted by permission of Time, Inc.

Chapter 3 first appeared in the November 12, 1955 issue of *The Saturday Evening Post*. Reprinted by permission of Curtis Publishing Co.

Chapter 4 first appeared in the April 20, 1956 edition of *The Columbus Dispatch*.

Chapter 10 first appeared in the November 21, 1969 issue of *Life*. Reprinted by permission of Time, Inc.

Chapter 15 first appeared in the October 1974 issue of *Esquire*. Reprinted by permission of Hearst Magazines, Inc.

Chapters 18, 19 and 26-40 first appeared in *The New York Times*. Reprinted by permission of The New York Times Company.

Chapters 20-25 first appeared as newswire stories of United Press International and The Associated Press in The New York Times.

"GOD HELP ME. I LOVE IT SO."

General George Patton

Contents

FOREWORD / *i*

THE MAKING OF A DYNASTY / *1*
    Woody Hayes Gets Unanimous Vote Of School's Trustees / *3*
    The Ohio State Story: Win Or Else / *7*
    Phooey On Popularity / *17*
    O.S.U. Won't Appeal Probation / *29*
    Agony Instead Of Roses In Columbus / *33*
    You Love Woody Or Hate Him / *36*
    Cut 'Em Off At Forward Pass / *50*
    Something To Shout About / *55*
    Defense And Rex Make A King / *60*
    The Reincarnation Of Woody Hayes / *64*
    Ohio State: Alone At The Top / *70*
    A Freshman Named Archie / *76*
    An Oak Leaf Cluster For General Woody / *80*
    And The Reason Is Woody's Machine / *84*
    Woody Hayes Makes War / *100*
    Still Alive And Kicking / *111*
    O-High-O Buckeyes / *116*
    Ohio State's General Loses His Command / *122*
    In Columbus, Tears and Relief / *125*

THE MEMORABLE GAMES / *129*
    Buckeyes Subdue Wisconsin / *131*
    O.S.U. Overcomes U.S.C. And Weather In Rose Bowl / *133*
    Ohio State Rally Halts Iowa / *137*
    Buckeye Field Goal Beats Webfoots / *139*
    O.S.U. Outduels Iowa / *142*
    Buckeyes Romp Over Michigan / *144*
    Buckeyes Overthrow Purdue / *146*
    Michigan Routed By Buckeyes / *150*
    Buckeyes Rally To Beat Trojans In Rose Bowl / *153*
    Buckeyes Get Revenge On Michigan / *156*
    Stanford Upsets Ohio State / *160*
    U.S.C. Trounces Ohio State / *163*
    O.S.U. Routs U.S.C. In Rose Bowl / *166*
    Buckeyes Boot Michigan / *169*
    U.S.C. Rallies To Beat Ohio State / *173*
    Buckeyes Triumph On Late Touchdowns / *176*
    U.C.L.A. Stuns Ohio State / *179*
    O.S.U. Turns Back Colorado In Orange Bowl / *182*
    Sooners Beat O.S.U. On Last-Minute Kick / *184*
    Alabama Conquers O.S.U. / *187*
    Gator Bowl Melee Ends Woody's Reign / *190*

APPENDIX / *195*

WOODY HAYES
THE MAN & HIS DYNASTY

Foreword

He was bigger than life to most Buckeye football fans.

In a career that spanned 28 seasons at Ohio State University, Wayne Woodrow (Woody) Hayes gave the alums much to be proud of. He gave them national championships and mid-winter trips to Pasadena for the Rose Bowl. He gave them Big Ten titles and emotional come-from-behind victories. He gave them prestige and glory. He also gave them frequent wins over arch-rival Michigan.

Woody Hayes was a man who walked his own path in life, yet he attracted the curiosity of an entire nation. Football fans either loved Woody Hayes or hated him. There was no middle ground.

His friends were U.S. presidents, Marine generals, noted scholars and children recuperating in the hospital who had been visited by him. His enemies were the press or those fans from that "School Up North" — Michigan.

When Woody Hayes arrived at Ohio State as the new head coach in 1951, he had been the third choice in a 71-day courting match held by university officials. Don Faurot, the head coach at Missouri U., had turned down the job and the university board of trustees couldn't get a majority to vote favorably on the hiring of Paul Brown, the highly-successful Cleveland Browns' head coach and a former head coach at Ohio State who previously had delivered a national championship for the Buckeyes in 1942 during his earlier stint. The university board of trustees then looked to a brash, young coach at Miami University named Woody Hayes to lead the once-proud Buckeyes out of their valley of despair.

For a meager salary of $12,500-a-year and a handshake deal on a 5-year contract, little did the university board realize what they were getting for their money. In four seasons, he gave them a Big Ten title, a national championship and a Rose Bowl victory over Southern California. And in the 3 years that followed, Hayes added two more conference crowns, another national title and a rain-soaked victory over the Oregon Fighting Ducks in the 1958 Rose Bowl.

By the mid-1950s, the Ohio State football program had been nicknamed "The Machine" by both sports writers and jealous rivals. The big money in Ohio lined up in support of Hayes' winning ways and the athletic department coffers began to be enriched with generous contributions. And a zealous group of Buckeye alums known as "The Frontliners" was organized to make sure that every promising high school football star in Ohio made his way to Columbus to play for the Scarlet and Gray.

Suddenly, it seemed, that to be a Buckeye football fan was to be life in Fat City. At post-game cocktail parties noted sports writers often were forced to give a puzzled response when asked, "Isn't this the same school that only a few years ago was known as 'The Graveyard of Coaches.' "

Yet with this burgeoning climb to the elite club of college football's fraternity, Hayes and his Machine rolled over many egos. In 1955, the brash upstart sports magazine *Sports Illustrated* wrote an exposé on Hayes and his football juggernaut. The story, entitled "The Ohio State Story: Win or Else," portrayed the Buckeyes as a rising phoenix on the college football power scene who, while under the intense pressure of demanding alumni, would break all of the rules and crush anyone in its path in an attempt to achieve big-time success.

Based on the information revealed in this article, the following spring (1956) the Big Ten slapped Hayes' program with a 1-year probation penalty and Hayes, himself, was personally reprimanded for loaning money to players.

Then in 1961, after winning another Big Ten title and a Rose Bowl invitation, Hayes' program was given another setback when the university's faculty senate voted 28-25 against the O.S.U. football squad from accepting the Rose Bowl invitation.

For the next six seasons, Hayes' teams wandered aimlessly in mediocrity.

Then in 1968, while armed with a youthful squad of sophomores, Hayes & Co. smashed their way back into the limelight with an undefeated season and dethroned defending national champion U.S.C., who was led by all-America tailback O.J. Simpson, in the 1969 Rose Bowl. It was the beginning of Woody's 10-year dominance of the Big Ten, the Rose Bowl and the penthouse of college football.

His critics branded him for his furious temper, his emotional outbursts on sideline yard markers, football officials and newspaper and television cameramen, and his boring "three yards and a cloud of dust" grinding offense. Yet Woody's system worked. It worked very well.

This book, *Woody Hayes: The Man & His Dynasty,* is a celebration of this great dynasty that Hayes and his teams built together. It is a collection of the best articles which were written on this era. They were penned by the best writers in America.

It also is a look back at a special time which created many wonderful memories that are forever preserved in our minds and in our hearts.

Woody Hayes was a great coach. More importantly, he was a great teacher. And the subject he taught us best was how to win.

Mike Bynum
August 21, 1991
Birmingham, Alabama

The Making Of
A Dynasty

1

Woody Hayes Gets Unanimous Vote Of School's Trustees

February 19, 1951

By KAYE KESSLER
The Columbus Citizen

Columbus' little world within a world today was ready to again recognize the world situation, the onrushing baseball season and the outrageous price of pepper — Ohio State had named its new football coach.

Wayne Woodrow (Woody) Hayes, a broad-shouldered guy with an intense desire to win football games, was booked as the 19th Buckeye head grid boss Sunday night. He succeeds Wesley Fesler, who resigned last Dec. 9 because of "excessive pressure for winning football games," and who has since taken a three-year lease on the head coaching job at Minnesota.

Hayes, second-youngest head coach in O.S.U. football history at 38, seems equipped to tote the load and weather impending reverberations.

Paul Brown, 35 at the time of his appointment in 1941, was the youngest.

Ohio State's board of trustees ended the 71-day suspense program by endorsing unanimously the former Miami University mentor at 8:11 p.m. Sunday — after one hour and 26 minutes of deliberation.

Announcement of the trustees' approval of Hayes was made by Dr. Howard L. Bevis, the university president. It was the second attempt by the trustees to pass judgment on Hayes. They received the recommendation of the O.S.U. Athletic Board last Monday, but tabled the issue at that time because only four of the seven members were present.

Only missing member Sunday was Warner M. Pomerene, but the meeting was delayed two hours and 45 minutes by the late arrival of Sen. John W. Bricker. Bricker was flying in from Albuquerque, N.M., after a speaking engagement and his plane was grounded in St. Louis because of the fog. He arrived at 6:42 p.m. and the meeting started at 6:45.

Hayes, who was in the O.S.U. athletic offices with Athletic Director Richard Larkins while the trustees pondered the problem, will take over his new assignment March 1. He will receive $12,500 a year and a full professorship in physical education. (Fesler also received $12,500 his first season, but received $15,000 last year, the highest salary ever paid a Buckeye coach.)

"Hayes has a one-year agreement, like all our contracts," Dr. Bevis said, "but it's a general understanding that it's to be a continuous agreement."

There are no strings attached to Hayes' appointment according to the O.S.U. president, who said, "He has a free hand in selecting his assistants."

Larkins expressed relief and delight that the turbulent problem had been solved. In his office with him during the trustee meeting were all but one of the Athletic Board members. They were on "stand-by" orders in the event the trustees didn't approve Hayes.

When Dr. Bevis called Larkins at the conclusion of the meeting to confirm Hayes' appointment, Larkins said, "Thank you very much." And a round of applause issued from the Athletic Board members.

"I think that's wonderful," Larkins told Dr. Bevis. "I want to thank you and the board of trustees for the confidence you vested in me and the Athletic Board."

Hayes said he was "tickled to death" to get the job and showed a tremendous desire to start his new duties. With spring grid drills only five weeks away (March 27), Woody was anxious to iron out problems with Larkins and meet the squad.

His biggest problem will be to convert the Bucks from a single wing to a T-formation team, but facing problems seems to be a habit with the new Buckeye coach.

Although he was born in Clifton, Ohio, near Springfield, Woody claims Newcomerstown as his native home. His father, Wayne Benton Hayes, was school superintendent at Newcomerstown from 1920 until his death in 1939. Woody starred in football, baseball and basketball, captaining the team his senior season.

Hayes graduated from Denison University in 1935 with a major in history and English and a minor in physical education. He continued graduate work in phys ed and gained his Master's degree in educational administration from Ohio State in 1948. He played three seasons as a tackle at Denison.

In eight seasons as a head coach, Hayes' teams have compiled 51 victories, 22 losses and two ties.

His first coaching job was at Mingo Junction High School as assistant to John Muth in 1935-36. He moved to New Philadelphia High School as an assistant to John Brickels in 1937 and took over his first head coaching job in 1938 at New Philly, where he remained three seasons until enlisting in the Navy in July of 1941. He was discharged as a lieutenant commander in 1946, having commanded the PC 1251 in the Palau Island invasion and the destroyer escort Rinehart in both the Atlantic and Pacific operations.

Hayes returned to his alma mater, Denison, as head grid coach in 1946. The school had discontinued the sport during the war and he had a disastrous debut as a college mentor, losing the first eight games. But his Big Red won the final game of 1946 and blazed through the following two seasons undefeated, winning nine games in 1947 and eight in 1948.

Woody took over at Miami University in 1949 and the Redskins won their opening game to give him a 19-game winning streak. The Redskins won five and lost four in his first season, but turned in a sparkling exhibition last year by winning eight of nine games and establishing a new Miami scoring record of 322 points in copping the Mid-American Conference title.

Miami capped the 1950 season under Hayes by trouncing Arizona State of Tempe, 34-21, in the New Year's Day Salad Bowl game.

Hayes produced a Little All-America selection in each of his undefeated seasons at Denison and his 1949 and 1950 Miami elevens dominated all-Ohio and all-Conference selections. The 1949 Redskins ranked second among the nation's major colleges in pass defense (good news with S.M.U. the opener for the Bucks this fall) and they finished second in total offense and third in pass offense this past season.

The new Buck boss is a stickler for training and his traits include a year-round devotion to the game. Asked once how much time a coach must spend on the job to produce a winner, Hayes replied, "I try to get six or seven hours' sleep a night, and try not to miss a meal. The rest of the time goes to football."

Hayes has been married nine years to the former Anne Gross, a New Philadelphia girl and graduate of Ohio Wesleyan. They have one son, Stephen Benton, age 5.

Hayes' appointment ends a nine-week search for a successor to Fesler. Hayes had been rumored for the past two weeks to have the inside track over six other cadidates singled out by the screening committee as candidates.

In all 14 candidates were interviewed with seven actually in the running. Others in the picture until Hayes took over were Paul Brown, the former Buck coach, now of the Cleveland professionals; Warren Gaer of Drake; Jim McDonald of Springfield High School; Harry Strobel, the O.S.U. freshman coach; Chuck Mather, the Massillon High School coach; and Sid Gillman of Cincinnati.

2

The Ohio State Story: Win Or Else

October 24, 1955

By ROBERT SHAPLEN
Sports Illustrated

Every Saturday afternoon during the football season, while a scar-let-jerseyed quarterback of Ohio State University barks signals on the field, 425, 000 additional quarterbacks in Columbus and another 8 million throughout the state are sure to think, at some point during the game, that each of them could do a better job. By Monday morning, the traditional time for quarterback sniping, these millions of signal callers will have replayed the game several times over in their own minds, and will then start replaying it in groups. Along about Wednesday or Thursday the coming Saturday's game will come up for discussion, and all of Ohio will decide in advance just how *that* one ought to be played.

To a certain degree this sort of thing goes on all over the country, but in Ohio football is super-serious business. Few are the games at Ohio Stadium, rain or shine, that are not attended by capacity crowds of 82,000 screaming, back-pounding, bottle-sipping, pigskin-pixilated customers. The rest of the quarterbacks in the state — those who couldn't get tickets — do their second guessing on radio or TV (a half dozen radio stations make sure the game is brought into every home). And if O.S.U. loses, the separate and collective wrath of these millions of proprietary partisans will be leveled against the man behind the quarterback — The Coach.

Big Brother to everybody when he's on top, but candidate of candidates for the salt mines when he's not, a head football coach at O.S.U. has been described as having, next to the Presidency, the toughest job in the United States. Not only does he have to direct the fortunes of his squad, but he is at the constant beck and call of all the quarterback organizations in Ohio, to whom he must make full accountings. The coach's postgame confessions of sins are regularly delivered in a manner reminiscent of a defendant at a Soviet trial. "I was wrong there," he will say, hanging his head abjectly. "I shouldn'ta done that." The fact that he may have been right, or that the point in questions is at least debatable, makes no difference. The boys in the backroom want blood.

The man on trial this week (for losing 20-14 to Duke) is an oddly wound-up individual named Wayne Woodrow (Woody) Hayes, who is both a charming and frightening product of what, in these years of postwar prosperity, is more of a bountiful big business and a mass hysteria than it ever was before. In many respects Hayes is the perfect man for the job. Beyond replaying the game cozily with the manifold quarterbacks in mufti, he is bumptiously tough and is far from a hypocrite. Hayes is completely, in fact devastatingly, aware that in the struggle for survival he must produce a winning team or lose his $15,000-a-year position and, even more important, his prestige as a big-time coach, which happens to be Woody's total *raison d'être*.

"I love football," Hayes says, with his slight lisp and almost with tears in his eyes. "I think it's the most wonderful game in the world, and I despise to lose. I've hated to lose ever since I was a kid and threw away the mallets when I lost at croquet."

This perhaps unadmirable trait has the unalterable approval of every man Buckeye, but Hayes gets no points for mere enthusiasm. Each week of the season brings on a public reincarnation of himself, in the image of hero or villain. If, as usual, there are nine games to the schedule, he lives nine unpredictable, breath-taking, spine-tingling lives. Depending on how much of a winning edge he has at the end of November, the reincarnations can be terminated in one tremendous, popularly applied, postseason kick-after-lack-of-touchdowns — OUT!

So far, Hayes has hung on, but it's been close. He is now in his fifth season and until last year he was more often a bumbling devil incarnate than a gridiron Galahad. But in 1954 he dismayed his most ardent detractors by producing an unbeaten team of national champions. For the moment at least, all the angry and frustrated Walter Mittys in Ohio had to stay on the bench.

By the end of this season, Hayes may be in for fresh trouble. But if he doesn't talk too much, a habit he's had considerable difficulty controlling in the past (last winter at a Cleveland alumni meeting he couldn't resist asking, "How many of you were here last year?" and demanding a show of hands), the consensus is that he earned himself enough insurance in '54 to survive a likely so-so '55 record.

In four and a half years at O.S.U., Hayes has won 28, lost 11 and tied two. If he should fail two years in a row to win more games than he loses, he will automatically be a flop as a coach and a foolish fellow to boot. That's how it is in these fickle flatlands, and that's how it will be, with Hayes simply a Frankenstein of the system, until football ceases to be a vast profitmaking amusement enterprise with amateur dressing.

There unquestionably is a great demand for this kind of game. The demand isn't hard to diagnose. Ohio is a heavy populated state but, unlike New York or California, it has comparatively little outlet for the hungry and abundant entertainment dollar. Since O.S.U. now claims to have the biggest single-campus enrollment in the country, more than 21,000 students, it seems only natural to Ohioans that it also ought to have the best football team, year in and year out; that, in the immortal words of one college president, repeated tongue-in-cheek by O.S.U.'s President Howard L. Bevis, "We should have a university of which the football team can be proud." Not only do the alumni demand perpetual gridiron greatness, but so does everyone else, which is where things get blurred. When the barber, the cab driver and the waitress all express themselves firmly on the matter, they are doing more than getting a vicarious thrill out of identifying themselves with the university they were never able to attend. They are helping form what is obviously a professional atmosphere — and it is the atmosphere and the attitudes that are important — in which Dem Bucks (and dem bucks) play a role highly similar in the mass mind to Dem Bums in Brooklyn.

"If football is a plaything for the community and nothing more, if we can't prove that the program is three-fourths education and one fourth circus, then we should cut it out," says Dick Larkins, the university's personable and efficient athletic director. "But we think we can steer the ship in such a way that we have a fair measure of success and still uphold the best principles of academic life." Somewhat defensively, Larkins adds: "I don't know of any football player who doesn't go to class."

Jack Fullen, the alumni secretary, who is an outspoken opponent of big-time football, turns the argument around. "The football tail is wagging the college dog," he maintains. "Larkins has to meet an $800,000-a-year budget in the athletic department. If he doesn't fill that stadium every Saturday, he won't be able to make ends meet. Like Woody, Dick is a creature of the system. Little by little his ideals are disintegrating as he has to use football receipts to pay off the bond issue on the new field house. We'll never be off the hook until we stop worrying about attendance."

Since attendance depends on the quality of the football, both Larkins and Hayes are staunch defenders of the recruiting methods that each year bring two or three dozen of Ohio's best high school players to the university. Says Larkins: "If athletics are forced to pay the freight for a program that ought to be defrayed by the state, then you've got to produce a winning team for the community as well as for the alumni." To which Hayes adds: "The only way we can justify college football is to see that the kids get their due educationally, that they get here and then stay here."

If a high school football star does meet O.S.U.'s academic requirements, he can get himself a state scholarship of a few hundred dollars a year and either a part-time state office job, paying about $60 a month, or a considerably better one working for such wealthy alumni as John Galbreath, the real estate man and sportsman, or Leo Yassenoff, a Columbus contractor.

Galbreath and Yassenoff are probably the two best-known members of the Frontliners, an organization comprising some one hundred alumni in the state whose prime function it is to recruit young high school stars. Ironically, the Frontliners were organized eight years ago by Fullen, who figured if he couldn't beat the system he'd string along with it and at least "try to sell O.S.U. to players instead of trying to purchase them."

The fact that there have been abuses of the system of encouraging and supporting players is essentially the public's fault, Fullen feels. Because football is a state-wide institution, with everybody getting in on the act or wanting to, the opportunities for evil begin back in the lower echelons. "What we've got in Ohio is the guaranteed annual B for high school football stars," Fullen says. "Can he run, can he pass, can he punt? — that is the question. If he can, the wherewithal and the consciences can be easily provided and appeased."

Fullen may exaggerate, but a couple of recent, celebrated cases would seem to prove his point, and perhaps an axiom — that abuses are inevitable once the goal (read touchdown) is established in the image of a constantly victorious football machine.

The first concerns a young man with the odd name of Hubert Bobo, a handsome, Atlas-type fullback who came from the tough little town of Chauncey, Ohio. There, according to Fullen's research, he seldom went to classes more than three days a week and was awarded his high school diploma by the school board over the protests of the principal because Bobo promised to put Chauncey on the map. At O.S.U. he was a terror, both on the field and off. A tremendous blocker and an astonishingly fast, helter-skelter runner for a big lad, he played a big role in O.S.U.'s great '54 record. He also openly boasted of having four tutors, and he got involved in a paternity suit. Bobo finally flunked himself out, and since then he's turned down some good Canadian pro and southern college offers. Today he has a job and Hayes, sore beset as he is, would be delighted to welcome a reformed Bobo back to O.S.U.

The other case has to do with Russ Bowermaster, a young end from Hamilton, Ohio. Bowermaster played fine freshman football at O.S.U. last year but then he, too, flunked out. This past summer he failed a make-up course, so he wasn't available this fall. While he would hardly seem to be meeting the academic standards Dick Larkins and Hayes proclaim, patience is called for because, as Woody says, "This kid's a helluva football player." Now, like Bobo, Bowermaster is expected back when he finally catches that elusive academic pass.

Despite the Bobos and the Bowermasters, many gridmen *do* attend classes, and some of them, Hopalong Cassady included, get better than average marks. Hayes particularly seeks quarterbacks with straight-A averages so he at least won't have to worry about *their* flunking out. "Woody is refreshing in his frankness," Fullen adds, "but his conscience, like that of all the others involved in this mess, is caught in the compulsions of survival. 'Don't give me any of that character building business,' he's told me. 'I could build all the characters in the world and lose enough games, and I'd be out of here, but fast.' "

In recruiting, Hayes gets some help from his wife and some from the frank expenditure of the approximately $4,000 a year he earns doing a TV stint in Columbus. The Hayeses often entertain prospects in their home (Big Ten rules forbid coaches to recruit outside). Once signed, a recruit can count on some financial help from Hayes if he is "in need." Woody insists that he never forks up for a luxury — another narrow line — but it's certainly also true that he makes sure he won't lose any valuable men by financial default.

Hayes has all the respect in the world for the bona fide bird dogs in Ohio. His troubles spring from the fact that so many of them turn into wolves. Actually, the wolves were prowling at his doorstep the moment he talked himself into the job his best friends warned him not to take.

He came into a climate that was anything but congenial. A powerful alumni faction had demanded the return of Paul Brown, who had coached at O.S.U. before going off to the Navy and subsequently becoming a pro coach — and if Brown wasn't available another big-time name coach was wanted. Hayes, these alumni contented, was pretty small potatoes when you looked at his record.

Who, indeed, was Hayes?

At least, he was unadulterated Ohio. Born in Clifton in 1913, he grew up in Newcomerstown, where his self-educated father was superintendent of schools. Both his parents were adamant, as far back as Woody can remember, about his getting a college education. As a pair of husky country boys, Hayes and his brother, Ike, were naturally interested in more robust pursuits. Stemming from a line of tough mountaineer fighters, they carried on the tradition. One evening Superintendent Hayes went out to deliver a speech and found himself in an empty meeting hall. He was told about "the big fight" going on, and rushed over to discover that his competition was his two sons, putting on a bout under assumed names.

Woody went to Denison University in Granville, where he majored in English and history — he was a top-grade history student — and played varsity football as a tackle and varsity baseball as an outfielder. After graduating from Denison, Hayes spent a year as assistant football coach at Mingo Junction High School and then took a similar job at New Philadelphia. The head coach there was John Brickels, whom Hayes credits with teaching him more than anyone else about the game.

"Woody was always subject to temperamental outbursts," Brickels recalls. "Maybe it's because he was smart, quick and a perfectionist. I'd let him know what I wanted done and he'd do it, pronto. He lacked patience. I tried to tell him that when he corrected a kid he shouldn't make an enemy of the boy, but Woody had a hard time controlling himself and he drove the kids too hard. He'd swear a lot, and I also told him he was the last guy who should, that it didn't fit his personality, what with that little lisp of his. He kept improving, though, and when I left I recommended him for the top job."

Through 1938 and 1939, Hayes won 18, lost one and tied one at New Philadelphia (after succeeding Brickels as head coach). In 1940, he won only once though, and got into trouble with the superintendent over his harsh methods. At the end of the season he went into the Navy.

During the war, Hayes commanded a patrol chaser and a destroyer escort. When he was discharged, as a lieutenant commander, he got the football coaching job at his alma mater, Denison, and after a poor first season his teams won 19 games in a row over two years.

Hayes still had his troubles though. His nerves were strung together with football laces. On more than one occasion, his assistant coach, Rix Yard, and his close friend, Mike Gregory, a local hardware man, had to intervene to maintain harmony between him and his players.

"Woody drove himself as hard as the rest of us," Yard says. "The secret of his success has always been that he sticks to what he believes is right, even if he's wrong. He never stopped thinking football. One afternoon he caught me reading. 'What the hell d'you mean, reading a book during football season?' he shouted."

In 1949, Hayes moved on to Miami University in Oxford, Ohio, where he won five and lost four. "Woody will have trouble in his first year wherever he goes," his friends say. "It takes time to get to know him and his ways." The next season seemed to prove the point. Miami won eight out of nine and climaxed the season with a Salad Bowl victory over Arizona State.

As far back as Denison, Hayes had his cap set on O.S.U. "In 1951, when the job was open, I spent an hour and a half trying to dissuade him, telling him about the wolves," Mike Gregory says. "But he wouldn't listen. It was a challenge."

After 71 days of deliberation, the O.S.U. trustees were won over by Hayes' oratory (later Hayes said: "Before I went to see them, I didn't think I had a chance, but after talking to them for three hours I knew I had the job.")

He started building up public confidence in himself at once. "We may not win 'em all, but we'll show you the fightingest team you've ever seen," he said in the first of many speeches. "I promise you we'll never be outconditioned."

That last was an understatement. Hayes' obsession for condition and discipline almost ruined his first year's team. While he continued to treat the Frontliners and the others with kid gloves (more than one subdued wolf was heard to murmur, "If he can coach like he can talk, maybe he *will* be our man"), he drove his squad mercilessly.

The players came to hate him.

"I believe in overlearning," Hayes maintained. "That way you're sure." One of his favorite gimmicks was "gassers," six or more laps around the field at the end of each grueling practice session. "The fellows don't think too much of all this running," Woody joked at one of the downtown alumni gatherings, "but they'll thank me for it once the season starts." During one drill one hot afternoon, far from thanking him, three men collapsed from heat exhaustion.

When he wasn't running them ragged, Hayes was talking his players deaf. "We set a record for meetings," tackle Dick Logan said later. "We had meetings about meetings and when we weren't in a meeting we were out running some more. When we finished running, we had a meeting about that too."

The bitter feeling between Hayes and his players reached such an impasse that they locked him out of the dressing room before the Illinois game, then went out and played the favored Illini to a 0-0 tie. Another tie, four victories and three losses marked that first season of dissension. Quarterback Tony Curcillo, a standout single-winger, having been awkwardly switched to Hayes' T formation, said: "He had me so fouled up I didn't know what he wanted. If I passed, he jerked me out and said run. If I ran, out I came and he said pass. You couldn't call the right play." Halfback Doug Goodsell added: "I'd rather be playing jayvee ball. How would you like it, with 82,000 fans screaming at you while you were on the field and the Bull (Hayes) ranting and raving at you when you came off it?"

After archrival Michigan clipped the Bucks, 7-0, "Goodbye Woody" banners were flying over Columbus, and several members of the wolf pack were taking about raising $25,000 to buy up Hayes' contract. One wolf kept calling the Hayes home at 4 a.m. every day. Mrs. Hayes would answer the phone. "I just called up to say goodbye," he'd say. "We're not going anywhere," she'd reply. "Oh, yes, you are," the wolf would persist.

The next seasons didn't start off much better. In the dressing room between the halves of one game, a halfback reportedly took a sock at Hayes, missed him and crashed his fist into his own locker. Maybe it was then that Hayes began to see the light. At any rate, he calmed down. Wins over Illinois and Michigan at the end of the season saved his job, giving him a record of six wins and three losses.

But in '53 the clock was set back, even though O.S.U.'s overall record was the same. The team suffered from fumbleitis, a malady that drives Hayes out of his mind. ("It's just plain carelessness," he insists. "It's antisocial.") One practice episode nearly proved disastrous. Freshman fullback Don Vicic had been making steady gains through the varsity line. As he ripped off a large one, a vicious tackle made him drop the ball.

In front of Larkins and several businessmen who happened to be watching, Hayes blew his top. "Get out of there, Vicic," he stormed. "We don't stand for fumbling on our team. Get out and stay out until you learn how to hold the ball." Vicic tried to stammer a reply but Hayes raged on and finally, reddening, the kid tore off his helmet and tossed it in Hayes' direction as he headed for the sidelines. Later Hayes saw him stretched on the ground and renewed the attack. "Get up, Vicic," he yelled. "Who told you to lie down?" Vicic was ready to quit O.S.U. that night but assistant coach Ernie Godfrey, who tries to maintain a homey, family atmosphere not unlike that of his famous radio and TV namesake, intervened. Vicic had dinner at Hayes' home, where things were patched up. Today Vicic is O.S.U.'s best fullback.

At the end of '53, in losing to Michigan, 20-0, O.S.U. played miserably and it looked as if Hayes was through. But Larkins and other rallied to Hayes' defense. Larkins won't admit it, but he started Woody on the road back by talking to him like a Dutch uncle about temper tantrums and sideline gymnastics (Hayes still punts and passes in pantomime), and by arranging for Lyal Clark, one of the finest defensive line coaches in the country, to return to O.S.U. (he had been there from 1947 to 1950 but had gone to Minnesota with Wes Fesler, Woody's predecessor).

For the first time in his life, Hayes began delegating authority, not only to Clark but also to others on his staff. With his customary candor, Hayes is the first to admit his faults. "I never worked under a big-time coach, so I naturally grew accustomed to doing everything myself," he says. "It's taking me a long time to learn, and I've still got a long way to go. But I'm getting there."

As an offensive specialist in a rushing game — he uses 14 basic ground plays — Hayes' delegation of authority to defensive experts is especially important. The difference in technique was apparent to the naked eye in '54, as it has been this season when, except for Cassady, who is one of Hayes' strongest admirers, O.S.U. lacks not only depth but concomitant talent. Cassady, an all-America star in anyone's book, calls Hayes "the best coach in the world," but there are few others on the squad who would yet rate him on a par with Bud Wilkinson of Oklahoma or Ivy Williamson of Wisconsin as a player's pal.

Hayes is still criticized for working his men too hard — the 6-0 loss to Stanford, in the second game of this season, was attributed to overwork — and the self-styled quarterbacks in town figure he conducts far too many meetings and tends to leave his game at the blackboard. "He underestimates the intelligence of the boys," says one. "His intensity doesn't allow him to get a good grasp of the problem."

His dedication to football to the exclusion of anything else has made Hayes a lonely man. He has no more than half a dozen close friends and he doesn't see them very often. It is one of his contradictions that he can charm an audience at a banquet but is a bad social mixer. "He hasn't got time for both friends and football," says one of those who knows him well. "But if you are his friend, he'll do anything for you, and so will you for him."

Hayes' wife is a football widow — he calls her his "buffer" or "blocking back" and his son, Steve, now 11, is virtually fatherless. Away all day during preseason practice sessions — he even moves into the dorms with his players — Hayes will spend every Saturday night during the season in his office, studying the films of the day's game. On Sunday, with the whole coaching staff attending, there's a re-run of the movies, and Monday starts the next week's grind.

With his fat season behind him, Hayes is a more relaxed man today even though the wolves are still around and the old compulsions remain. But instead of being defensive, Woody these days is more like an absent-minded professor.

When a visitor spoke with him two weeks ago, Hayes was in a fine mood. He had just come from a luncheon of the Agonis Club, another of the countless quarterback groups, where prayers for President Eisenhower's quick recovery were blended with prayers for an O.S.U. victory the next day over Illinois. It was raining, and Hayes had already decided that his team was fit and ready — which proved to be the next afternoon. Strolling to his dressing room, he stripped down to his shorts and undershirt, talking volubly.

Suddenly he stopped and, with a sheepish grin, scratched his head. "What the hell am I getting undressed for?" he said. "There's no practice today."

3

Phooey On Popularity

November 12, 1955

By JACK CLOWSER
The Saturday Evening Post

If there ever was a football man who couldn't be neatly typed and classified, it is Wayne Woodrow Hayes, the dedicated coach of Ohio State University. Woody Hayes is a gentleman of beaming personality and eloquence. He has charmed innumerable gatherings of alumni and other constituents. Yet his career has been punctuated by episodes such as:

Driving his first squad at little Denison University so hard that authorities told him to ease up — or else.

Smashing a trophy in rage on the floor of his boss' office at Miami University, of Ohio, before the startled eyes of the local mayor and booster-club officials.

Blowing his top on two occasions at Ohio State last season in unsuccessful attempts to have the bands barred from the playing field on rainy game days.

In 1951, Woody's first year at Ohio State, his players came close to mutiny. They held grievance meetings and openly expressed dissatisfaction. Yet in 1954 his boys twice carried Hayes off the field on their shoulders after winning games. Athletes can pay a coach no higher tribute than that.

Hayes wound up last season with his squad behind him, not to mention a streak of ten consecutive victories. Ohio State won the Big Ten title, the Rose Bowl game and a national-championship award. Ordinarily, achievement on such a scale quiets all opposition and brings an era of harmony. But the usual formulas don't apply to Woody Hayes. There still is less than unanimous enthusiasm for Woody among his fellow coaches, the Ohio State official family, the alumni boosters and even the Columbus sports writers — a group fanatically devoted to the university's football well-being.

However, it is doubtful that Woody Hayes expects universal admiration or even wants it. He places a higher value on plain-speaking frankness than on calculating diplomacy. And he can take it as well as dish it out. This is a priceless attribute for a coach in America's most rabid college-football community, where the team habitually is up among the leaders in attendance and a halfback's fumble may rank in importance with the Yalta papers.

Think that's an exaggeration? One Saturday in November of 1944, with the Allied forces penetrating Hitler's Europe and history's bloodiest war rushing to a climax, a Columbus newspaper carried this eight-column streamer headline on its front page: THE DAY HAS COME — OHIO VS. MICHIGAN!

In riding out the inevitable squalls at Ohio State, Hayes has shown more than a thick hide and a strong will. He has demonstrated a wholesome readiness to admit mistakes and to adjust accordingly. He also has a far from incidental asset in his wife, Anne, a delightfully effervescent woman who seems completely undismayed by the pressure that surrounds a coach's family. For instance, Woody's immediate predecessor at Ohio State, Wes Fesler, had an unlisted phone number. He and his family couldn't endure the abuse when the team had a mediocre season. It finally drove him into resigning — he subsequently served three years at Minnesota. In contrast, W. W. Hayes has been in the telephone directory since he moved to Columbus, although there were times during 1951, his first and worst year, when the phone must have seemed like a device of the devil.

"I remember answering it at four o'clock one morning," Mrs. Hayes says now, laughing. "The man said he was going to ring us and say goodbye to Woody every week until the season ended. I asked him if he had a wife, and since it was nearly morning, invited them both to come to our house for coffee while we talked over the football situation. They didn't appear, and the man didn't phone any more. As far as we're concerned, things like that are part of the job."

It is no job for anyone who likes things calm and peaceful. Even last New Year's Day, when Woody's team climaxed its big year by running up a 20-7 score on Southern California in the Rose Bowl despite a drenching rain, there was discord along with the rejoicing.

One controversy started because Hayes had stormed both before and after the game about the bands "being permitted to tramp all over the field and damage the playing surface." This promptly brought Woody under attack from an influential quarter. John B. Fullen, Ohio State's national alumni secretary, dictated a biting editorial for his alumni magazine after getting back to Columbus.

"A coupon of events since returning have convinced me our football is getting out of hand," Fullen wrote. "One was to find a number of persons agreeing with Woody Hayes that the bands should not have been allowed to perform. . . . The football tail now seems to be wagging the university dog visibly. Since when is the training of musicians less educational than the training of football players?"

Hayes set off another rhubarb after the game, when a West Coast newspaperman asked how Woody thought Southern California compared to the leading Big Ten teams. Most coaches would answer a question like that in cautious generalities, but Hayes responded with his customary candor.

"In addition to us," he declared, "I'd say that Michigan, Wisconsin, Iowa, Purdue and possibly Minnesota — although we didn't play them — were better than Southern Cal."

Next morning there were headlines: HAYES INSULTS WEST COAST FOOTBALL.

Woody had no apologies. "What was I supposed to do, lie about it or tell them what I really believe?" he demanded.

His public outspokenness is the chief reason why there is considerable antagonism to Hayes in the football trade. In particular, many coaches resent his flouting of one cherished custom. As a matter of self preservation, a coach is supposed to be ultraconservative in discussing his team's prospects. But Hayes goes in for cheery optimism.

This kind of talk does not win a man favor in the coaching brotherhood. It is significant that when national honors were being determined last year, Woody Hayes and Ohio State lost out on those awards in which football coaches have the final say.

The Buckeyes were voted the national championship by the sports writers in the Associated Press poll. But the United Press ratings, determined by a board of thirty-five coaches, gave first place to Red Sanders' unbeaten U.C.L.A. team, which took the Pacific Coast Conference title, but was ineligible for the Rose Bowl, having played there — and lost — the year before. And in the balloting by the American Football Coaches Association for the Scripps-Howard Coach-of-the-Year prize, Sanders was the winner with 173 votes. Hayes was second with 134.

Midwesterners and many others who consider the Big Ten the strongest league in the country — it has won eight out of nine Rose Bowl tests with the Pacific Coast Conference — will never understand how anyone could rank U.C.L.A. over Ohio State last year. But then, it was a big surprise to find Woody Hayes and his Buckeyes in the national-championship picture at all. Few people had expected Ohio State to go very far in 1954.

This may have helped. For once, the Buckeyes were spared the pressure that goes with a big preseason build-up. Another fortunate development was the return to the coaching staff of Lyal Clark, a defensive specialist who had followed Wes Fesler from Ohio State to Minnesota.

In the sixty-five years since Ohio State organized its first football team, the university had enjoyed only two perfect seasons prior to 1954. Probably not even Woody Hayes thought there was much hope of a third one last year. However, he did say privately that if Ohio State could win two out of three from Illinois, Iowa and Wisconsin, who were being met on successive Saturdays, then the Buckeyes would have a good chance for the conference title.

The first of these games turned out to be no problem. Illinois' sparkling backfield received insufficient help in the line, and the Illini collapsed. Hayes was able to reset his stars most of the afternoon as Ohio State won, 40-7.

Against Iowa and Wisconsin, the Buckeyes earned a come-from-behind reputation, with a grinning redhead named Howard (Hopalong) Cassady, who was to become an all-America consensus halfback, engineering the clutch plays. In the Wisconsin game, which wound up as a 31-14 victory for Ohio, the Buckeyes stopped Alan Ameche, Wisconsin's tremendous fullback, for the fourth straight year. Ameche never did score on Ohio State in his entire college career.

After the Wisconsin win, Rose Bowl fever was surging throughout the state. Fans swarmed into airline and railroad offices to make reservations for California. This was a trying period for the coaches and the squad. They still had four games to play — three of them against conference opponents.

"We played 'em one at a time," Hayes recalls. "We had a secret agreement among ourselves that anyone who mentioned roses would get a punch in the nose — unless it was a lady over eighty."

Despite all precautions, Ohio State had a natural letdown the next week against lowly Northwestern, but survived, 14-7. Then the Buckeyes thumped a couple of potential spoilers, Pitt and Purdue. That left dangerous Michigan, Ohio's oldest and most bitter rival. More than ever, the Michigan game was the big one.

Hayes received a letter, purportedly from a Michigan student, asking if he would be interested in learning something about the Wolverines' special preparations for the game. Woody didn't want that kind of information, of course, but he began to worry about the possibility of spies in his own camp, since he was installing new plays himself.

Hayes went to extraordinary lengths to keep unauthorized observers from his workouts. He issued spare Ohio State football shirts to all noncombatants, including the sports writers and Dr. Walter Duffee, the team physician for thirty-five years. Woody gave strict instructions to campus police and team managers that no one was to be admitted unless he wore the identifying garb. "Then, when I glance over toward the sidelines, I won't have to fret about who so-and-so is," Hayes said.

It was on the day of the Michigan game that Hayes staged his first dust-up about the bands. It had rained steadily all morning. Two hours before game time Woody marked into the office of Richard C. Larkins, Ohio State's director of athletics, and demanded that the bands be kept off the field to protect the turf.

It so happens that next to their football teams, Ohio State partisans take greatest pride in the outstanding Buckeye band shows. Hayes got nowhere in his attempt to get the musicians out of the act at the 1954 Michigan game. "I listened to Woody carry on for a while," says athletic director Larkins. "Then I told him I wouldn't think of ordering off the bands. But it seemed to me he was working himself into a state of mind where he might not be able to direct the team to best advantage during the game. So I told him that if he wished, we would put it up to the president" — Dr. Howard L. Bevis — "who was at a pregame luncheon in the stadium dining room. Woody said he was all for that. We got Doctor Bevis' ear. Both he and Doctor Hatcher" — Michigan's president — "said it would be unthinkable."

Once the game began, Hayes had other things to worry about. An inspired Michigan team tore Ohio State apart in the first quarter.

Another demonstration of rallying power was needed before the Buckeyes pulled ahead. When the game ended with Ohio State the winner, 21-7, there was the wildest celebration since the great gray stadium at Columbus was erected thirty-three years ago.

A blizzard of shredded paper fluttered from the top deck. Ohio's bench-warmers engulfed their teammates. Rooters stampeded and mobbed the squad in unrestrained joy. Hayes was hoisted on his players' shoulders and borne off in triumph.

Much farther up, in the jammed press box, ticket manager George Staten squirted gusts of rose perfume into the air-conditioning system. The Ohio State band, purple-cheeked, blared the modern happiness song of Big Ten teams, "California, Here I Come."

Inside the training quarters, Buckeye players howled and jumped, embracing and pounding backs. Finally they were quieted by Hayes' call for their regular postgame prayer.Then the husky coach addressed them. Pride and overwhelming joy shook his voice as he called them "the greatest team with the finest fighting heart I've ever known."

When he stopped, the players thrust him, fully clothed, under the showers. He had to dash to his locker for dry togs before he could hold his press conference.

It was one of those supreme days in a man's life. Not many people thought that Woody Hayes would last long enough to experience such a day when he was struggling through his first Ohio State season in 1951.

Woody has had a history of early difficulty on new jobs. His impatience with anything short of outstanding success and his burning desire for quick improvement have driven him to outbursts which shocked his players.

At his first college post in 1946 as head coach of his alma mater, Denison University, in Granville, Ohio, he had a difficult situation. The school had abandoned football in 1943 and was having a hard time getting back to its normal strength.

"That 1946 season was a nightmare," he says. "We won only two games. I guess they thought I was being too tough on the boys then. They darn near threw me out."

But Hayes was undefeated in his next two years at Denison, running up an eighteen-game winning streak. This brought him an offer to move to Miami University, at Oxford, Ohio, in 1949. Hayes took the job — Miami was a bigger school in a more powerful league, the Mid-America Conference.

"I'll never forget the first year Woody was with us," relates John L. Brickels, Miami's director of athletics. "We roomed together in a dormitory during fall practice before classes began. He insisted on living football, night after night, until about 3 a.m. He'd talk until I could stay awake no longer."

After a shaky start, Hayes' 1949 and 1950 Miami teams won fourteen of nineteen games, rolling up 322 points the latter season. It was after the 1950 season that Wes Fesler resigned at Ohio State. Hayes entered a contest for the job that was to rock the university.

Seven men were interviewed before a decision was reached. Included was Paul Brown, whose famous Cleveland professional teams have yet to miss their league championship playoffs. Ohio State's president, three vice-presidents and the board of trustees, goaded by the tremendous public interest in Ohio, became parties to the deliberations.

Some trustees even attempted to get Gov. Frank J. Lausche to enter the controversy.

When Woody Hayes finally was named, he beamed. "I wanted this job badly," he said. It's the greatest coaching opportunity in the country."

He automatically acquired a full professor's status. His starting salary was $12,500. Only last spring it was raised to $16,500, and he was given a five-year "gentlemen's agreement." Employees of the state university may not legally be signed for more than a year at a time.

Hayes immediately began capturing alumni audiences with his magnetic personality, good looks and enthusiasm. He reorganized the coaching staff, substituted the straight 'I' formation for Fesler's single wing, and worked at a fantastic pace.

Much was expected of the new coach. He inherited a veteran squad, including the celebrated Vic Janowicz, the Heisman Trophy winner and all-America halfback of the previous season. But Janowicz, like several of his fellow players, was not averse to extracurricular activities. There were other complications. Hayes was a rookie coach with a largely green staff. He was installing a brand new system of offense. And the fact that Ohio State was a favorite for the conference championship made the Buckeyes a prize target for upsets.

The opening game was a success as the team checkmated Fred Benners, Southern Methodist's passing ace, in a 7-0 win. However, Michigan State edged out the Buckeyes the next week with a last-quarter maneuver, 24-20. When a 6-6 tie with Wisconsin followed, querulous Buckeye fans began second-guessing.

Indiana, frequently regarded as an automatic victim for Ohio, really gave the complainers something to scream about the next Saturday. Ohio State was drubbed, 32-10. By this time opponents had completed sixty out of ninety-one passes. Hayes was bitter and edgy. So were his players. The squad held a "grievance meeting," and delegated team captain Bob Heid to tell the coach that they felt they had been "driven to long too hard."

Hayes did ease up on his whipcracking. He had been telling the players, "I want you thinking and living football." Now he made such concessions as relaxing his ban on singing in the showers. The tension was further eased by an unprecedented mid-week party staged by some members of the Frontliners, the booster organization which does so much to recruit football players for Ohio State.

Temporarily, things were better. That Saturday, Ohio State laced Iowa, 47-21. Hayes then delivered a brief talk to the players, telling them, "You taught me a lesson today."

But the team was unimpressive again the next two weeks. Ohio State barely got by Northwestern, 3-0, and winless Pittsburgh, 16-14. The Pitt performance brought on another crisis. In his press conference afterward, Hayes blew up.

One Pittsburgh newspaper used an eight-column headline to report, OHIO COACH CALLS TEAM MUSCLEHEADS. In Columbus papers, Hayes was quoted somewhat more delicately as saying, "The thing that hurts me is, a lot of kids are sitting on the bench who never get a chance. They have to watch those other clowns out there."

With Hayes in that mood, no one asked why he didn't substitute the bench-warmers for the "clowns." When this reporter, who had been at another game that day, asked Hayes if he had been correctly quoted, Woody displayed his usual frankness.

"Yes, I was," he said. "But I intended only to castigate a couple of players who had been making the same mistakes over and over again."

Then ensued a week of great strain. Ernie Godfrey, the veteran assistant coach, had a phonograph put in the training room. The records he played included one of Knute Rockne's famous pep talks at Notre Dame, and music such as the Ohio State marching song, "Fight the Team Across the Field."

Practice procedures we're lightened. The coaches instead of the players whacked the tackling dummy. Again morale rose, although the next opponent was unbeaten Illinois, destined to reach the Rose Bowl. Ohio State fought the Illini to a scoreless tie.

Hayes was in a reflective mood after the Illinois game as he reviewed the season to date. "We shot the works back against Michigan State," he said, "and were licked in the best game we played — until today. After Michigan State, we worked too hard and the boys went stale. We pushed and pushed when we should have let up."

Ohio State finished with a controversial 7-0 loss to Michigan to round out a generally frustrating season. The overall record of four wins, three losses and two ties was far below expectations. At the annual "appreciation dinner" for the squad two days after the season, Woody Hayes stood up, squared his shoulders and said, "If people don't criticize me, there's something wrong with them. I passed a mirror this morning and almost took a swing at myself. You should learn something from getting licked, and I've learned a lot this year."

But many of his listeners where unappeased. One of the backfield stars, before stepping up to receive his varsity letter, told me, "I never would have believed I'd live to see the day when I'd be glad my college football was over."

It is from this dismal low that Hayes has fought his way back to win the respect and admiration of his players. Both in 1952 and in 1953 his Ohio State teams had six-and-three records. A 27-7 triumph over Michigan delighted Buckeye fans in 1952. Only a 20-0 loss to the ancient rival prevented the following season from being exceptionally pleasing.

Athletic director Larkins was quick to announce, "The coaching staff, headed by Woody Hayes, will return next fall. I say that in case there is doubt in anyone's mind." When Ohio State loses to Michigan, there often is.

After the grand-slam season of 1954, of course, there no longer were any grounds for speculation about Woody Hayes' immediate future at Ohio State. This forty-two-year-old coach is now at the crest of a career that has covered a lot of years, although not much distance. He has spent all his football life in Ohio, where he was born, near Springfield, on February 14, 1913. His father, Wayne Benton Hayes, was superintendent of schools at Newcomerstown, Ohio, until his death in 1929.

"For twelve years I went to school where my dad was superintendent, and that can be difficult for a youngster," Woody says. "My grades were not exceptional. I'm afraid I was too darn ornery — always getting into fights."

Woody does admit to a special liking for history — a subject he later taught in high school, and which still interests him. He says his only outside activities as a kid were in athletics. At one point he took up amateur boxing and had something like ten bouts, of which he lost two.

In high school football, he has a lightweight center and tackle. He weighed only 157 pounds when he entered Denison University. There he played three years as a varsity tackle. His top weight was 185. After graduating in 1935 he became an Ohio high school coach, putting in a year at Mingo Junction and then going to New Philadelphia as assistant to John Brickels, later his boss at Miami. Hayes cites Brickels as his chief model. "John was a fine morale builder and disciplinarian," Woody declares. He was rough and tough, but extremely fair. I tried to pattern myself after him. You know, many of the very successful football dynasties have been headed by stern men, like Earl Blaik at West Point, Bernie Bierman at Minnesota, Frank Leahy at Notre Dame and General Neyland at Tennessee. But I believe you must maintain close contact with your boys off the field. Then you don't lose many. On the field it has to be on a rough-and-tough basis. That's the nature of football. Off the field we try to be a big family here."

During the time that he was at Brickels' home being interviewed for the New Philadelphia job back in 1936, Hayes noticed a charming girl who came to leave a May basket of flowers, in observance of an old custom.

"We had known Anne Gross for a long time," Brickels relates. "Woody seemed interested immediately. We phoned Anne at her home a little later and introduced her to Woody over the wire. He asked her for a date that evening."

Anne fills in the details. "I already had a date. And when I did start going out with Woody, we dated for six years, but never kept steady company. In fact, we never were engaged. Woody proposed over the phone one day in 1942, after he was in the Navy. He had some leave time due. I accepted, he came home and we were married."

Hayes' service record is unusual. He enlisted six months before Pearl Harbor and stayed in for five years, until the ship he commanded was mothballed in 1946. Woody was no land sailor. He got out of the Tunney and Hamilton physical-fitness programs and asked for more active duty. At sea, he rose to lieutenant commander. He was skipper of Patrol Chaser 1251 in the Palau Islands invasion in the Western Pacific in September 1944, and of the destroyer escort Rinehart in both Atlantic and Pacific operations.

"People talk about how devoted Woody is to football," Mrs. Hayes observes. "He was just as dedicated to the Navy. Why, we had been married only five days when he asked for sea duty. He didn't get it at once, but he did request it. Stevie" — the Hayeses' only child — "was nearly nine months old before Woody saw him for the first time."

An impulsive man like Hayes is fortunate to have an understanding wife and friends. John Brickels describes him as the sort of fellow who flares up occasionally, but is sorry soon afterward.

"One day," the Miami athletic director relates, "we had a misunderstanding about an assistant coach's assignment. The mayor and a couple of Boosters Club leaders were in my office, but that didn't stop Woody from picking up an intramural sports trophy and smashing it to pieces on the floor. I knew he'd feel differently soon, and he did. The next morning he came back and said he wanted to pay for the trophy."

Like all successful modern coaches, Hayes is a good executive who stresses basic principles. This extends to the off-field conduct of his players. On road trips, Woody and Anne Hayes make sure of such things as that the boys don't miss church, and that they dress impeccably. "We try to pick boys for character and smartness," Hayes says.

Woody Hayes had no hope this year of catching any opponent napping. He suffered a real personnel loss in June when Hubert Bobo, a sophomore fullback star in 1954, was suspended from school for academic reasons.

In early-season games this fall, it quickly became evident that Ohio State had an ineffective passing game. Nebraska, supposedly a pushover, was beaten only 28-20. Stanford, a ten-point underdog, brought off a major upset with a 6-0 triumph over the Bucks. Stanford stacked its defenses to stop Cassady's sweeps, and O.S.U.'s overhead game was too weak to compensate. The next week Cassady broke loose despite continued passing inadequacy to lead Ohio State to a 27-12 victory over Illinois, but on October 15, Hayes' team fell back into the losing column, with a 20-14 setback at the hands of Duke.

If Woody Hayes were ever going to resort to the time-honored device of bewailing his chances in advance, this was the year for him to do it. So what did he say? "Our problem now is staying on top," he declared. "But don't worry about us. We're going to come back and play great football again."

In college football — and in other fields, for that matter — you just don't find many men with the uncompromising forthrightness of Ohio State's Woody Hayes.

4

O.S.U. Won't Appeal Probation

April 27, 1956

By PAUL HORNUNG
The Columbus Dispatch

Ohio State football, reeling from its first disciplinary punch since it entered the Western Conference, April 6, 1912, Friday totaled up the box score in this manner:

It will make no appeal of its one-year probation, handed down Thursday by Western Conference Commissioner Tug Wilson;

It had not completely doused the final glimmer of hopes for regaining Rose Bowl eligibility, despite the specific wording of Wilson's statement;

It was under "continuing investigation;"

It was shocked, not denying its guilt, but pledging its efforts at getting its house in order quickly; and,

It had a privately unhappy, but publicly restrained football coach with a slightly disappointed, but newly determined football squad.

Athletic Director Dick Larkins said flatly: "We have no appeal" and Faculty Representative Dr. Wendell Postle stated: "We will not take advantage of our right to appeal within the 5-day period allowed."

However, university officials apparently do not believe the door on possible participation in the 1957 Rose Bowl has been locked and sealed. Dr. Postle added in his statement: "When we are satisfied that all matters pertaining to our probation have been corrected, we may appeal to have the period of probation shortened."

Speaking on the strength of his experience in conference matters, Dr. Postle explained: "It's my understanding that we do at any time have the right to appeal. Maybe there is no chance (of the Rose Bowl ban being lifted), but I like to think there is a possibility. We want to shorten the probation if possible."

He revealed that he had received a telegram Friday morning from Wilson commending Ohio State on its official reaction to Thursday's announcement.

Wilson's directive to Ohio State President Dr. Howard L. Bevis was rather specific on the issue. It said: "Ohio State University shall be placed on a state of probationary membership in the Intercollegiate Conference for a period of no less that one year. The terms of the probationary status shall include:

"An express understanding that during the period of probation Ohio State University shall under no circumstances be considered a representative team eligible to represent the conference in the Rose Bowl football game."

Michigan State was slapped with a similar probationary penalty on Feb. 22, 1953, "for its delinquencies in permitting to exist an organization, the Spartan Foundation, known to have solicited funds for assistance to Michigan State athletes." Yet, on Dec. 10, 1953, the probation was lifted and the Spartans defeated U.C.L.A. in the Rose Bowl, 27-14, Jan. 1, 1954.

The Michigan State probation was announced as "for a year," but there was no mention of the Rose Bowl. In fact, it was understood that the Spartans would go to Pasadena if they earned the bid, regardless.

Another condition of Wilson's directive placed in at least temporary jeopardy the eligibility of "about 15-20 football players." Wilson's final verdict was that "none of the athletes who were beneficiaries of the irregularities in the work program which permitted them to draw pay in advance of performing work thereof shall be presented for eligibility until I have approved satisfactory evidence that they have actually repaid fully in services the wages received."

The commissioner, who, along with his special investigator, Jack Ryan, made a 10-week probe of Ohio State, added that "a thorough investigation has satisfied me, however, that the athletes involved have repaid or are. . . engaged in the process of repaying the wage advances."

It's understood that the ruling does not affect other sports and that the only two footballers participating in other sports at the moment, Hopalong Cassady and Galen Cisco, have been cleared. It's also understood that Wilson's severe rap doesn't affect other sports; does not the rule football players in question out of spring practice or the May 5 intra-squad game; that it will have no affect on the fall schedule of Ohio State eligibility to be recognized as champion, should it win its third straight next fall.

Wilson listed two reasons for his decision:

1. "Coach Hayes has acknowledged assistance to unnamed members of the Ohio State football squads from his personal funds in amounts which are said to total approximately $400 annually over a period of five years."

2. "A serious irregularity in the off-campus work program for certain football players. . . ." The players "were being advanced monthly wages for either two or three months with no enforceable liability to repay in kind or in services."

The general reaction at Ohio State to Wilson's final decision was summed up picturesquely by a high official who declined to take credit for the remark: "We violated the rules; the sooner we go to the woodshed and take our whipping, the better."

Dr. Howard L. Brevis, the Ohio State president, set policy in the future with "Any violation of the rules of which we have been guilty will be stopped. We mean to live within the rules."

Coach Hayes' statement was one of restraint, but of obvious distaste for the final verdict.

"All my life, " he said, "I have been taught respect for properly delegated authority, and for this reason I do not believe we should appeal the decision. This, however, does not infer that I agree with the severity of the penalty, nor the manner in which the investigation was made."

Hayes held a meeting with his squad prior to Thursday's practice. The players had been counseled not to comment on the probation, but locker-room discussion — what there was of it — centered around the possible Rose Bowl situation and Michigan State's probationary experience.

Hayes said, "the kids have been swell. They went out and worked hard. They never worked harder."

The Buckeye gridders scrimmaged for most of their hour-and-a-half practice.

Wilson, who made the announcement from his Chicago office, although he had apprised Ohio State officials here Wednesday of the decision, revealed that his investigation is continuing. This is based not only on the work-pay status of the unnamed football players, but because of "Mr Hayes' refusal to provide an accounting of this assistance (personal loans to players)."

The invesigation was touched off by an article in Sports Illustrated (October 24, 1955), which said that "a recruit (for Ohio State football) can count on some financial help from Hayes if he is 'in need.' Woody insists he never forks up for a luxury... but it's certainly also true that he makes sure he won't lose any valuable men by financial default."

Wilson made his first trip to the campus in February to open the probe. He said at that time that no Big Ten school had asked for an investigation of Ohio State, but that because of the widespread publicity he, as commissioner of the Western Conference, felt obligated to investigate. He also mentioned that the N.C.A.A. had shown interest.

After the investigation was well under way, it branched off into the job program.

The conference rule on compensation for athletes states:

"No student shall be eligible who receives compensation from any employer unless (1) he is performing useful work, (2) he is being paid at the going rate in his locality for the work performed, and (3) he is working on the job all the time for which he is being paid."

The accusation against the university, Wilson said, was that it had been "lax" in enforcing the rule.

Hayes' refusal to name the players who received his personal "loans" obviously stemmed from a fear that these names might become public to the embarrassment of the players, especially if the N.C.A.A. stepped into the case.

Wilson's stern action probably will preclude any action by the N.C.A.A.

5

Agony Instead Of Roses In Columbus

December 11, 1961

By WALTER BINGHAM
Sports Illustrated

Ohio State football coach Woody Hayes did not hear the news until he arrived at the Hollenden Hotel in Cleveland to make a speech. When reporters told him he dropped his bag and walked out. For an hour and a half he roamed the Cleveland streets, trying to compose himself. But back on the campus the Ohio State students were making no such effort to count 10. They burned members of the faculty in effigy, snake-danced down the main street, surrounded the capitol building, broke windows, besieged and insulted their professors and generally raised the most hell that has been raised in Columbus since V-J day. Over what? Over a faculty decision not to permit the football team to go to the Rose Bowl.

Such matters are not taken lightly in the capital city of Ohio and the home of the finest grind-it-out college football team in business. The local TV and radio stations, without exception, joined in the denunciation of the anti-Rose Bowl faculty members, some of them in violent terms. *The Columbus Dispatch*, in an act of dubious public service, printed a list of those professors voting against the joyous trip to California, complete with addresses, salaries and amounts of money spent this year on out-of-state travel at state expense. The result was that the offending professors were jeered, scowled at, browbeaten, telephoned day and night and greeted with messages in Anglo-Saxon monosyllables on blackboards all over the campus.

In a sense, the whole witches' brew seemed a contradiction in terms. Here was Ohio State University, a frankly football-minded institution which spends something like $1,300 a head to recruit good ballplayers, sends them through Woody Hayes's hard-but-clean football school, treats them like idols and gains a national reputation for football excellence. Why not carry the theme out to the end and go to the Rose Bowl?

The reason is that Ohio State is ripped and torn by an internal battle over football, a battle which has been going on for several years and will most likely continue for many more years. Ultimate control of the athletic program rests, by Big Ten law, with the faculty, and more and more the faculty has become exercised over the concept of Football *über Alles*.

Last year a United States Senator visited the O.S.U. campus and innocently blurted out, "I don't know much about Ohio State, but I do know you have a good football team here." Certain professors boiled. As one explained:

"We're upset over the fact that the image of Ohio State is that the school is merely an appendage to the football team. When we go away for meetings, we're kidded about this by people from other schools. We don't dislike football, but the feeling is that things are out of proportion."

Came last week and an invitation to play U.C.L.A. in the Rose Bowl. Into the Faculty Club marched 53 members of the all-powerful Faculty Council to debate the issue and make a final decision. Indignant debate raged for an hour and 25 minutes. There was a "secret" ballot, followed by University President Novice Fawcett's intonation: "28 against, 25 for." Bang. The demonstrations began.

To the amazement of followers of Ohio State's internal dogfights, the forces of law and order were led by — of all people — Woody Hayes. For years now Coach Hayes has been at the storm center of all the squabbles, laying about him right and left with strong epithets and, at least once, a rap in the chops. But this time he gained prestige by adopting what, for him, was almost a Nehru stance. "I don't agree with those 28 'no' votes," Woody told 1,000 O.S.U. alumni at the hotel in Cleveland, "but I respect their integrity, if not their intelligence." He made it plain that he was not going to quit over the action (as had been rumored). "We have had to learn to accept defeat under pressure and that may help us now," he said, "although it is difficult to explain to the boys when, after 15 years, the Rose Bowl is jerked out from under them."

The picture of a Woody Hayes speaking moderately did not escape the notice of the diehards back in Columbus, who always had looked upon him as their General Patton. By the second day the public demonstrations began to simmer down. They came to a halt when football co-captain Mike Ingram announced to the crowds through a police loudspeaker, "They're not going to change their minds. We might as well face it. We're not going to the Rose Bowl. Go home before somebody gets hurt." There were a few boos, whereupon husky linebacker Ingram pulled out his last stop. "The team did all the damn work!" he said. "If they can accept the decision, you certainly can. You college kids leave and let the police pick up the high school kids hanging around." Telephone calls excepted, that was the end of anarchy in Columbus.

6

You Love Woody Or Hate Him

September 24, 1962

By ROY TERRELL
Sports Illustrated

Woody Hayes will be 50 years old next Valentine's Day, if he makes it, and sometimes you wonder. Football is a happy game, even in the Big Ten. Chrysanthemum sales boom, old grads have a good excuse to get squiffed, hardly anyone goes to class, and if the halfback gets a black eye his girl will kiss it. Only Woody Hayes must suffer. To him, football is less a game than a 20th century torture device, and on his own private rack, on a hundred Saturday afternoons in the vast stadiums of the Midwest, he has been subjected to agonies that would make your hair look like Harpo Marx's.

While the avalanche of sound from 80,000 hysterics rolls down upon him, he stands alone, a short, powerful man with a barrel chest and a barrel stomach. It is cold, but he wears no coat. His hands are balled fists below his shirt-sleeves, and perspiration streams from beneath the old gray baseball cap with the scarlet letter O, as in O-HI-O, that he has worn so long it now seems a part of his head. He prowls the sidelines like a bear in a pit, shouting in fury at the officials, snarling in frustration at his team, at his coaches, at himself. Deprive Woody Hayes of victory and he would die, just as surely as a man in space suddenly deprived of his oxygen supply; and so, until victory is assured, Woody dies. With each Ohio State mistake, with each fumble and penalty and interception, he dies. It would be a pitiful sight were it not for one thing: at the rate at which

Ohio State makes mistakes, no one should have to worry about burying Hayes for at least another 132 years.

There was a time when the thought that Woody Hayes might go on forever would have set off only limited celebration in the Big Ten. In his 11 seasons at Ohio State, the Buckeyes have behaved more like Mongols, spreading devastation throughout what the Big Ten, with dissent only from the Southwest, the Southeast and sometimes the Big Eight and Pacific Coast, like to call the toughest football conference in the land. Hayes has won four of the last eight Big Ten championships, including last year's. He set a record of 17 consecutive conference victories, and the Southeast may note that the Buckeyes were not playing Chattanooga and Richmond and Memphis State. In one remarkable stretch, Ohio State won 24 of 26 Big Ten games. The only losing season under Hayes came in 1959, when he tried to get fancy, a lapse that he now attributes to temporary insanity. Outside of that, Hayes has lost just nine games in the last eight years and, in one poll or another, Ohio State has three times been named the national champion. Now the Bucks are primed to win again. Success breeds its own antagonisms, and Woody Hayes would be the most surprised person in the world if the Big Ten should ever elect him Queen of the May.

But success alone can never explain the passion that Hayes has been known to arouse. You either love him or you hate him, and if you happen to be one of the few with no opinion you may just as well form one, since he probably has an opinion about you. He has an opinion about everything else. If you choose to disapprove of Woody Hayes, there is a wide selection of reasons.

He drives his players with a ferocity that would make a Marine Corps drill instructor look like Mary playing with her lamb. The football that he coaches — the crunching up-the-middle trap and off-tackle smash — is about as inspiring as a radish. It has furnished the sport with a now-tired phrase — three yards and a cloud of dust — and so far as you can discover in Columbus, Knute Rockne, Gus Dorais and the forward pass have not yet been invented. His own faculty complains that Woody's football success is distorting the academic image of a great university, and Hayes, a professor himself, sometimes attends faculty meetings to roar denunciations of his detractors.

Reporters assigned to cover the Ohio State dressing room decide to bury their grandmothers on days when it appears that the Buckeyes might not win. If Hayes is a bad loser — he has refused to shake hands with an opposing coach who beat him — he is also a bad winner, sometimes heaping scorn and humiliation upon a defeated opponent's head. He has a temper like a toothless cat. Most damning of all, he always says what he thinks. In fact, Woody Hayes passes up more opportunities to keep his mouth shut in one year than most people do in a lifetime.

In the middle of a game he once ran 60 yards, probably a record for fat coaches, in order to accuse Big Ten officials of allowing the defense to play dirty football. "You're overofficiating the offense and letting the defense get away with murder," he snarled. "The Bible says turn the other cheek, but I'll be damned if I'll tell my kids to do that when they'll just get it fractured!"

He once banned from his practice sessions, locker room and office for two years all reporters from a magazine — this magazine, curiously enough — because of a story that led to Ohio State's being placed on probation in 1956 by the Big Ten. Admitting that the story was accurate, he remained firm: "I just don't want you S.O.B.s around." Although not involved in the great musical chairs game of 1957, when many college coaches jumped contracts, Hayes had something to say on that subject: "Instead of blaming the coaches, they should blame the presidents of the universities who hire coaches away. They are equally at fault and the only ones in a position to control the situation."

He charged, in 1956, that Forest Evashevski had allowed the stadium grass to grow long at Iowa in order to hamper the Ohio State running attack, and he threatened to get a lawnmower and cut it himself. At a Big Ten press conference in Chicago, he was first on the schedule to give a rundown of his team's prospects for the season ahead. When Hayes stopped speaking, all the other conference coaches stood up and left. Hayes had covered each team in the Big Ten so thoroughly that there was no more to be said.

He beat Southern California, 20-7, in the 1955 Rose Bowl game, then told the local press corps that at least four other Big Ten teams could have done as well. "He was probably right," another Big Ten coach agreed, "but he might have been more tactful." Tact is the last thing the state of California seems to arouse in Woody Hayes. Before the '58 Rose Bowl game, both Ohio State and Oregon warmed up in the end zones to save wear and tear on the rain-soaked field. When the bands were allowed to march on this same field just before kickoff, the residents of Pasadena thought that it had begun to thun-

der again. Hayes hasn't cared a great deal for bands since. Nor for
Southern California's assessment of its climate. "They should have
covered that field. They never admit it's going to rain out there," he
said.

After the 17-0 loss to U.S.C. in '59 he was less than gentle with
one West Coast reporter. "He slugged me," the newspaperman
claimed. "I just barely brushed him," said Hayes. "Well," said one of
the Ohio State assistants, "you might say that Woody showed him to
the door."

Not even sports writers infuriate Hayes quite so much, however,
as an athlete who fails to play up to his maximum ability. At an Ohio
State basketball game during the time of Frank Howard, the all-
America behemoth who now plays right field, in a manner of speaking, for the Dodgers, Hayes was sitting with members of his football
squad in the stands. He decided that Howard wasn't putting out. "He
got madder and madder," one of the players remembers, "until finally he jumped up and ordered us all out of the arena. 'I'm not
going to let you watch this,' he said. He took us outside and lectured
us for an hour and a half on always trying to do our best."

Two years ago, as a spectator at a game in Cleveland between the
Indians and Yankees, Hayes suffered through the one-handed artistry
of Vic Power at first base until he could stand it no more. "You're
showing off," Hayes yelled from his box near the Indian dugout.
"Why don't you use both hands and help your team win?" Power,
whose ears are as good as his hands, dropped over and invited Mr.
Hayes to discuss the matter further after the game; Hayes, probably
figuring that much of the 230 pounds he carries these days is relatively useless in hand-to-hand combat, went home instead. He didn't
go back to watch the Indians again until they traded Power to Minnesota. "That guy makes me sick," he says. "What's he got two
hands for?"

The man who can make Woody Hayes sickest of all is the archen-
emy, Jack Fullen, alumni secretary at Ohio State. Fullen once proposed that the school give up all pretense at amateurism, hire a
professional team and control it under a bureau of football. Hayes
feels that Fullen has been trying to get him fired for years; he can
understand this well enough, since he would like to get Fullen fired
and is currently engaged in a campaign to accomplish just that. What
makes him furious is that in the process he thinks Fullen is sabotag-
ing Ohio State football.

Through the years, Hayes has been in more scraps with opposing coaches, officials, reporters, university administrators, alumni and fans than he can count, if he bothers to count at all. He has not changed a whisker in all this time, but a strange thing has happened: the people *around* Woody Hayes are beginning to change. A former assistant, Rix Yard, once said, "Woody sticks to what he believes is right, even when it's wrong." In retrospect he has proved to be wrong so seldom (at least about football) that a slew of people who once opposed him are now on his side. He is suddenly in danger of becoming one of the most popular men in all Ohio, a fate that horrifies Hayes no end. "I'm trying to win football games. I don't like popular people. I like tough, honest people." Apparently others do, too.

Hayes grew up in Newcomerstown, Ohio, where his father was superintendent of schools, and he played tackle three seasons for Denison University in Granville. He received a master's degree from Ohio State and coached in high schools at Mingo Junction and New Philadelphia before going off to command a destroyer escort during World War II. As the head coach at Denison in 1946-48 he won 18 games in a row; at Miami University in 1950 he won eight of nine and beat Arizona State in the Salad Bowl. In 1951 he became head coach at Ohio State.

In the years preceding Hayes, some very good football coaches had fled this job like rabbits, unable to stand the ridicule, the abuse, the unremitting pressure to win every game. The last of these was Wes Fesler, a sensitive, kindly man who lost seven games in three years. When Fesler's wife began to shudder every time the telephone rang, he decided to retreat, too. The telephone was unlisted, but this hardly slowed down the Columbus fans.

"Not one big-time coach was interested in coming to Ohio State," says Hayes. "They approached Earl Blaik and Don Faurot, and a number of others. Blaik wouldn't even listen. So they hired me."

At first they laid odds in downtown Columbus on how long this new guy would last. Then they began to find out things about Woody Hayes. Criticism had about as much effect on his hide as a spitball against a charging rhinoceros. For a man who was virtually a recluse, he was the most compelling speaker since Daniel Webster reclaimed a soul from the devil. "If this guy can coach as well as he can talk," said one dazed alumnus after a speech, "we're going to have a hell of a football team." Woody Hayes, they soon discovered, could coach.

"I get along fine with the fans," Hayes says. "They want to win, and I can understand that. So do I. That's the idea of this game. The only idea. Anyway, I'm just a little bit meaner than they are." His telephone number has always been in the Columbus directory.

The sincerity that flows out of Hayes like beer from a barrel and the absolute honesty of the man have made him one of the most spectacular recruiters in college football. Ohio State is the only Big Ten school in Ohio and sits smack in the middle of what Michigan State's Duffy Daugherty calls "the most fertile talent area in the Big Ten." This area Hayes covers like a midwestern blizzard, charming parents, preaching the advantages of Ohio State, looking for what he calls "the quality boys." He is the first to admit that a great deal of his coaching success reflects the type of boy that he gets.

"We concentrate on character," he says with the slight lisp that sometimes startles you, coming as it does from such a tough man. "We talk to their parents, their teachers, their principals, coaches, ministers, priests. If a kid doesn't have character, you don't have a chance."

Jim Parker, the all-league guard of the Baltimore Colts, went to Ohio State after being interviewed, as he says, "by about 25 major colleges and I don't know how many minor ones. I was promised the moon by some. Woody didn't promise me the moon. He told me, 'You don't get anything on a silver platter here,' and I didn't. But I sent my brother Al to Ohio State after I left so he could be coached by Woody, and I want my son to learn football under him, too."

"Woody gets the good material," says Jerry Burns of Iowa, "and he never misuses it."

Most of Ohio State's recruiting competition comes from the service academies and the Ivy League, but Hayes gets more than 50% of the good Ohio boys, the ones that he really wants, the exceptionally gifted athletes. Of the 132 boys on his three Rose Bowl squads — Woody considers last season a Rose Bowl year, too, since the team was invited although not permitted to go — 128 were from Ohio. "Ohio boys have more loyalty to the school and the state," he says. "It seems to work out well."

He believes that good students make good football players, but he is worried about the future of the Negro in the conference. "If we're not careful," he say, "these rules we have now are going to eliminate about 80% of the Negro boys. No one questions their intelligence; it's their educational background that slows them down. Just because Ohio high schools are integrated doesn't mean that all are academically equal. Some schools are in areas made up almost entirely of

Negro families. Those schools just aren't as good, and the boys don't have the preparation.

"Outside of that, the only problem I ever had with Negro football players at Ohio State was in 1959. We lost five ball games that year because we didn't have enough of them. They're great athletes and they're great kids. If those southern schools had a few of them at halfback I don't think the defensive records would look quite so good down there. I hope we never legislate Negro football players out of the Big Ten."

Football has been Hayes' life, and since he is not a religious man it may be the closest thing to a God that he has. But running a close second is the deep feeling that he has for education, a feeling that was planted early in life by his father, who never went to high school but earned a college degree and became an educator. Hayes, in fact, considers himself first of all a teacher. "What do you think a coach is?" he asks. "Why, we teach a boy more in two months than some professors do in three years."

While talk of educations sounds hypocritical on the lips of some coaches, no one can question Hayes' sincerity on the subject. "I've never heard him talk about how many all-Americas he's had, or how many undefeated teams," says another Big Ten coach, "but he'll drive you crazy telling you about all his boys who have become doctors and lawyers and dentists and engineers."

"He never let me forget that I was at Ohio State for an education first and to play football second," says Jim Parker. Dick Schafrath, the 260-pound tackle of the Cleveland Browns, grins when he remembers his last meeting with Woody. "You know the first thing he told me? 'You still need a semester to complete that degree. You'd better get back here and finish up,' he said."

"I don't guess there is anything that I believe in more than this university and the value of the education that a boy receives here," says Hayes. "If I can convince my kids of what a degree means to them, then I don't have to worry about them quitting school. I don't have to worry about any of them getting involved in this damned bribe business that almost ruined basketball. I show them the statistics: a college degree is now worth about $180,000 over a working lifetime.

"Of the 27 freshmen who came here on football scholarships in the fall of 1959, 24 will be around this fall. Normally you can expect 40% of the students entering a big university to graduate. On the

Ohio State football squad we graduate 70% to 80%. How can anyone condemn college football when they see a figure like that?

"When I came here 11 years ago I was determined that you don't cheat the kid who plays football for you. You see those two buildings?" and Hayes waves at the gleaming mass of steel and concrete that is St. John Arena and at the huge field house sprawling alongside. "They cost $5.5 million to build. Where did the money come from? From these kids on the football team. They earned it. Football is a $2 million business at Ohio State — which means that the 22 boys on the starting team bring in almost $100,000 apiece in gate receipts each year. Think of that. And what do they get in return? Well, we're not going to cheat and give them a slice of the melon or anything else illegal, you can bet on that. What they get is $1,300 a year in room, board, tuition and books — the opportunity to get an education. And I'm going to see that they get that education. We certainly owe them that."

If Hayes feels that the university has a responsibility to the boy, he also feels that the boy owes something to the university. This payment he extracts, often in Churchillian terms, on the football field. When Woody Hayes gets through conditioning a team for the season ahead, it could probably beat the Washington eight-oared crew rowing a Roman galley.

"I hope I work my teams harder than anyone else," he says. "I sure hope so. I try hard enough." How the players feel about this, he doesn't know. "Frankly," he says, "I don't give a damn." Instead of sending boys away from Ohio State like a flock of pigeons, this treatment nails them to the campus — and to Hayes — in some manner incomprehensible to the normal jellied soul. Under his lash, boys who would faint at the thought of walking to the grocery at their parents' request run a mile in full football equipment in less than six minutes flat; if they don't, they keep running until they learn how. Eventually the relationship between Hayes and his players reaches a state bordering upon the spiritual. Mike Ingram, last year's co-captain, who ran his first mile in 7:40 — he is 5 feet 9 inches tall and weighs 220 pounds — and his last one in 5:40, calls Woody Hayes "the fairest guy I've ever known." Tom Perdue asked Woody to be his best man. Hopalong Cassady, still considered by Woody the best football player he ever coached ("He put out 100% on every play," says Hayes, offering his greatest tribute), points out that the man is a rarity among coaches, if for no other reason than that "he goes all out for you after you graduate. If he can help out when something happens, he'll be there."

It happened to Vic Janowicz after an automobile accident on the West Coast had ended his professional career. "I was in a Chicago hospital, recuperating but not well," says Janowicz. "Ohio State was playing Northwestern, and Woody asked me to dinner. 'You look terrible,' he said. I guess I did; it seemed to me that I wasn't getting the proper treatment. So Woody made arrangements for me to return to Columbus on the team plane. He put me in University Hospital and kept me there for a month of physical therapy. It was the turning point for me, the start of a new life."

Bob Vogel is a very large, blond young man who may be one of the two best tackles in America this fall; the other is his teammate, Daryl Sanders. Vogel has survived two years of Woody Hayes and, like a man who has become fond of hitting himself on the head with a hammer, looks forward to a third. "Playing for him is a challenge," Vogel grins. "If you get through his preseason two-a-day workouts, you get the feeling that you can handle most of the other things you are going to run into in life."

Hayes sees nothing unusual in this stoic acceptance of his coaching. "The boys seem to welcome discipline," he says. "Success is the only motivational factor that a boy with character needs.

"When he sees that he's getting in shape, that all this work is good for him then he doesn't grouse about it anymore. He begins to drive himself. Hell, he wants to win as much as I do. There's a lot of silly talk about building character in college football — and I happen to believe in it. In our society there aren't too many the things that a boy can do anymore. Football is one of the few. He has to whip that guy across from him and he has to do it as a member of a team, playing within the rules. But a coach doesn't go out to build character, he goes out to win. The character will take care of itself."

The only other thing Woody Hayes demands of his players, besides condition and character, is perfection. So far it has eluded him, though opposing coaches agree that his boys sometimes perform the fundamentals of the game so well that it frightens them. "No one comes close to him in coaching blocking and tackling," says Minnesota's Murray Warmath. "You always know what his teams are going to do," says Jerry Burns, "so you set your defense to stop them. But they do what they do well enough and often enough to beat you. They know how to block and carry out assignments."

Actually, Hayes has a theory that the only team that can beat

Ohio State is Ohio State. "Eliminate the mistakes in football," he says, "and you'll never lose a game." As a result, an Ohio State practice session looks like a day in the salt mines. "We're not out here to laugh," Woody says.

An official, in uniform, stands over every play, whistle in mouth, red handkerchief in hand. When he spots a boy beating the snap count, when he detects holding on a block, when he sees a rule infraction of any kind, he blows and throws. This discourages sloppy practice habits and contributes to the Buckeye record of leading the Big Ten in fewest penalties in most years. Hayes does not approve of fumbles, either. "No back in the history of football was ever worth two fumbles a game," he says. If an Ohio State player fumbles twice in a practice he has to run a mile to the Olentangy River dike. If he fumbles in a game, he might just as well jump in.

"To eliminate mistakes you have to pick the right quarterback," says Hayes. "That's why I may keep a superior passer on the bench and play a boy who is less spectacular but steady and sure. The five big mistakes in football are the fumble, the interception, the penalty, the badly called play, the blocked punt — and most of these origi- nate with the quarterback. Find a mistake-proof quarterback and you have this game won."

Hayes does not necessarily consider a pass, in itself, a mistake, as has been charged, but he feels that a football in the air only too often winds up in the wrong hands. "The pass is still primarily a weapon of surprise," he says. "Your first pass play in a game should succeed 75% to 80% of the time. The second attempt should succeed 60%. The third time you run that same pass play, watch out. Interception."

At Iowa in 1958, the Buckeyes beat the Hawkeyes 38-28 in a football game that many people — including Forest Evashevski and Woody Hayes — consider one of the most exciting every played. Randy Duncan and Iowa threw 33 passes that afternoon, completing 23 of them for 249 yards and a Big Ten record. Ohio State threw exactly two — but gained 397 yards on the ground. "When you get fancy, you get beat," says Hayes, after the game. Evashevski, who had already won the Big Ten championship, just shook his head.

The Ohio State offensive unit may devote 50% of its practice time to the famous off-tackle play, No. 26. "It may be Right 26 or Left 26 or Bingo 26 or Double 26," says Hayes, "but it's still 26. We run it until we get it right. Then in only 3% more time, we can teach the quarterback keep wide off this same play and with 5% more time than that, half a dozen pass patterns that begin the same way.

"Actually, we work very little in complete teams. We spend most of the time with the individual or small unit. Today you coach the individual. The greatest improvement in football has been not in the plays themselves but in coaching the plays. And how a boy is taught is far more important than what he is taught. The game of football is one of strategy and tactics. Compared to the strategy of football, tactics on the field amount almost to nothing. A fleabite."

The primary Ohio State tactic is to run a play until the opponents are crushed flat or else get bored and go away. Last fall Hayes sent his all-America fullback, Bob Ferguson, into the T.C.U. line 36 times, which may be a bad example, since T.C.U. tied the Buckeyes, 7-7, and Hayes doesn't like to remember that. Usually Ohio State will probe and test the other team until it finds a weakness. "When we are stopped," says Hayes, "we don't go to another play. We change the blocking angles in the line until the play works. Maybe that is why we don't look very spectacular early in the game. But we look pretty spectacular sometimes in the fourth quarter."

"Just when you think that two-three-four yard offense is dull," says Duffy Daugherty, "he burns you with a 50-yard breakaway. Woody is primarily an offensive coach — he believes you should score — but in recent years he has paid more attention to his defense. Now his defense is dull, too, but it works."

Woody Hayes' contributions to the game of football do not stop with winning games and boring spectators on a Saturday afternoon. He has been one of the leaders in the study of injury prevention, developing something of a mania on this subject, just as on most others in which he gets involved. Ohio State takes a preseason electroencephalogram of each player, for comparison if a head injury should occur later. "This is sometimes the difference between spotting something dangerous and ignoring it until it is too late," he says. His players undergo a series of neck exercises that play havoc with collar sizes but increase resistance to head blows to a marked degree. In the spring practice of 1962 not one Ohio State football player was even dazed from a blow on the head, and they do not play patty-cake in an Ohio State scrimmage even in the spring.

If Ohio State were not such a rich market for equipment manufacturers, their salesmen would never go near the place. Hayes drives them wild with demands for better helmets, better pads, better uniforms. For two years his boys have been wearing a plastic helmet cushioned on the outside to protect others as well as on the inside. "Of course this outside padding isn't doing us much good," he grumbles. "Everyone should use it."

The Buckeyes frequently change uniforms halfway through a hot early season game or practice to avoid a form of heat prostration known as water-blanket suffocation. Hayes has even plotted the area of greatest incidence of knee injuries — it is an arc 20 yards laterally from the point where the ball is positioned to start play — and says this is another reason why his teams run inside the end most of the time. "You don't get hurt," he says, "when you run straight ahead." Even when an Ohio State halfback gets loose, he is instructed not to hug the sidelines but to stay at least a yard inside the field. When penned in, the runner has room to ride with, and better absorb, a hard side tackle.

"We're so far ahead of other schools in the matter of protecting our players that it's pitiful," Hayes says. Last season only two Ohio State boys were unable to start games because of injuries.

No Ohio State football player ever drops out of school because of lack of funds, either, if Woody Hayes can help it. The 1956 probation came about because Hayes was helping some destitute athletes out of his own pocket, a well-intentioned practice that happened to be at variance with the conference rules. "We've got to do something to help those kids," Hayes roared. "One of those boys came to me and said he had only one pair of pants. 'Can't you get a loan?' I asked him. 'I tried,' he said, 'They told me it would take four months.' Hell, a pair of pants can get to be awfully dirty in four months. Sure I gave him the money." Hayes roared so loud, in fact, that the Big Ten authorized conference schools to set up loan funds that now furnish needed financial assistance almost immediately.

Money apparently means nothing to Hayes. His salary is $20,000 a year, and on at least two occasions he has turned down raises, requesting that the money be split up among his coaching staff. Once he refused a new Cadillac after a winning season. He lives in a pleasant two-story house in a quiet residential section five minutes away from the campus by Chevrolet; it is the same house into which he moved upon arriving in Columbus more than 11 years ago. The drive needs a new surface, but Hayes figures that he will do it himself, with the help of Steve, his 16-year-old son, who would rather play baseball or go swimming or bowl than play football or pave driveways. Hayes' wife, Anne, plays bridge and belongs to things; she also answers the telephone and placates the furious fans who call and ask why in the name of Robert Taft doesn't Ohio State throw a pass once in a while.

"I love 'em," Anne Hayes says. "You can't blame people for getting mad, but you can't let them stay that way. Sometimes I ask them to come on over and have a cup of coffee and we'll talk this all out. It breaks them up."

There is nothing unusual about a coach being dedicated to his job — it would be highly unusual if he weren't — and still successful, these days, but Hayes spends more time at football than most. In fact he spends all of his time at football. "He doesn't play cards, he doesn't play golf, he doesn't fish," said one assistant, thinking hard. "He doesn't smoke, he doesn't drink. You know, now that I think about it, he doesn't do anything at all." Actually Hayes plays hand-ball once in a while, trying to stay under 230, and although he knows little about golf, he will drive halfway across the country to follow Jack Nicklaus around a big tournament. "The boy grew up just around the corner," Hayes says. "You listen to Woody," a friend says, "and you'd think he taught Nicklaus all he knows about the game."

Most of Hayes' time away from the practice field, his office and home is spent at football clinics, where he is in constant demand. He reads a great deal — history, economics, current events — and is a nonstop talker on all these subjects. Forest Evashevski once walked up to Hayes to congratulate him after a game. "I wanted to tell him what a great game Ohio played," says Evashevski, "but I made the mistake of asking him what time it was. I never got another word in; he spent 30 minutes telling me about his new watch."

Last spring an Ohio State alumnus named Ed Garman invited Hayes to make the annual Memorial Day address at Oakwood Cemetery in Cuyahoga Falls, a rather unusual request for a football coach. Hayes couldn't get there fast enough. "It was the biggest crowd in history," says Garman, "and for 35 minutes they didn't move a muscle while Woody talked to them, without notes about what this country means to all of us. They were spellbound. Later he thanked me for the chance."

But the greatest speech that Woody Hayes ever made was deliv-ered before an Ohio State alumni group last fall at the Hollenden Hotel in Cleveland. Arriving from the airport, Hayes was met in the hotel lobby by reporters. "The Ohio State Faculty Council has just voted 28 to 25 against letting the team go to the Rose Bowl," he was told. Hayes dropped his bag and walked out. For two hours he paced the streets alone, thinking what this meant to his players, who had been working for the championship for four years, thinking what the decision meant to the Ohio State fans, the school, to himself. When

Woody Hayes, the new O.S.U. head football coach, in a tense moment on the sidelines of the 1951 Michigan State game.

(*left to right*) Vic Janowizc, Hayes and Walt Klevay pose prior to beginning of 1951 spring practice.

An excited Hayes shouts words of encouragement to his team during the 1954 Wisconsin game.

Two famous Hopalongs, Howard Cassady of Ohio State and Hopalong Cassidy of the movies, meet on the practice field prior to the 1955 Rose Bowl game.

Hayes and his son, Steve, greet Buckeye fans prior to the departure for the 1955 Rose Bowl game against U.S.C. in Pasadena, Calif.

Bob Watkins romps for big yardage against U.S.C. in the 1955 Rose Bowl.

Howard Cassady makes a hole for Bill Leggett near the U.S.C. goal line in the 1955 Rose Bowl.

Howard (Hopalong) Cassady won the Heisman Memorial Trophy in 1955.

Howard Cassady chats with Ed Sullivan prior to an appearance on The Ed Sullivan Show in 1955.

Vice President Richard M. Nixon gets a few pointers from his friend, Woody Hayes, at the 1958 N.C.A.A. Convention.

Hayes in the press box while scouting Rose Bowl opponent Southern California at the 1954 Notre Dame - U.S.C. game.

he finally arrived at the speaker's platform, he was remarkably composed, for Woody Hayes.

"I don't agree with those 28 no votes," he said "but I respect the integrity of the men who cast them, if not their intelligence. I would not want football to drive a line of cleavage in our university. Football is not worth that."

Not everyone has fallen in love with Woody Hayes, even yet. He still pops off, he has a terrible temper, and defeat, when and if it comes, will jar him as before. This season he may not throw even a pass. But the old joke — "The football team should have a university of which it can be proud" — does not sound absurd now.

7

Cut 'Em Off At Forward Pass

October 19, 1964

By WILLIAM BARRY FURLONG
Sports Illustrated

Playing Ohio State is a little like volunteering for a waterfront rumble. It isn't just a sporting event; it's a benefit for bone surgeons. Teams that play Ohio State go into the game feeling that the best that can happen is that they will merely become uninsurable. The worst that can happen is what happened to Illinois' Rose Bowl champions at Champaign last Saturday. They not only lost the game, 26-0, but also their status, their pride, their illusions and — in all probability — their Big Ten football title.

The illusions were the hardest to part with. For four and a half years Coach Pete Elliott has been trying to get Illinois football players to accept winning as naturally as breathing. It was not easy. They once lost 15 consecutive games under him, and the crowds began to dwindle. Against Michigan State in 1962 Illinois drew only 19,547 fans ("They didn't have enought people to hear your echo when you yelled," says one fan). But Elliott carried out one of the most effective recruiting programs in Big Ten history and put together a team that caught the winning idea as if it were virulent. Before it was over, Illinois had won the Big Ten title, gone to the Rose Bowl and left Washington looking like a bunch of guys who had just fallen through a skylight.

Since his arrival at Illinois, Elliott has patterned his teams in the Ohio State image. He wanted — like Ohio State — players so big that seismographs trembled when they walked on a football field. Dick Butkus, who plays linebacker with the authority of a Marine sergeant, weighs 243 pounds; tackle Archie Sutton weighs 260. He wanted them tough and hard-nosed but filled with compassion for their fellow man; they were always to frisk their victims for signs of life before throwing them away. Fred Custardo won the first-string quarterback job this year on the day when — as a freshman — he stuck his hand under the face mask of a lineman, mashed him in the face and snapped: "Nobody talks in the huddle but me." It was a little like courting oblivion but the lineman took it — and Custardo took command.

Illinois' style of football became much like that of Ohio State. Nothing fancy — just good wholesome gang war in the interior of the line. Like Coach Woody Hayes of Ohio State, Elliott stressed the quarterback-fullback offense. In Illinois' last 12 games — 10 last season and two this season — the quarterback and fullback handled the ball on 72.5% of the plays, letting the halfbacks have it only when the rest of the team went home to eat. Elliott also preferred a defense that gave ground like it was money. On only four plays all last season did the opposition gain more than 20 yards. The other 99% of the time Illinois yielded ground by the inch. To be sure, Illinois didn't have the snap and drill-team precision of Ohio State. Nor did it score big; only once last season did Illinois get more than 20 points in a game. But it was, like Ohio State's offense, enough to suffice — and to win the conference title.

The irony is that as Illinois became more and more a mirror image of Ohio State, Ohio State itself was changing. More and more Woody Hayes was accepting the existence — even the possibilities — of aerial warfare. Last year Ohio State attempted more passes than Michigan State, and completed more, on the average, than Illinois. In practice, the Buckeyes worked on a "volleyball defense," in which a ball is tipped in the air by one player and snared by another. It wasn't the first time that Woody Hayes had tried passing. When he first came to Ohio State he embraced the pass as cordially as any other coach: In 1951 Ohio State threw 172 passes, upped it to 217 the next year, and in 1953 threw another 181. But Ohio State won only 11 out of 20 Big Ten games during those seasons, and the alums were parodying one of their own alma mater's songs:

Come let's sing Ohio's praise;
Say goodbye to Woody Hayes.

So the next year, 1954, Woody became more conservative. Ohio State threw only 125 passes, and reduced that figure to 50 and 51 in the next two years — or just a few more passes in those three seasons than it had thrown in 1952 alone. It was clear that Woody much preferred grinding away at the middle of the line with the belly series and fullback smashes. Sometimes the action was so thick at center that trying to locate the ball was a little like trying to pick up a token in a subway turnstile during rush hour. Rivals jeered at everything but the results. Ohio State won the conference championship in three of those five years, and in one of them became the only team since 1913 to capture the conference title with seven consecutive wins.

But this season the substitution rule became almost as free as in the postwar years. That means teams could platoon, develop offensive and defensive specialists. Relieved of the burden of teaching both offense and defense to the same boys, Hayes decided to use the bonus time teaching the offense blocking on pass defense, how to run pass patterns and even so alien a concept as how to throw and catch the ball. Hayes became so enamored of the pass that he put two quarterbacks, not just one, into his backfield. One of them, Tom Barrington, plays left half. He is a strong, versatile boy who can — in the tradition of Ohio State quarterbacks — run better than he passes. The other, Don Unverferth, breaks that tradition. He is a quarterback who can pass better than he runs. Unverferth has large hands — he wears a size 13 glove — and he puts the index finger of his right hand on the rear tip of the ball, like a man about to throw a dart. ("You see, my brother was a quarterback, and we'd play catch and he'd always pass it to me, but I'd just throw it back to him any way I could," he says. The result is a quick, hard pass that in Ohio State's first two games led to completions 60.6% of the time.

Hayes went about preparing for the Illinois game as carefully as a Prussian general. First he circulated a dirty rumor about Butkus — that he was merely mortal. This was not easy to prove. Last year Butkus nailed Ohio State halfback Paul Warfield with a tackle that separated him from the football and set up an Illinois touchdown. Then he rattled Unverferth around on blitzes that set up another touchdown. But now Woody was shrewd enough not to test Butkus or the rest of the burly Illinois defense in head-to-head combat. Instead, he decided on a subtler tactic. Its seed could be found in a book on military strategy that Woody tucked into his luggage as he descended on Champaign. Part of its message was the indirect ap-

proach to combat delineated by Hanson Baldwin, the military analyst of *The New York Times.*

The translation from battlefield to ball field became clear in the
first few minutes of play when Ohio State intercepted one of
Custardo's third-down passes with its volleyball defense. The pass
hit the receiver's fingertips, and an Ohio State defender, John Fill,
picked it off and ran it back 49 yards to the Illinois 23-yard line. On
the first play Illinois was set for a wide halfback sweep or a pass;
that's what Ohio State customarily does after a sudden turnover.
Woody gave them the illusion of the sweep but not its substance. He
set up the whole flow of the play to the right and then sent Unverferth
bootlegging inside left end. Butkus and the whole Illinois defense
followed the play to the right, searching the various Ohio State backs
for the one who had the ball.

"Nobody even touched me until I got to the two-yard line," said
Unverferth later. That gave Ohio State its first touchdown and set the
tone for the whole game. Thereafter, the counteraction plays and
bootlegs had Illinois lunging hopelessly in the wrong direction.
Butkus' superb instinct for football was entirely neutralized by this
direct approach. When he wasn't frozen by the action of a counter-
play, he was wrestling desperately with fullback fakes into the line.
"Hanson Baldwin," said Woody, "would have been proud of us today."

So would Sammy Baugh or any of the high priests of passing.
Ohio State ran twice as many ground plays as pass plays, but the
team netted more yardage in the air than on the ground. On the cuff
of adhesive tape that Woody wears on his left forearm during a game
was printed his "short list" of plays. Illinois had seen only seven
different plays in scouting Ohio State against Indiana. Now Woody
had 15 running plays printed in blue ink on the cuff. "And I hate to
admit it, but almost that many passes," he said. One of them was a
tackle-eligible play that worked twice for 37 yards. "We got burned
by that play in the past," said Woody. "I'll tell you, if they want to
come and crowd us again, we'll pass next week, too."

But it was, finally, defense that won the game for Ohio State.
Hayes had worked hard on defense. He put the first-string defensive
team against his first-string offensive team for 25 minutes on
Wednesday and "they (the defense) really cut us up." (To the offense he said: "You guys look like Andy Gump.") By Friday night
the defense was so keyed up that a few of the players whiled away

the hours throwing up. On Saturday afternoon, however, the defense did not allow Illinois to get any closer to the Ohio State goal than the 31-yard line — and even that boldness did not come until midway through the fourth quarter when Ohio State held a 26-0 edge. In fact, Illinois got into Ohio State territory only four times all day, once in each quarter. The Ohio State defense repeatedly took the ball away in Illinois territory. Four of the five scores came with turnovers in Illinois territory — interceptions, recovered fumbles or the forcing of poor punts. "Our offense simply took advantage of the opportuities that our defense bought for us," said Hayes.

It stands to reason that if Woody Hayes can fall in love with the forward pass, anything can happen in the Big Ten, even at Michigan. For the last five years the Wolverines, under Coach Bump Elliott, have played such unsuccessfully conservative football that they have been accused of stealing Ohio State's worst plays. But last Saturday it finally became clear to even the most sullen and rebellious rooters of Michigan that a change has taken place. The Wolverines, ranked seventh in the country, beat Michigan State, ranked ninth, 17-10, for the first time since 1955, and in the process looked just about as exciting and powerful as the revamped Buckeyes.

Take the play that won the game. Losing, 10-9, with less than five minutes left, Michigan scored when quarterback Bob Timberlake pitched out to halfback Rick Sygar — pretty daring stuff right — who in turn lofted a 31-yard touchdown pass to end John Henderson. Unheard of. The victory kept Michigan undefeated and marked November 21 as a banner day in the Big Ten, the day that razzle-dazzle Michigan meets hipper-dipper Ohio State in the game that will likely mean the Rose Bowl, if not the national title.

8

Something To Shout About

November 11, 1968

By WILLIAM JOHNSON
Sports Illustrated

More than once he has been accused of being an anachronism —
a latterday Neanderthal charging into battle swinging the jawbone of
an ass against opponents equipped with Sidewinder missiles. In recent years, when his fortunes as a football coach ebbed, some con-
signed him to a dinosaurs' boneyard, a man outdistanced in his own
time. But Wayne Woodrow Hayes of Ohio State University refused
to be declared extinct. He thrust out his brawny paunch, squared his
incredible shoulders and spoke word written by his own personal
seer and philosopher, Ralph Waldo Emerson: "No law can be sacred
to me by that of my nature."

Last Saturday the contemporary justification — to say nothing of
the late-model reincarnation — of Woody Hayes was on display for
all to see. Before a record crowd of 84,859 at Ohio State's dreary old
hulk of a stadium in Columbus, his Buckeyes cut up and then beat
down Michigan State, a team that only a week earlier had defeated
high-ranked Notre Dame. The 25-20 victory proved that O.S.U.'s
stunning mid-October upset of Purdue was no fluke and heralded the
return of Hayes and his teams to fame and fortune. It was the Buckeyes' sixth straight win this season and it solidified their hold on the
No. 2 spot in the national rankings (No. 1 1/2 might be more like it,
considering the constant tribulations of top-ranked U.S.C.). More-
over, the Buckeyes are favored to win the Big Ten title, a Rose Bowl

trip and perhaps a chance to beat U.S.C. themselves — though all that will not be decided for certain until a climactic clash on Nov. 23 with that other upstart in the Big Ten, Michigan.

The success of Woody Hayes 1968 Buckeyes has generated excitement even within the booster club complacency of Columbus where, despite legends to the contrary, wild-eyed football fever long ago took a backseat to more cosmopolitan undertakings. Beyond the current victory string itself, the very style of Ohio State football this year is a stimulating sight — especially for eyes made sore in years past by the dust clouds raised as Hayes-built juggernauts slogged to dozens of victories with numbing repetitions of the fullback plunge.

Suddenly in 1968 Hayes has found speed to burn and the forward pass besides. His team has 16 sophomores who play consistently, and there is flair, flamboyance and a happy-go-lucky outlook that might have been put down as treason on Ohio State teams of yore. But Hayes is a wise and flexible man; he knows how to flex with a good thing when he sees it, and this fall on his Columbus practice fields he has seen it every day.

Saturday, Michigan State saw it, too. O.S.U.'s first-string sophomore quarterback, Rex Kern, opened the game — from his own 17, no less — with three quick passes. Then after setting up an 18-yard run of his own with some polished fakery, he threw another pass for 39 yards and finally sent fullback Jim Otis in for the first Buckeye score with only 1:43 gone in the quarter.

There was still scarcely a speck of O.S.U. dust in the air late in the first quarter when sophomore safetyman Mike Sensibaugh recovered a Spartan fumble. Kern immediately threw twice for long yardage and then lofted a 14-yard pass to sophomore end Bruce Jankowski in the end zone. With a mere minute gone in the second quarter the score was 13-0, Kern had completed 10 of 13 passes for 148 yards, and — in another break with Hayes tradition — had called nearly all of the plays himself. But the touchdown pass was Kern's last play of the day; he was taken out with a severely sprained ankle and spent the afternoon slouched sadly on the bench with a bag of ice taped to his foot.

This might have mattered a lot, but not to the modern model of the Buckeyes. Besides speed, youth and style, Hayes has accumulated around him a shocking number of attentive wunderkinder. When Kern went out, in came another child quarterback, sophomore Ron Maciejowski. He displayed neither the grace nor aplomb of Kern, but he was more than adequate as he took O.S.U. for an easy touchdown and a 19-7 lead as the half ended. From then on it was a matter of Michigan State almost catching up — only not quite. When the score eventually narrowed to 25-20 at the end of three quarters the defense stepped into the act and all over the chest of Spartan quarterback Bill Triplett. Again and again Triplett was pressed into fumbles and bad handoffs, primarily by O.S.U.'s Mike Radtke and Dave Whitfield who make a specialty of falling on the ball once it was loose. Three times in the fourth quarter the Spartans lost the ball on fumbles, and O.S.U., though it never scored again, secured its victory ably enough. The clock ran out with the Buckeyes punching at the center of the Michigan State line on play after play — bringing to mind old times under Hayes.

But this is obviously a shiny new era in Ohio — a time of resurrection. Oh, Hayes is not exactly playing the phoenix, rising with a smile from his own ashes of disaster. Things have never been that bad for him. Seventeen full seasons have passed since he was first hired at Ohio State, then infamous as America's leading cemetery for football coaches: O.S.U. had had four in the 10 years preceding Woody's arrival. Despite the funeral prospects, he prospered, compiling a fine 107-41-7 record that included four Big Ten championships and two Rose Bowl wins. He has had some dismal years. There was a 3-5-1 in 1959 and 4-5 in 1966 when a small plane was seen flying over the O.S.U. stadium carrying a sign that read: GOODBYE WOODY. He has easily survived such disloyalties, but he has not been really in the limelight since 1961 when his team went undefeated on the football field, only to fall crushed and beaten beneath a faculty committee that voted to ban Ohio State participation in that season's Rose Bowl.

Then renowned for his rages, culminating in such acts of personal damage as shoving his head through a wooden locker door or pounding his skull with his fists hard enough to make knots rise, Hayes took years to cool his fury over that episode. Indeed, even today he blames the relatively lean records of his teams in the mid-60's in part on that faculty vote. "All our rival recruiters had to say to a boy was, 'Son, if you go to Ohio State, you probably won't ever see the Rose Bowl,' and the boy would go off to another school."

Around Columbus there are people who claim Hayes has mellowed, that he has so softened his approach to life he is wearing a Thermal undershirt beneath the short-sleeved T shirt that he favors for practice, even on sub-freezing days. ("Being cold, like being determined to win, is just a state of mind," he has always told his teams.) Of course, Woody Hayes is no mean psychologist, and he has even been accused of pre-planning some of his wilder tantrums for maximum impact on his team. For example, he wears a baseball cap to practice every day and, periodically through a season, he will seemingly go berserk with anger over some error. He will bellow, snatch the cap off his head, twist it in his huge meaty hands and then fling it on the ground — tattered, shredded, destroyed. But occasionally, those wise to his ways contend, he has used a razor blade to slice some threads in the cap before practice so that it tears apart more dramatically, and easily. There was a time, too, when Woody punctuated his practice-field rages by ripping a watch from his wrist and jumping on it while springs flew all over the ground. On such days, it is said, he tended to wear cheap, dime-store watches. But the man was impressive, regardless.

Those who think that this phase of Woody Hayes has passed, that he is turning sophomore quarterbacks loose while pastorally sniffing life's flowers, just don't know their man. They might understandably be deceived by his always turning to the bracing words of Emerson, reaching for his dog-eared paperback of the *Essays* so that he can read aloud front dozens of passages he has underlined. " 'Blame is safer than praise,' " he recently quoth. "And that's what I tell the boys' all the time — that this niceness from people complimenting you can be what kills you. It can be deceiving. Yes, sir, Emerson was hitting the ball square when he said, 'As soon as honeyed words of praise are spoken for me I feel as one who lies unprotected before his enemies.' "

And so it was not too surprising when Hayes recently became infuriated and wasted no honeyed words over what he considered lax officiating. All season, he said, people have been beating up his quarterback. He told the press that too much piling on was permitted in Big Ten games, and he promised to complain officially to the league office. He never did file any complaint in writing, and Big Ten Commissioner Bill Reed, irked at Woody's public tirade, snapped to reporters last week: "We haven't heard much from Woody lately because his teams haven't been so good. Now he's unbeaten and talking again. He reminds me of what Winston Churchill said about General Montgomery — indomitable in defeat, insufferable in victory."

"Listen," said Hayes himself last week. "I'm not mellow. I'm the same guy I've always been and I'll tell you this, the minute I think

I'm getting mellow, then I'm retiring. Who ever heard of a mellow winner!?"

That's Woody. Indomitable, insufferable, unmellow, thoroughly

9

Defense And Rex Make A King

January 13, 1969

By DAN JENKINS
Sports Illustrated

The many theories of Big Game Winning in football echo through the sport like the growls of Woody Hayes. Big games are won on defense, it is said. Big games are won on preparation. Big games are won "up front" with emotion, with momentum, by the better quarterback, by coaching, on the fewest mistakes, with field position, with the kicking game and sometimes by the One Great Scorer who comes to write against your face mask. And, finally, it is said that big games are usually *lost* and not won, but this is normally the lament of a loser. The truth is that big games are decided by a combination of these things and the truest thing of all is that what *should* have happened in this season's Big Game, ahem, in fact, uh, did.

What should have happened in the Rose Bowl contest last week between No. 1 and No. 2 is that Ohio State should have beaten U.S.C., 27 to 16. This final score is somewhat irrelevant because the game really ended on the third play of the fourth quarter when the Buckeyes roared ahead by 20-10. An additional Trojan mistake added to Ohio State's total, and an official's mistake donated a meaningless touchdown to U.S.C. at the end, but the big game really lasted only 46 minutes and eight seconds, which was the time elapsed when Rex Kern — the better quarterback — threw a scoring pass to put Ohio State up by 10.

With the wondrous O.J. Simpson running 80 smog free yards to the foot of the Sierra Madre, U.S.C. had been a good enough team to take a 10-0 lead in the second period and offer up the possibility that this one peerless back might just be dazzling enough to overcome the team strength of Ohio State throughout the beautiful afternoon. But this was asking too much. It takes a strong team to chew its way back from 10 points down to 10 ahead, and O.S.U. was that strong any way you wanted to measure it.

Rex Kern proved to be a more effective quarterback than U.S.C.'s Steve Sogge. Ohio State's corps of runners — Jim Otis, Leophus Hayden and Kern — counterbalanced O.J. and the Ohio State defense, front, back and sideways, made the big plays that U.S.C.'s did not.

It is only the esthetics of football which says that the offense not the defense, should make the turning-point play in such a game. It would have been seemly and thrilling if Simpson could have burst loose again, and if Ohio State could have won with a long drive at the finish — if, in other words, the game had not ended prematurely. That would have been the suspense drama that the Rose Bowl's 102,000 flag wavers and Nixon-watchers might have been happier with. But the Ohio State defense was simply too impatient. When the Buckeyes' Bill Urbanik, an unesthetic tackle, rammed into Sogge's back, forcing him to fumble at his own 21-yard line, and when Vic Stottlemyer recovered for Ohio State, the play of the day had occurred. Not an 80-yard run or a leaping pass catch. Just a passer dropping back, being smothered and losing the ball. An ugly play, really, as unglamorous as Woody's white fishnet jerseys but part of what football is all about — taking the ball away from the other team.

At this point the score was 13-10, with Ohio State leading in an ultraclose, thoroughly stimulating affair that was as far from being settled as Columbus, Ohio, is from Pasadena. No one could have been more aware than the suddenly desperate Trojans that to let Ohio State seize this opportunity to score, to jump ahead by 10 points, would be catastrophic. Nor was there any guarantee that U.S.C. would allow it to happen. Earlier, in the first quarter, the Buckeyes had driven to a first down at the Trojan 14, but Coach John McKay's forces had held.

Yet this could be the ball game, this fumble, and Rex Kern was personally going to see to it that it was. One of the first things Kern did was get away for a crucial gain on what Hayes calls his quarterback's "third dimension."

Kern drifted back to pass at the U.S.C. 18, saw himself being enclosed by crimson shirts on both sides and quickly looked for the third dimension — the open alley in the middle. It was there, so Rex ran. For 14 huge, golden yards he ran. Momentarily after this it seemed U.S.C. had a chance to escape by giving up only a field goal, for two plays netted Ohio State zero. Now it was third down for the Buckeyes at the U.S.C. four-yard line. With McKay's defense dug in for the run, or perhaps the dropback pass, Kern had another key play — a first dimension. He faked the middle, rolled to his left and threw a perfect little pass to Leophus Hayden, his halfback, who had sneaked lonesomely into the left-hand corner of the end zone.

These two plays — the run and the pass, both in clutch moments — demonstrated Rex Kern's superiority at quarterback. He is a bigger, stronger, faster and more instinctive football player than U.S.C.'s Steve Sogge, so Kern certainly should be a better quarterback. The amazing thing about Sogge is that he took the Trojans as far as he did. He is a kid that John McKay never thought would make it. But few coaches ever got more out of a player than McKay got out of Sogge, so he will just have to be excused for the Rose Bowl loss.

So will O.J. Simpson. The Heisman winner committed a pair of important errors during the afternoon, but they were not his two widely discussed fumbles. These did not hurt that much, although fumbles never help anything. One fumble came when the score was still tied, and Ohio State did not capitalize on it. The other came after the game was lost. What Simpson did do — which almost nobody noticed — was underestimate the speed of Jack Tatum, Ohio State's demon cornerback, on a swing pass that should have been a touchdown, and then on the same series he overthrew a cinch touchdown pass to end Ted DeKraai, the kind you complete to your 6-year-old son in the backyard.

These plays came on U.S.C.'s initial significant drive. On the first, Simpson took the pass from Sogge for 16 yards down to the Ohio State three-yard line. He was breezing into the end zone, he thought, when out of nowhere flashed Tatum. The Buckeye sophomore saved four points, the difference between a touchdown and a field goal, by bouncing O.J. out of bounds. O.J. was not burning speed or he would have scored. He just didn't see Tatum coming, he said later, and he didn't know Tatum was that fast, anyhow, although McKay respected the Buckeye defender by shaping his game plan to work away from him. Three plays later O.J. overthrew the pass, and U.S.C. came away with three points instead of seven.

This did not seem to matter much moments thereafter when O.J. got loose on a pitchout to the short side of the field, broke two tackles, faked a third man dizzy with a 180-degree cutback and sprinted 80 yards to a touchdown on the prettiest run of any Rose Bowl ever. It seemed then that O.J. was going to close out his splendid two years in the grandest of style.

He did, in fact, wind up with 171 yards, which is hardly an argument that Ohio State stopped him. He repeatedly kept the game rocking with good runs and pass catches. In his whole two years at U.S.C. he never stopped being the best collegiate runner that most of us have ever seen or will be seeing for quite a while.

But as the reign of O.J. ends, the reign of Ohio State's Woody Hayes and Rex Kern begins — or continues. Woody has been proving all season that the game has far from passed him by, and he made this unmistakably clear in Pasadena. His preparations were superb, right down to not letting his squad overeat or be overimpressed by the scenery, an attitude that outraged local boosters. Woody was tough in practice, and the California press thought even tougher with them. Offensively, he believed he could run U.S.C.'s middle, and he did. "We knew if they studied us, they'd want to stop us outside first, and they did a good job of it. But that gave us the inside running and the curl-in passes. They couldn't stop everything," he said.

Woody claimed, shortly before leaving on his annual visit with the troops in Vietnam, that he was not rattled or stunned when he trailed by 10 point. "We'd found out that we could run on 'em," he said. "And I didn't figure O.J. was going to break another one. I still thought we'd win."

One of the rather frightening aspects of the victory, for Ohio State's future opponents at least, is that Woody gets back Rex Kern and almost everybody else. True, he loses his big tackles, Dave Foley and Rufus Mayes, and a terrific linebacker, Mark Stier, and a few others from around the trenches, but Ohio State has never had a problem filling the trenches. Some of Woody's past teams looked like 11 tackles who had flipped a coin to see who took the snapbacks. But the throwers and the catchers and the runners and such superb defensive backs as Tatum and Mike Sensibaugh all come back to Woody for 1969 and most of them for 1970 as well. "They never made a mistake," said a discouraged U.S.C. player afterward. They may not for two more years.

10

The Reincarnation Of Woody Hayes

November 21, 1969

By WILLIAM BARRY FURLONG
Life

Sun Tzu is his god, and *Ping Fa* is his bible. "Deviation — it's all in the deviation," says Ohio State football coach Woody Hayes. He is describing the art of successful warfare as handed down by the Chinese military strategist Sun Tzu (4th Century B.C.) in his classic *Ping Fa,* as well as the style of football now prosecuted by the team that was No. 1 in the nation going into last Saturday's game. ". . .after enticing the enemy out of the way, and though starting after him," counseled Sun Tzu, "to contrive to reach the goal before him, shows knowledge of the art of deviation." That is exactly how Woody Hayes does it, in this particular incarnation.

For a long time, Woody Hayes was renowned as the Field Marshal Joffre of college football, dogging straight ahead through enemy trenches. Part of it was because of a trait he still has: his militaristic perfectionism. For years he expressed his frustration when plays misfired by tearing off his cap or his watch, throwing it on the ground and stomping on it. (Cynics insist he wears cheap watches.) This year, his 19th at Ohio State, he added a new tactic: he bites into the fleshy heel of his hand until the blood flows. At times, he cannot restrain his more visceral instincts. "Woody's idea of sublimating," says an acquaintance, "is to hit someone."

Over the years, he belligerently bellied up to everybody from rival coaches to his own players, as much to motivate the latter as to intimidate the former. A year or so ago, he publicly pushed, shoved and then battered one of his finest players on the pads and helmet so fiercely that the kid ran off around the track crying. He was not hurt — he was frustrated that he could not hit back. The result was that on Saturday the kid played his finest game, and this season he is almost certain to become an all-America. "So he sublimated exactly the way Woody wanted him to," says a friend.

But Hayes's Joffrean reputation was rooted most deeply in the style of football his teams played. For years Ohio State fielded behemoths who dug in and fought for every inch of ground. Woody recruited big, strong kids who had only one kind of compassion: they always frisked their opponents for signs of life before throwing them away. Woody taught them trench warfare and little else. It was not uncommon for Ohio State to spend an entire day's practice on one play — No. 26, fullback off right tackle. . . and then spend the next day on fullback off left tackle.

Hayes sought real running ability at only one position — quarterback. That's because he didn't want the boy to be tempted to pass. It was Woody Hayes who first said, "There are only three things that can happen on a pass, and two of them are bad." His style was celebrated as the ultimate in dull, enormously successful football. In those days, under Hayes, Ohio State won pieces of two national championships, two Rose Bowl games and three Big Ten titles in four years. In the process, it put together the longest winning streak in conference history: 17 consecutive games.

However, some eight years ago Ohio State's "three yards and a cloud of dust" offense began producing more dust than yards. Over the six-year period that followed, the Buckeyes lost or tied 19 games. This was not good enough, as far as Woody Hayes was concerned, even though Ohio State continued to lead the nation in attendance. Then Woody got to reading Sun Tzu and digging deviation.

Hayes studies military affairs the way a lepidopterist studies moths. In one brief discussion of football recently, he strung together quotes from General Rommel, Patton, Guderian and Sherman ("Sherman ran an option play right through the South") and mixed them with a dash of philosophy from Santayana. For a long time, his favorite text was *Strategy,* a book by the British military analyst B. H. Liddell Hart. "I've been carrying that around with me for years." In it he found reference to Sun Tzu and his *Ping Fa.* Woody turned to the English translation by Samuel B. Griffith, called *The Art of War* and studied Sun Tzu's "indirect approach."

And, presto, a few years ago Ohio State adopted it. Woody began recruiting boys who were fast, agile and who might — under strong cross-examination — admit that they'd heard of the forward pass even if they denied they'd ever committed it. He also began attacking on a broad front instead of trying to penetrate a massed defense: he used his fullback on end sweeps, option plays and pass patterns. For the offense as a whole, he used speed and deception — "deviation" as he and Sun Tzu like to call it. Indeed he turned up with a quarterback named Rex Kern who isn't big, isn't strong and who runs like a man standing still. But he can throw the football. "Kern gives our attack all the same offense principles General Sherman used. . . ."

Having subdued his art, or at least reduced it to manageable proportions, Woody Hayes last season used deviation to take Ohio State to the Rose Bowl and the national championship. Through the first seven games of this season, the Buckeyes were again undefeated. Going into last Saturday's game with Purdue, a rugged team with a long-standing reputation as spoilers, Ohio State had a chance to tie its own Big Ten record for consecutive victories.

Woody Hayes bore into this season the authentically melancholy stigmata of the successful football coach. He is compulsive, direct, narrow in interest, quite free of high sophistication and so serious that success has failed to wrench joy out of him. He has never learned to take a formal vacation; some years ago he went on a 12-day outing his wife planned, only to give up in exasperation after three days. Nor can he let his assistants take a vacation. A year or so ago, Hayes tracked down one assistant vacationing in the South, then flew to Atlanta, checked into a hotel and phoned the assistant to say he just happened to be in the neighborhood. Then Woody asked, ever so casually, "Can you come over so we can talk a little football?"

The game occupies all of Woody's waking moments and most of his sleeping ones. He frequently sleeps overnight on a hard-cushioned bench in his office, a cubicle as large as a nun's cell, so that he can get up during the night and study game movies. In the course of a year he sees more film than Darryl F. Zanuck, studying and restudying every possible detail of an opponent's game. Occasionally he becomes concerned about ignoring his family. "So after one game," says his wife, Anne, "Woody said we'd forget football that night and he'd take me to dinner and the movies. He took me to dinner all right. But the movies were four hours of game films."

Hayes sees this remorseless preparation as a lugubrious reflection on himself and his intellect. "I was always third in line in intelligence and personality among the children in my family," he says. One of three children of the school superintendent of a small Ohio district, Woody felt overshadowed by his sister, Mary Hayes ("She became a leading lady on Broadway opposite George Jessel"), and his late brother, Ike ("He was the most colorful character I ever met").

As a youth Woody felt terribly insecure about anything but his willingness to work. He still feels he has no spontaneous insight or brilliance; indeed, some critics have said he gets stuck in a game plan and can't adjust to changing conditions. "It's when I hurry into something — that's when I don't do very well," he says. "That's why I'm a hermit, a recluse during the football season. I have to work harder to do what comes easily to other people."

In his lonely disciplined struggle, Woody Hayes has learned how to handle people without learning how to relate to them. Last year, after a great Ohio State victory, he was suddenly touched by the poverty of some black kids who hung around the stadium long after the game. Hayes wanted to do something for one of them but he couldn't think of anything to give him. Woody never carries money; he doesn't really care about it. (He's the most successful and most senior coach in the Big Ten but he is only the fourth highest paid.) He paced in agitation for a while, then finally sat down and took off his shoes and socks. His gift: the sweaty socks he had on.

Unlike most coaches, Woody disdains the usual home-team cocktail party after a game. "He doesn't drink, he doesn't smoke and he wouldn't come anyway," says his wife. His pleasures are more private. "He reads for at least a half hour every night, no matter how late he gets home, if he gets home. One summer I decided I'd read whatever he was reading," says Anne. "The first book he gave me was *Skylines of the World*." He relates all his reading, which is omnivorous and indiscriminate, to business, no matter how distant the association. In talking football, he has quoted everybody from Doenitz to Disney, from Herodotus to Sir Joshua Reynolds. His favorite nonmilitary author is Ralph Waldo Emerson. "For every strength," Woody says of football, "there is a consequent weakness." His source: Emerson's essay on compensation.

Hayes is such a compelling speaker that, as a longtime associate says, "if you want to hate Woody Hayes, then you must never let yourself hear him make a speech." But many people have always wanted to hate Hayes. When his first teams at Ohio State won only 11 of 21 Big Ten games, alumni started singing, "Come let's sing Ohio's praise / Say goodbye to Woody Hayes." Since then success has calmed alumni — but not the coaches who oppose him. That hardly bothers Woody Hayes. "I'm not trying to win a popularity poll. I'm trying to win football games," he says, "I don't like nice people. I like tough, honest people." His own tough honesty has all the tact of a keelhauling.

He is a poor loser — he has refused to shake hands with coaches who beat him — and an insufferable winner. Some years ago, after Ohio State beat the then champion of the Pacific Coast colleges in the Rose Bowl, which were just beginning to enjoy the conceit that they were back in bigtime football, he said that he could think of four Big Ten schools better than the one he'd just defeated. That made him as popular in California as an earthquake.

"What was I supposed to do — lie to them or tell them what I really believe?" he says. It never occurred to him to explore the alternative of simply not answering. "Keeping it in," Hayes says, "is the way to get an ulcer."

There are those who feel he has mellowed with age — he's 56 now — and success. Hayes denies it, saying, "I don't want to be known as that nice old man." He changed his strategy but not his method. He is still excruciating about details. He takes a dentist, as well as a doctor, on road trips, and every year he has all his players take an electroencephalogram so that he will have something to measure against the possibility of a head injury. He is still militant about mistakes. He has a special practice jersey with restraining straps for the hands of linemen given to offensive holding, and he pays an official to work at every practice — in striped shirt with red flag — to call penalties just as he would in a ball game. (And just as he would in a ball game, Hayes sometimes charges the official to express his outrage at a particular call.) He is less militant on social change: "I'm not a law-and-order man," he says, "I'm a law-and-orderly-change man." He has not resisted the new style in college kids. He has only one player on the traveling squad with a crewcut. Most of the other players have extravagant sideburns and wear large, wildly colored "Clyde caps." "We control by attitudes rather than rules," he says.

He has a growing sensitivity to the attitudes of the kids, even in his most emotional moments. The new breed, for instance, is not altogether submissive about his physical approach. One player, very large and very mean, confided to intimates that if Coach Hayes ever laid a finger on him, he'd kill him. The consensus was that he would; it's the new spirit on campus.

So when Hayes began getting worked up about this kid's performance in one practice, the rest of the squad gathered around, like auto-racing fans at a treacherous turn. At the very peak of his outrage, Hayes drew back his hand and everybody flinched — to avoid the splattering of Woody's blood. But then, in the last microsecond, something clicked in Hayes and he sensed a better move. He turned and hit the pads of the kid standing next to his target.

11

Ohio State:
Alone At The Top

Nobember 24, 1969

By DAN JENKINS
Sports Illustrated

This is just the seed of an idea, gang, but you can go ahead and slap it on the side of your helmet with all those Buckeye leaves and see if it will stick. The deal is this. On New Year's Day when even Notre Dame is in a postseason football game for the first time in 45 years and when Texas and Penn State are struggling to present their cases for No. 1, let's all go back out to gray, icy contemptible old Columbus, Ohio, and play us the game of the decade, which we would call the Woody Bowl. We'll take that Ohio State offense with Rex Kern all wound up and put it at one end of the field, and we'll take that Ohio State defense with Jack Tatum pawing at the turf — and by now wanted for manslaughter in Lafayette, Ind. — and put it at the other. And then on a signal like, say, the dropping of a few assorted No. 1 trophies at midfield, we'll let them come screaming at one another while we, being careful, somewhat like Purdue last week, press our forefingers to our ears and turn our heads away just before impact.

It would be some crash, boy, but it might be the only way this dazed collegiate world of 1969 would ever find out what the best team in the country is. The other major undefeateds can howl all they wish but if the Buckeyes do it to Michigan this week they will be the national champions for the second year in a row — and what the college game will have on its hands is another of those dynasty things, one of those Oklahomas of the mid-1950s which won 4,000 straight games or something.

And the only question left will be this one about whether Ohio State's offense or defense is the more magnificent. There are these two teams out there in Columbus, you see, as most everybody in that disaster area once known as the Big Ten can tell you. There is the offense belonging to quarterback Rex Kern and occasionally to Coach Woody Hayes — when Woody can get the plays in before Rex can call the snap. It is perhaps the only attack in the nation that makes a defense hear footsteps. It is an offense that rages for about 46 points a game and already is the highest-scoring team in Ohio State history even though the first unit wouldn't know a fourth quarter from chemistry lab.

And then there is the defense belonging to cornerback Jack Tatum down on the field and assistant coach Lou McCullough up in the booth. This is a destruction outfit that encourages itinerant ballcarriers and pass receivers to slip down and crawl under the grass before the redshirts arrive, one that goes around limiting opponents to just over a touchdown per Saturday in an era when touchdowns are cheaper by the dozen.

All season long it has been impossible for Buckeye watchers, who travel in groups of 86,000, give or take an extra mackinaw, to decide which of the two units is more responsible for Ohio State's success or, as a matter of fact, which is the more fun to be awed by.

Last Saturday, the Purdue game was supposed to furnish the big answer for everyone. Ohio State would be meeting a good team at last after seven consecutive rag dolls. Purdue was a 7-1 team averaging 37 points a game, a laughing conqueror of Notre Dame, a team with a devastating history of concocting upsets over No. 1s; indeed, a team led by the brilliance of Mike Phipps, who was merely the total offense leader of the U.S., perhaps the top draft choice of the pros and a very serious candidate for that coveted, oversized paper-weight known as the Heisman Trophy.

Some answer. The game worked out pretty much the way Woody Hayes confidentially told a close friend it would. "You don't think our kids are gonna let this slip away from them now, do you?" he had said. That philosophy gradually worked its way around Columbus last week and everybody believed it to the point that when Purdue was discussed Buckeye fans would hold up five fingers and say, "We win by this — and I don't mean five points."

They were right, of course. It was about 70-7 in tone and 42-14 on the scoreboard, but it did nothing to settle the gnawing question about the relative stupendousness of those two separate teams that Ohio State has — Kern's and Tatum's. Both played out their roles as friskily as usual, knocking so many Purdue guys backwards and sometimes out you would have thought that Woody had scheduled Hanoi.

With Kern running, passing, faking, blocking and in spare moments looking around for concrete portals to run into, the offense got its usual quota of six touchdowns, four of them before the half, by which time the game was of course over. The 186-pound, 6' junior, who has one of those squinty-eyed expressions like the neighborhood prankster and always seems to be smiling, did everything so expertly he made most of his worshipers forget that their feet were frozen.

On a day when a lot of mistakes would have been excused because of the stadium's refrigeration, young Rex wrought not only those 42 points but some 436 yards in total offense as he personally ran for two touchdowns and hurled a 38-yard pass for another. He was so frenzied out there at times that he had the team racing out of the huddle and lining up before Hayes could shuttle in the call.

"Sometimes the plays from the bench ruin our momentum," Kern explained later. "We had 'em on the ropes and I wanted to get it in there."

Nor was the defense bothered by the cold, the 23 degrees and the 20-mile winds that forced Woody Hayes, who always wears shirtsleeves, to put on a jacket. The defense not only had the killing presence of Tatum — another of those boisterous juniors, roaming the secondary to make Purdue's receivers believe they were hearing the Chinese army marching down the Olentangy River Road — but it also had a lot of special tricks Lou McCullough had worked up for stopping Mike Phipps. It had floating zones, concealed man-for-mans and surprise blitzes, a variety of defensive innovations with such marvelous names as "Eddie Go" and "Cindy Crash." With it all, the Ohio defenders practically gave a daylong demonstration of how to set the passing game back to 1912.

Five interceptions it got. Three fumbles it got. A punt return for a touchdown it got. And a miserly 29 yards rushing it allowed poor old Purdue, which tried to use exactly what Ohio State figured it would try to use. "They'll send five men out," McCullough had said. "They'll try to catch us in double cover on the outs and hit us in the seams, and pretty much at 20 and 30 yards, but we'll be there. I might guess wrong with him a few times but maybe our kids can pick it up."

Much of the game nowadays is played upstairs in isolated booths. Up there a coach calls a play to the bench where another coach signals to the quarterback who takes it to the line and then uses it or an audible. Meanwhile, another coach calls a defense to the bench, which is signaled to the field, whereupon a defender uses it or changes it at the last second by hollering out such things as "Stay, stay," or "Go, go."

At Ohio State the defense is entirely in the mind and yelling of McCullough, a little Southerner who has been with Woody since 1963. Hayes almost never sees the defense, and there is this joke that he hardly knows the players' names. The last time he even spoke to Jack Tatum, the story goes, is when he was a freshman who one day returned a punt zigzag about 60 yards for a touchdown against the varsity, and Woody, on the verge of ripping up his cap or biting his wrist, or whatever he has been known to do out of the intensity that consumes him, went up to Tatum and said, "Son, at Ohio State we run straight for the goal line."

Well, it really might not matter whether Woody's offense or McCullough's defense is the more spectacular. They combine to make up one of the most imposing teams of any season, one that carries a 22-game winning streak into Michigan this week, one that has piled up 371 points in eight Saturdays and, just as important as anything, one that will lose only seven players out of the top 22 for 1970. Kern and Tatum and a lot of other fierce individuals will be back, which suggests that the only thing the Buckeyes have to fear in the immediate future is their preseason scrimmages.

This is such a good team, in fact, that one must pause for a moment and think about what it all means. First, there is this business of winning a second straight national title, which will come, either unanimously or in shares thereof with a victory over Michigan. If it is pretty much unanimous, then that will not have been done since Bud Wilkinson's Sooners of 1955-56, the Tommy McDonald-Jerry Tubbs crowd.

Next, with so many Kerns and Tatums returning next season, one has to assume that the prospects are certainly bright for three in a row, which hasn't been accomplished since the Glenn Davis-Doc Blanchard forces at Army in the 1940s. Bright isn't a bad word for it. The Buckeyes open with such dandies in 1970 as Texas A&M and

Duke and then they go into the sadly weakened Big Ten for the same staggering lineup of foes, except that improving Michigan and troublesome Minnesota must come to Columbus.

Woody felt, incidentally, that the Minnesota game (a paltry 43-7 victory) was this year's team letdown, but he likes to blame it on a Friday night movie. "The kids went to see that *Easy Rider*," he said, "and they were so depressed by it they didn't play well."

This becomes more amusing when one scans the Buckeye squad and notices all the deep sideburns, mustaches and shaggy hair, which Woody permits as a bit of an irony to his nature. Hayes may be an enthusiastic hawk, one who is returning to Vietnam this Christmas (for the fifth year in a row), but he is a realist who knows ballplayers have to stay happy. Happiness is winning with sideburns today. He has also avoided any problems with his black athletes, primarily by using them even when he shouldn't. Example: he started John Brockington at fullback once this year ahead of Jim Otis, his leading scorer and ground-gainer. Brockington was delighted and Otis was so annoyed he started running tougher than ever. Wily old Woody.

Another national championship this season would mean something special to this most cantankerous and yet fascinating of coaches. It would give him four such titles, tying him with people like Frank Leahy and Bernie Bierman as having the most ever—and it would put him safely and surprisingly up on a number of coaching geniuses like Bear Bryant, Knute Rockne and Wilkinson, who each won only three. And next year of course Woody would have a chance to make it six, given the good health of Rex Kern and Jack Tatum.

Kern was involved in three plays against Purdue that demonstrated precisely what kind of athlete he is. On one of them he proved he has as good an arm as anyone when he drifted back to throw that long touchdown pass to end Bruce Jankowski. The Purdue rush, big and tall, was bearing right into him, right there in his face, but Rex let sail a beauty that must have traveled 40 yards in the air and Jankowski, who never broke stride, took it between two defenders who were half a step late. This was the play that made the score 28-0, a runaway, for it also proved not only to Purdue but to the national television audience that Ohio State can beat you every way there is.

Kern does a lot of running on intentional option keeps but he rambles just as well when he darts out of a passing pocket and improvises. Doing both he got nearly 100 yards on the Boilermakers, but he gave back a whole bunch of it the one time the Purdue rush trapped him. Anyhow, there was this one special time when Rex came out of the pocket and steamed upfield and hurled himself head-long into a clutch of defenders. It took one of them a couple of moments to get up while Rex bounded back to the huddle clapping his hands.

The other time, when Kern showed what kind of iron framework he has, was when he unleashed a long incompletion under another furious rush. The instant the ball left his hand a big Purdue end, Bill McKoy, who happens to be 6' 4", 230 and mean, popped him so hard Kern did an absolute backward flip and sort of skidded to a halt. At first it looked as if several things had been broken because Rex held his chest and moved slowly. In a minute, however, he was running as fanatically as ever, looking for somebody to hit.

Although he has splendid help from players like Otis and Leo Hayden and Larry Zelina, Kern is the player who gives Ohio State a great attack, just as Jack Tatum stands out among Lou McCullough's glittering array of defenders, which include the nose guard Jim Stillwagon, the other stars in the secondary such as Mike Sensibaugh, Ted Provost and Tim Anderson and linebacker Phil Strickland. All of their headgear are littered with those leafy decals for valor. Buck-eye leaves. They get them all kinds of ways, and as many as 42 have been awarded in a single game. They wear them only on the right, which may or may not have any significance.

The unfortunate thing about this Ohio State team, as we all know, is that it has no place to go on New Year's Day. Woody has said that if — if, he stresses — his team winds up No. 1, it will be a shame to hide it, this being the centennial year of college football. He would go back to the Rose Bowl if the Big Ten would waive the no-repeat rule, or he would even go somewhere else to play Texas or whoever winds up No. 2. The chance remains slim, however, that the Big Ten faculty representatives will permit it. College football might be 100 years old, but books and lectures are older.

And anyhow, it might not be so bad to spend the holidays the way halfback Larry Zelina expects to spend them in Ohio.

"It might be kind of fun to sit by the fire on New Year's Day and watch all the games," Zelina said. "Knowing you're No. 1."

12

A Freshman Named Archie

October 9, 1972

By DAN JENKINS
Sports Illustrated

Somewhere back in the history of college football there was a stereotyped coach, complete with growl, baggy canvas pants, baseball cap and whistle around the neck who conjured up the myth that freshmen cannot play varsity ball because they are inexperienced and undeveloped. Innocently, the world has lived with that myth for quite a while, without questioning it, except during the periods of the Second World War and the Korean involvement. Freshmen cannot play. Not ready yet. That's it.

Well, here we all now sit in Ohio Stadium, all 86,000 of us, right here on the banks of Woody Hayes' Olentangy River in Columbus, in utter and complete shock at the whirling, dashing sight of 18-year-old Archie Griffin, a freshman tailback, three days in classes at Ohio State, who has just ripped off a record 239 yards inside a 50-year-old cement edifice that has seen the cleats of the very best. Archie Griffin has just spun off wicked runs of 55 yards and 22 yards and 20 yards and 11 yards and assorted runs of six and eight and nine yards. He has sneaked through tiny little holes in the line and he has slid outside and tiptoed down sidelines. He has bumped into people from North Carolina and knocked them down. He has burst into the sunlight of the secondary and darted this way and that. He has scored a touchdown and set up other touchdowns and a field goal and won a game for the Buckeyes, the final score being 29-14.

This is essentially a fullback park. Ohio Stadium belongs to all of those fellows from Woody Hayes' past who run a thing called the Robust-T and who send thunder into the minds of visitors. This is a place where the 86,000 are accustomed to watching gentlemen like Hubert Bobo and Matt Snell and Will Sander and Bob Ferguson and Jim Otis and John Brockington go bang-crash-crunch into people while most of them are wondering why they keep coming out to see it and agree that they probably wouldn't if Woody's teams didn't always win much more than they lose.

But into this fullback's paradise, and in front of the roaring crowd, came this teenager last Saturday to break a 27-year-old Buckeye rushing record with astonishing ease, and break the Tar Heels along with it. As North Carolina's Bill Dooley said afterward, "We came here not even knowing Archie Griffin existed, and now you tell me he's a freshman!"

Griffin was most likely a happy surprise to Woody Hayes himself, although Woody outfought Navy and Northwestern to recruit him last spring. Probably talked him into staying home during lunch one afternoon at Woody's favorite eatery, the Big Bear Supermarket.

Ohio State played an opening game two weeks prior to North Carolina, and in that 21-0 victory over Iowa, Archie Griffin, a freshman, had appeared for only a moment. Toward the end. Now he's averaging 119.5 yards a game.

Anyone following Columbus high school football might have guessed on Friday evening that the weekend would belong to the Griffin family. James, who is a factory laborer, and his wife, Margaret, have eight children and live on Kenview Road, across town from the Ohio State campus. On Friday night in a smaller stadium and a smaller game, Ray Griffin, who is a high school junior, sped through the rain for touchdowns of 68, 19 and 16 yards, as Eastmoor High defeated Central High, 30-14. So it would seem that Woody Hayes, as well as the football world, can look forward to seeing alot of Griffins in the future. It would seem unthinkable now that Archie and Ray wouldn't want to play in the same Ohio State backfield.

Archie did not get in the North Carolina game last week until Ohio State trailed by 7-0, thanks to a blocked punt, and until starting tailback Morris Bradshaw had shown he could not gain any yardage. Archie, who is only 5' 10" and weighs 185, came in, just an insignificant No. 45 on your program, a tailback in the Power-I that Woody runs when he isn't in the Robust-T.

First play, Archie Griffin goes outside for six yards. Second play,

Archie goes inside for six yards. Another play, Archie goes inside for six more yards. Griffin got the call only once after that, so Ohio State stalled. Ah, but the next time. On first down, there went Archie, wriggling, turning on the speed, 32 yards. Ohio State was finally untracked.

A rare Hayes-ordered pass, from quarterback Greg Hare to Rick Galbos, worked, and then it was Archie Griffin for six straight carries to what wound up being a field goal, mainly because Archie didn't carry anymore.

In the second quarter it was Griffin's 22-yard run that set up the go-ahead touchdown for Ohio State and a 9-7 lead at halftime. It was Archie's 20-yard squirm in the third quarter that got the Buckeyes started on the drive that made the score 16-7. And it was his dazzling 55-yard run later in the period that set up the score that made it 23-7. Game over, for all practical purposes.

Along about then it became obvious that Archie Griffin could break Ollie Cline's 1945 single-game rushing record at Ohio State — 229 yards — a record that past halfbacks like Vic Janowicz and Hopalong Cassady (who had his own big day as a freshman, scoring three touchdowns) had not been able to approach. All he needed to do was be lucky enough for Woody to let him carry the ball in the fourth quarter. He was.

After an interception, Archie ripped for four, six, six, six more and finally nine yards, breaking two tackles, dancing on the sideline, for his very own touchdown and the rushing record. He left the field to a standing ovation, and the announcement that the record was his.

"I don't know what it is that makes a player that good," Woody said later. "He's not big but he has power. He has speed but not great speed. He's just hard to catch. He has a natural knack of knowing what to do, where to run."

And then Woody talked about the new freshman rule. "Freshmen may revolutionize college football. They give you a bigger squad to work with. They can give your squad a vitality and an enthusiasm it might not have. Everybody is going to have those few who can play, the exceptional kids. Take Archie. All you have to do is hand him the ball."

Woody went on, "I have never known whether I was for or against the freshman rule until now. Archie has convinced me it's O.K."

Archie Griffin himself is a quiet lad, and certainly a little bewildered about the whole thing. Although he had been on the squad since spring training began, he never expected to become useful so quickly. "It's all new," he said. "This is a big campus, and I don't even know my way around. I was lucky. I got in the game when the line was starting to open up the holes. I just ran. That's all."

That was enough. And Griffin's presence threw a whole new perspective on this 1972 Ohio State team. It's a young team, still finding its way. Physically, it resembles those Rex Kern-Jack Tatum teams, only it appears to be even deeper. There's muscle in the line and abnormal speed everywhere else and Greg Hare, only a junior, looks like a running-throwing quarterback who can lead it.

There's not much in the way of Ohio State in the form of a schedule. The Buckeyes are 2-0 and, until they meet Michigan on Nov. 25, it's just so many Northwesterns and Minnesotas. "We've got more depth and more potential than we've ever had," Woody said a couple of days before North Carolina showed up.

He went all through the depth that he had, and guess what? He never even mentioned Archie Griffin. But why should he? We all know you cannot depend on a freshman.

13

An Oak Leaf Cluster
For General Woody

December 4, 1972

By RON FIMRITE
Sports Illustrated

Woody Hayes, for all of his bombast, is a man of modest aspira-tions. All he seems really to want is for his bosom pal, General Lewis Walt, to emerge from retirement and lead a victorious Marine division into Hanoi, for all dope fiends to vanish in a cloud of their own wicked smoke and for his Ohio State football team to beat Michigan every year.

All things considered, Woody came rather closer to fulfillment than he had any right to expect last weekend in cold and damp Columbus. His football team not only beat arch-rival Michigan in a chiller, 14-11 — thereby earning it an invitation to the Rose Bowl and the dubious honor of playing undefeated Southern California — but it did it the Woody way, which is without benefit of the forward pass and by Holding That Line. That line was held, in fact, as it has not been since the salad days of Walter Camp. Furthermore, General Walt, former assistant commandant of the Marine Corps, was there to share the triumph with him and to acclaim Woody as "one of the greatest leaders our country has ever had." Finally, Hayes proved, at least to his own satisfaction, that good old-fashioned locker room oratory can transport a group of youngsters higher, as he put it, "than any drug can."

"Woody told us before the game that this would be the most important thing we'd ever do in our lives," said fullback Harold

(Champ) Henson, recalling the moment. "And I agreed with him." Thus convinced of the gravity of the occasion, Henson went out and scored a touchdown in the second quarter, his 20th of the season, an Ohio State record.

The fullback was hardly the only Buckeye high on words from Woody. His teammates, led by an arm-waving co-captain, John Hicks, raced onto the field before the kickoff like so many Warner Bros.' Apaches. At the 50-yard line they staged a veritable free-for-all of well-wishing that was interrupted only by the announcement of the starting lineups. The game itself must have seemed a peaceful interlude after this riotous display.

Highest of all was the defensive team. It gave ground — or, rather, Astro Turf — between the goal lines: Michigan ran off 83 plays to Ohio State's 44 and gained 344 yards to 192. But when their backs were to the wall the Buckeye defenders were not to be moved.

Three times the Wolverines had first downs on or inside the Ohio State five. Only once did they score. In the closing seconds of the first half Michigan drove to a first down on the O.S.U. one. Chuck Heater, the hard-running tailback, lost a yard on first down. Heater slipped on the rain-soaked artificial turf but gained a yard on second down. Bob Thornbladh made it almost to the goal line on third, but on fourth down quarterback Dennis Franklin fumbled the center snap and lost two yards. Ohio State's ball.

Midway in the third quarter, after freshman halfback Archie Griffin had scored Ohio State's second touchdown on a virtually unimpeded 30-yard run to make the score 14-3, the Wolverines moved to another first down on the five. This time they squeezed across on a one-yard plunge by fullback Ed Shuttlesworth, but it was a bitter and painful four-down journey. Franklin passed for a two-point conversion to conclude the day's scoring, although Michigan was to test the gallant goal-line warriors one more time. Early in the final quarter, the Wolverines reached familiar ground again — the Ohio State five-yard line on first down. Three times tailback Harry Banks hurtled forward. Net gain: four-plus yards. The on fourth and a foot, maybe two, Franklin tried a sneak. He was stopped short by what appeared to be 11 muggers. By now, the 87,000 spectators in Ohio Stadium were convinced they were witnessing a return to primordial football. Either that or a rerun of a Jack Oakie campus potboiler.

Emotional as these triumphs of negativism were, they were as much the result of guile as grit. Hayes is not one to take a goal-line stand lightly. "They shall not pass" is for him both an offensive and a defensive admonition. When the enemy is at the gates, he removes two defensive backs and replaces them with tackles — on Saturday, Jeff Davis and Rich Parsons usually went out and Charlie Beecroft and Pete Cusick went in. With only, as it were, passing attention to the threat of a pass the reformed Buckeyes bunch into the equivalent of an 11-man line. This goal-line strategy differs from that employed by other teams only in that the Buckeyes work harder at it and it works. One reason it worked against Michigan was that Cusick, normally a regular tackle, was able to play at all. He had been hospitalized earlier in the week with a virus attack but was on the field with the other zealots on Saturday.

Michigan Coach Bo Schembechler was criticized by some for not attempting a field goal on at least one of his deep penetrations — when he had the ball on fourth and one on the Ohio State 20 early in the fourth quarter. His kicker, Mike Lantry, had hit from 35 yards in the second quarter, and Michigan, which had entered the game undefeated, needed only a tie with once-beaten O.S.U. to win the Rose Bowl invitation. Schembechler tried for a first down instead and, naturally, was stopped.

Hayes was not in the least surprised by his opponent's strategy. There was no reason why he should be, for Schembechler was a Hayes assistant for six years and is so faithful a copy of the original that Big Ten people have taken to calling him "Little Woody," a sobriquet he deplores. Indeed, Michigan and Ohio State normally play the same type of anodiluvian football. Neither throws the ball, except in dire emergencies, and both prefer defense to offense.

On this day, however, Schembechler's offense was positively rococo in comparison with The Old Master's. The Wolverines ran out of a variety of offensive formations, including the so-called pro set, and Franklin, a black quarterback who is as extraordinary a faker as he is an ordinary passer, threw 23 times, while completing 13 for 160 yards. That constitutes an aerial circus in the conservative Big Ten these days. Franklin's Ohio State counterpart, Greg Hare, threw but three times, completing one to teammate Griffin and another to Michigan defender Randy Logan. The third was dropped. Hayes, who like Schembechler called every play, admitted that the intercepted pass was a bad choice. The pass just is not Woody; the past is, and, as he advises his young charges, those who ignore it "are condemned to repeat it."

When the game was almost over, the multitudes spilled onto the field, dismantling the "tear-away" goal posts specially erected for the game and milling among the combatants. There in the middle of them, shooing them off the premises, was the portly coach himself. Woody is no one to fool with, so the fans went back where they belonged. All this exertion on behalf of law and order cost Hayes a pulled leg muscle, the only serious injury in the game. What was he doing out there playing cop? Was he afraid someone would get hurt?

"There were six seconds left," he said, rubbing the gimpy leg. "I didn't want there to be any question about this game. I wanted to finish it. I wanted this game."

He managed to get that impression across to his players.

14

...And The Reason Is
Woody's Machine

September 9, 1974

By ROBERT VARE
Sports Illustrated

In the younger days they called him Johnny. As a kid in the tiny Ohio town of Derby, where his parents ran a small farm and raised a family of six, it was even Little Johnny. Then, as now, he was short but athletically inclined, a spunky baseball player who hoped to be coined a Hall of Fame shortstop like his hero, Honus Wagner. Instead he became one of the wealthiest men in American, owner of the Pittsburgh Pirates, breeder of championship horses, close friend of coach Wayne Woodrow Hayes and chief benefactor of the Ohio State Football Machine.

Today almost every Ohioan knows who John Wilmer Galbreath is. They know he changes the face of cities with the stroke of a pen, puts up skyscrapers, factories, warehouses, housing developments, and whole towns all over the world, and even now, at 77, may visit New York, California and Hong Kong within 24 hours to check on his holdings. And some are aware that next to concrete and steel, his heart belongs to the Buckeyes. It has been said that nobody, save Woody Hayes himself, has done more over the years for Ohio State football than John Galbreath.

Galbreath is an important component of the Ohio State Machine. He is the best known and one of the hardest working members of a group called the Athletic Committee, a predominantly alumni organization whose 300 active members in Ohio and across the country help recruit high school stars for the Buckeyes, provide Coach Hayes with his strongest personal support and contribute large sums of money to the football program. The Committee, founded in 1946 with 100 members, used to go by the name "Frontliners" until the Big Ten said it sounded too predatory and requested a name change. But its activities haven't changed much. It is the heart of the Machine.

"You want to know what my attachment is to Ohio State football," says Galbreath. "Well, you can't live in Columbus and not be part of it. We don't have big-league baseball, football or basketball, so the Buckeyes are *our* team.

"I have all kinds of ties to the university. I myself graduated from Ohio University in Athens but my son got a degree from Ohio State in business administration, and my daughter went there and my sister, too. But the main thing is Woody. You just can't turn him down when he calls up to ask for a favor. Especially when you see how dedicated he is to the young people. I'm the same way. I just love talking to the young people and helping out wherever I can."

Galbreath has been helping Buckeye players for years, rewarding their gridiron efforts with jobs that aren't difficult, hours that aren't demanding and salaries that aren't stingy. If a high school football star can just meet Ohio State's academic requirements, he can get a summer job working for Galbreath in one of his many many offices, on one of his many construction projects or at his 4,400-acre Darby Dan Farm.

In earlier days he could do much more. Players from poor families looked to Galbreath as a one-man welfare agency. He would tell them how to fill out their tax forms, find employment for the fathers, help pay their monthly bills. Sometimes a player would benefit more directly. He promised to lend money and give a job to Vic Janowicz if he would become a Buckeye. Later Galbreath admitted buying a convertible for Janowicz and a suit of clothes for him to wear in New York when he accepted the 1950 Heisman Trophy. N.C.A.A. crackdowns and conference rule changes forbidding players to hold jobs during the school year took away some of Galbreath's opportunities to aid the Buckeyes, but today there are still summer jobs to provide and blue-chip prospects and their parents to wine and dine at the farm. And rumors persist that even now, on occasion, he is not averse to throwing his arm around a high school star and promising to do all he can for him.

Galbreath is not a typical Buckeye recruiter, but he is not that unusual either. Most of the Committeemen are wealthy. Some, like Galbreath, are company presidents. Many are contractors, insurance men, doctors, lawyers and judges. Others run government agencies, stores and hotels. For all of them recruiting is a full-time avocation and a labor of love.

Each one keeps his membership in the Committee by flushing out and proselytizing the hot football prospects in his area. Most contribute to athletic department coffers and buy tickets to annual athletic department outings and dinners. And many enjoy doing favors for players, such as arranging lucrative summer jobs or giving stereos and clothes at Christmas or making loans that sometimes don't get repaid. Countless players have been made happy by their Committeemen, and they, with their performances on the field, have made countless Committeemen happy.

The recruiter's rewards are good seats at home games, status and identification with a successful football program. As long as he keeps finding and selling the prospects and Ohio State keeps winning games, it is an awful lot of fun to be a Committeeman.

Some Committee recruiters have helped land more quality players than they can remember. Take Frank Lafferty, who is in the motel business in Warren, Ohio. He has been recruiting in and around his hometown since the Hayes era began, and his track record is one of the best.

"We don't lose very many that we really want," says Lafferty, "and this is a great area for high school football. The idea is to keep after them and maybe help them find a summer job if they need it. We have contacts all over the area. Now, Paul Warfield (former Ohio State halfback and All-Pro receiver with the Miami Dolphins), we got him a job with the state highway department. We got Van DeCree, our starting defensive end this year, a job with Republic Steel. Randy Gradishar, the all-America linebacker. . . visited him about 25 times before we got him, but he didn't need a job. His father runs a supermarket. . . . Do we offer any other inducements? Well, we're not supposed to do it. . . uh. . . we don't do it."

Though men of vastly different resources and lifestyles, Galbreath and Lafferty perform key functions for the Machine. With every one of the nearly 750 high schools in football-happy Ohio covered by a Committeeman, it is almost impossible for an athlete with talent to go unnoticed. Upwards of 40,000 kids play varsity football annually in the state and they all have, thanks to the diligence of the Committeemen, an opportunity to move on to Ohio State. The better the player, the better the opportunity. But in general fewer than a hundred of them will be considered blue-chippers and thus prizes to pursue.

Texas, Pennsylvania and California might argue the point, but it has been said by experts that Ohio is America's most fertile football recruiting ground. Besides filling two-thirds of Ohio State's roster and sending nearly 150 players to the other nine Big Ten schools last season, Ohio high schools supply dozens of college powerhouses across the country. Ohio boys appear regularly in the starting lineups at Notre Dame, Penn State, Alabama, Tennessee, Arizona State, Tulane, Nebraska and Oklahoma.

With at least 75 major schools participating in the annual chase for Ohio talent and competition getting fiercer, it is only natural that some Committeemen are not above bending the rules. Big Ten regulations prohibit athletes from receiving financial aid beyond what is allocated for tuition and fees, room and board, and use of books. But it is tough to detect when a generous Committeeman lends an athlete a color television set for a couple of years or sells him a car for five dollars.

One Committeeman, a surprisingly candid wheeler-dealer who has helped recruit some of the best players in Buckeye history, is philosophical about the hanky-panky, concedes that it happens and even says: "A good Committeeman can find a way to help his players." However, he asserts, "We have a much cleaner operation than most places because we don't *have* to cheat to win. Woody has the name and reputation. People know he's a winner and that year after year he turns out players good enough to go on to the pros and star there. And that's what most of these kids are thinking about, even if it is a little unrealistic: playing pro ball. So we don't have much trouble finding kids who like the idea of playing for Ohio State. It's like recruiting for I.B.M. as opposed to a little 'Ma and Pa' outfit."

Above the Committeemen in the Machine hierarchy are the assistant coaches. Each of the nine full-time Ohio State assistants is assigned an area. Seven cover various sections of Ohio: one is responsible for Pennsylvania, the other the East Coast, where recruiting activities have been stepped up in recent years. Each assistant coach travels through his designated territory whenever he can, gathering tips from high school coaches and maintaining close contact throughout the year with the local Committeemen.

Since the assistant must know his turf, there is a good reason for who covers what. For example, defensive coordinator George Hill, who was born and raised in the Cleveland suburb of Bay Village, covers Cleveland as well as nearby Stark County with its football-famous tri-cities — Akron, Canton and Massillon; offensive end and tackle coach Ralph Staub, a native of Cincinnati who started at the University of Cincinnati in the early '50s and later coached there and at Cincinnati high schools covers Cincinnati; quarterback coach George Chaump, a native of Pennsylvania who coached high school football for a decade in Harrisburg, covers his home state; defensive backfield coach Dick Walker, who coached high school football in Cleveland for three years and is a Roman Catholic, covers Cleveland, concentrating on the city's talent-rich parochial schools.

The basic recruiting organization was devised a decade ago by Coach Hayes and an assistant coach named Lou McCullough. A short, tough and amiable man from Alabama, McCullough was surpassed only by Hayes himself in the ability to sell Ohio State to prospects in their own living rooms. After a decade of recruiting proficiency unparalleled in Buckeye history, McCullough quit in 1971 to become athletic director at Iowa State. But the recruiting army, now headed by assistant coach Staub, remains as strong and well disciplined as it was when McCullough left it.

"There isn't a better organization in the country," McCullough says flatly. "The key really is those Committeemen. Their devotion is unbelievable. They go to the high school games, read all the newspapers, talk to the kids, to their parents, to their coaches, to their teachers — to anybody who knows the prospect. They're willing to work their tails off, and it doesn't hurt that they're usually very influential in the community.

"So when the assistant coach comes to a town, the first thing he does is meet with the Committeemen in that town to get a thorough rundown on every decent prospect. And I mean it's thorough. Man, you find out everything about a kid right down to the brand of toothpaste he uses. You find out about the parents, too — what their likes and dislikes are. That gives the assistant coach a helluva head start. Recruiting is just like any other selling. You have to know what the customer likes and dislikes, wants and doesn't want."

Finding and selling are the gut work of the assistant coach and his committee recruiters. It begins in earnest in the spring of the high school prospect's junior year, when the assistants spend four weeks traversing their territories, talking to coaches and saying hello to a few players. In their briefcases are reports from Committeemen on each prospect: his speed, size, moves, arm, statistics, family, leadership, church and handshake. To supplement the data, the assistants send out questionnaires to the prospects, get game films and confer with principals about classroom ability. The boy's academic work is important. The assistants know that few things make Coach Hayes angrier than losing a player to scholastic ineligibility. By the end of May the inquiries will have yielded a list of 300 to 400 preliminary candidates.

Finding and selling. In the fall of the prospect's senior year the recruiting army swings into high gear. Only then can active recruiting between coach and player take place. The coaches would like to start sooner — say, in the cradle — but N.C.A.A. rules prohibit it. By early fall the grade reports are in and so are the recommendations from coaches and opposing coaches, from teachers and employers, and, in some cases, from social workers. Meanwhile, graduate assistants crisscross the state every Friday night, viewing the candidates in action. Before long the original list is pared to between 75 and 100 top prospects. Then come the months when they will be courted, flattered, wheedled, cajoled and badgered, until they either say no or put their signatures on a letter of intent. By early April, the end of the recruiting season, about 25 will have signed, always fewer than the N.C.A.A. maximum of 30. With such quality there is no need for quantity.

The Buckeye recruiting army does not wait until the high school season is over to start its assault. Soon after the first game the prospect is bombarded with more questionnaires, personal letters, brochures, then phone calls, house visits from Committeemen and assistant coaches. Mail, calls and bodies arrive according to a well-ordered timetable.

It is Coach Hayes' firm belief that there is no such thing as overselling. "Ring the doorbells" is his recruiting slogan. By ringing the doorbells, the Committeeman or assistant coach gets to know the prospect — every prospect — and is in a position to head-off any potential competition that might also be camping on the front lawn. It is no accident that in Hayes' 23 years as head coach, amazingly few top stars have eluded him. Wes Fesler, Hayes' predecessor, shied away from high-pressure selling because he thought it unfair to the "kids." This has not troubled Woody. His adage, on the lips of every Committeeman is: "Paralyze their resistance with your persistence."

There are rules in the Big Ten designed to keep a prospect from stumbling over recruiters during his senior year — and to keep the recruiters from stumbling over each other. In theory, recruiters may make only two visits to a prospect's home. Since the two-visit limit does not apply to people not on the official coaching staff, the rule favors schools with strong alumni recruiting organizations. Buckeye Committeemen can and generally do make all the visits the prospect or his family will allow.

Of course, there is another way to get around the rules. "Bump-ins," they are called, and they are not infrequent. A bump-in is when an assistant coach or Committeeman just happens to show up at the hamburger stand where the prospect hangs out, or at the bar his father patronizes.

If all the visits, prearranged and "accidental," accomplish what they are supposed to, the prospect's appetite will be whetted and he will be invited to spend 48 hours on the Ohio State campus. For this, the only expense-paid visit allowed, an ordinary blue-chipper and his parents can expect to be entertained lavishly, considering that Columbus is not New York or San Francisco. They can look forward to a guided tour of the campus, from the weight room to the library, a conference with a friendly dean or professor, tickets to a hockey or basketball game, cocktails with the coaches and dinner at a downtown rooftop restaurant, usually with Hayes and his wife, Anne. Sometime during the visit, the ordinary blue-chipper meets a few members of the varsity, and a player he might have something in common with is provided as an escort to a party where he can meet girls. If the blue-chipper is extraordinary, he can expect something more, namely a visit to John Wilmer Galbreath's Darby Dan Farm.

The farm is a vast stretch of landscape, 10 miles west of Columbus. The walls of Darby House are hung with the heads of game animals shot on East African and South American hunting parties. Where the stuffed animals leave off, the real ones begin. In Galbreath's very own game reserve roam zebras, impalas, water bucks, Thompson's and Grant's gazelles, sitatungas, lechwes and dozens of other exotic beasts. Nearby is the racetrack where his Kentucky Derby-bound thoroughbreds sometimes train. You almost forget it is really a farm until you see the 2,300 acres of corn, wheat and soybeans. For coming and going, there is a 6,000-foot airstrip, long enough to accommodate Galbreath's private jet. Surrounding it all are 35 miles of white plank fences that a lot of Ohio State players have painted for fun and profit. It is the kind of spread that might have dazzled Kubla Khan, not to mention a high school youngster who is just learning to shave.

Some prospects are impressed less by wealth than by sports figures they have been hearing about as long as they can remember. Jack Tatum, John Brockington, Rex Kern, Paul Warfield, Matt Snell, Jim Parker, Hopalong Cassady, John Havlicek, Jerry Lucas, Jack Nicklaus and many other premier ex-Buckeye athletes have been know to pitch in with phone calls and letters when called on by the Machine. Nicklaus once got on the phone with a prospect 40 minutes after winning The Masters.

When it comes to recruiting, the Machine can sometimes even count on Ohio's politicos. Quarterback Brian Dowling was watching television one afternoon his senior year in high school when a squadron of motorcycle police roared up to his front door. Terrified, Dowling opened the door to find his welcome mat occupied by Ohio Governor James Rhodes, who is best remembered for Kent State and his political rallying cry: "Profit is not a dirty word in Ohio." So impressed was Dowling with Rhodes' salesmanship that he enrolled at Yale. Such failures, however, are the exception.

The average head coach stays close to home during recruiting season. He may range afield for two or three exceptional prospects, but for the most part he assigns assistants to do the out-of-state work. As usual, Woody Hayes operates apart from the norm. He never seems to stop moving. From December to April he is likely to make eight trips to the New York area, six to Pennsylvania, two to Washington, D.C., three to the South and one to the Southwest, to say nothing of repeated forays throughout the Midwest. And despite the heart attack he suffered last June, no one who knows him expects the Hayes pace to slow.

Even the long-distance runner needs a finishing kick, and in the recruiting marathon few men run the gun lap like Hayes. Most coaches will sit on a prospect's living-room couch, rubbing their hands raw, looking nervous and wide-eyed, talking nonstop. Their pitch is predictable. They promise a starting spot by the youngster's sophomore year, at the latest, marvel at how he will fit in so well with their particular offense or defense, emphasize the big money such and such ex-player got when he turned pro, go on about why it is better to play on *their* artificial turf and in front of *their* fans and predict nothing but national championships and Heisman Trophies in the prospect's future. They harp on technical football, drawing diagrams of their pro-type offense or defense *ad nauseam*.

The low-keyed manner is disarming and it is meant to be. He knows that because of his reputation most recruits and their parents expect him to be all hot lava and rage. So when he shows up at the door bestowing benign smiles, nodding respectfully, asking light-hearted questions and exuding charm instead of being pushy and antagonistic or, God help us, breaking up the furniture, the hosts smile back gratefully. They are relieved, if not entranced. And after he leaves they may ask: "Now how in the world could that wonderful man be the same one we've always heard about?" With that question, ever so common, the hook is in, the sale assured.

Actually, Hayes has two approaches, one for the prospect and another, much stronger, for his parents. With the player himself he is direct and businesslike, hoisting up a challenge and promising nothing. This tactic is designed to appeal to the athlete's competitive instinct. He is negotiating from strength. Everybody knows Ohio State is a very large school, spends a lot of money for football, plays on television two or three times a season, produces plenty of all-Americas and professionals and has won big for many years.

"Now, son, we think you're a hitter," he will say. "We think you can play a lot for Ohio State."

Then the prospect may nod and timidly offer up the observation that Ohio State might already have enough good football players to keep the seat of his pants in touch with the bench. Hayes' answer never varies.

"Now we think you're a 110-percenter, son. You come with us, dig in your heels and prove you're the best. You just have to ask yourself whether you're man enough to be a Buckeye."

The message hits hard. But the real work is done on mom and dad, and, with them, there is seldom a mention of football. The talk is all about education, or at least what you can get from one — about how so many of his players graduate, about Ohio State's wonderful faculty, lofty academic ranking, magnificent placement bureau. "Ah, so your son wants to be a doctor. Well, we've got the best darned medical school in the country and here's something that will interest you: three years in a row one of our football players was the No. 1 medical student. . . . You say your son wants to go into business. Well, we've got a great business administration program. Oh, it's a dandy program. . . . He wants to be a veterinarian? We've got a fine department there. . . Law school? None better. And we can help him get in, too. . . . Ummm-hm. . . . Ummm-hm. . . . Don't believe what you hear about us being a football factory."

If the family still isn't convinced that Ohio State is a cross between Harvard and M.I.T., the educational line of talk will continue, with emphasis on practical advantages and end results. "Now if your son plans to live in Ohio, it just doesn't make sense to go anywhere but Ohio State. He can make the contacts he needs and we can help him. And at Ohio State, there's a good chance your boy will get his degree, because 84% of our ballplayers do and most graduate in four years." The claim is difficult to certify, since the O.S.U. registrar refuses to release the names of football players who graduated with their class, asserting only that "most of them did." A check of the 1973 *Football Register* shows that only five of the 24 former Buck-eyes on pro teams at the start of the 1973 season had managed to earn their degree.

Hayes will keep going until sunrise if necessary, with the loyal Committeeman at his side, to help the boy and his parents make up their minds. Recruiting is the name of the game, and each prospect represents an investment — months of visits, official and unofficial, dozens of letters, postcards and telegrams, and hundreds of phone calls. The payoff comes every Saturday afternoon in the fall when the touchdowns and field goals are totaled. If the Committeeman comes through he will be patted on the back by Hayes and used again next season. If he does not, he will be ignored, his name scratched off the active membership rolls. That hurts. "Those Committeemen really take pride in their work," says McCullough. "If a company has a man who doesn't produce, who isn't selling enough, they get rid of him for somebody else, don't they?"

Once or twice a year the Buckeye recruiting corps musters in Columbus. These gatherings exude the aura of a High Mass with the Committeemen sounding their praise of the Hayes regime. The Committee's "salesmanship school" in August, with Coach Hayes lecturing on how to recruit and passing out awards, is an example of organizational strength that should freeze the blood of opposing coaches.

"When you've got an organization like Ohio State, you're going to get the top prospects," says Duffy Daugherty, who coached at Michigan State for 19 seasons. "These sponsors take the boys under their wings and they have the resources to treat them royally. It's become the custom for them to arrange a job that will enable a boy to earn as much as $2,500 in two summer months. The small schools with piddling recruiting organizations don't stand a chance."

Besides the 300 core Committeemen in Ohio, Pennsylvania and points east, the Machine has contacts from Florida to California, from Texas to Canada, and even in Europe, a good place to look for placekickers. Most of the contacts are drawn from the ranks of alumni who have scattered throughout the Western world. They don't get to Ohio Stadium much anymore and they are not official members of the Athletic Committee, but their memories are long, and it is nice to know they can still contribute to the cause by tipping off the Buckeye coaching staff whenever a "good one" comes up where they live. Then, too, there are the former assistant coaches and players, many of whom have remained loyal to Hayes. They prove it be keeping a sharp eye out for prospects and, when asked, working to get them.

The expanding terrain of the recruiting army is reflected by the Ohio State roster. Fifteen years ago, only one of the top 40 players came from outside Ohio, and he happened to be from a Kentucky town just across the river from Cincinnati. Today fully one-third of the squad is from out of state.

Along with recruiting, another Machine component that has been precision-honed is tutoring. It too has contributed to be extraordinary success of the big-time football operation at Ohio State. The purpose of the tutoring program is simple — to lift the grade-point average of every player to "C" or better so he'll be able to keep putting on the pads. It works. According to Assistant Director of Athletics James Jones, who as head of the tutoring program occupies the position known in football jargon as "the brain coach," only one Buckeye player has been lost to academic ineligibility in the last eight years.

"Sure, we have a commitment to football and winning games," says Jones, who supervises nightly study halls and a team of two dozen tutors, while keeping his speech, hair and handshake in the Marine drill sergeant style of the '50s. "We have an investment in each kid, and if he's a flunk-out, we've lost our money. But we also have a moral commitment to each kid. Our revenues from football are just tremendous. Now if these kids don't get an education we've cheated them, because we live off their efforts. And we're proud, mighty proud, of the fact that eventually about 85% of our players get their degrees. We really feel equally committed to the two goals — the winning and the education."

A different version is offered by Greg Thomas, director of Ohio State's black education center and unofficial adviser to a number of black players. "That's so much jive. They hold up these high graduation figures and, dig it, they say, 'See what a fine education our boys get?' Well, damn, when they have to make the choice between eligibility and education, ain't no way they're going to pick the education. Like some of the black dudes have told me the coaches go through some changes when they ask to take courses that might be a little more demanding academically or ideologically oriented — that might mess up their head for football. They want the players taking popcorn stuff like physical education, recreation or business, which are easy and safe and where they know most of the teachers aren't going to give anybody a hard time, especially football players."

Another major component of the Machine is public relations. Ohio State has three full-time sports information officials and one unpaid publicist, Paul Hornung, who happens to be sports editor of *The Columbus Dispatch* and is no relation to the former Green Bay star. Hornung is Woody Hayes' idea of what a newspaperman should be, someone who is delighted to go along with Hayes' edict that local reporters be part of the team — a kind of propaganda arm of the Machine, parroting the official line and avoiding stories that could be distracting to Buckeye players or psychologically useful to the opposition.

If Hayes wants to see a certain story, he'll just tell Hornung, "Let's write this one up, Paul," and brief him on needed background. If the story is to be kept out, he will simply say "to hell with it" and go on with other work. Hornung never argues. He has been there since before the Hayes era began, a product of the Ohio State journalism department, sometimes even wearing the school colors, scarlet and gray, in the press box.

When an out-of-town columnist criticizes Hayes for tactics, temper or politics, Hornung will answer the charges by writing that the detractor is misguided and a fool. Then he will return to the bland player interviews, official pronouncements and dreary catalogs of how many Buckeye leaves the coaching staff awarded each player for his work in last Saturday's game. This is news that's fit to print, unlike blowups at practice, weaknesses in the passing game or disciplinary problems on the team. As Hayes so often says, "When I want to read about the bad things I look at the front page. When I want to read about the good things I turn to the sports page and Paul Hornung."

Other Columbus reporters are less friendly, but since they have to live with Hayes, they're rarely hostile. "Nobody ever really challenges Woody," says one. Tom Keys, sports editor of *The Citizen-Journal,* observes sadly, "You go to a practice. You see or hear something and the old man says, 'I don't want to see *this* in the newspaper' or 'I don't want to see *that* in the newspaper.' You make a choice: if you want to cover practice again, you don't put it in the newspaper."

Recruiting, tutoring, propaganda: each a vital component of the Machine. But the most important element of all — the fuel that keeps the parts running evenly — is money. Since most college football organizations spend more than they care to admit, finances are always a cloudy subject, and the situation at Ohio State is no exception. Only Hayes and a few administrators know precisely how much there is and how it is spent. As coach, Hayes controls the treasury and tells his athletic director what the budget will be, not vice versa as at most schools.

The spending is lavish. Even in a lean recruiting year, when most of the prospects are mediocre, Hayes may still shell out $100,000 for a recruiting campaign. Insiders say that Ohio State will spend as much as $50,000 just on its coaches' recruiting travel expenses, which is more than most Big Ten schools' entire recruiting budget. That, plus the long-distance phone call blitz and visits to the campus—another $50,000—means the money going out for recruiting easily surpasses that of almost every other school in the country.

So do the expenditures for nearly everything else, as the Ohio State athletic department's own figures attest. In 1972-73 the payroll for coaches and trainers ran to more than $350,000. Football scholarships cost another $260,000; clothing and equipment, $70,000; films for games and practice sessions, $37,000; meals and lodging for the team, $124,000; and transportation, $37,000. The spending is higher than nearly every other school's and going higher. And sitting on top of what is officially reported to be a $1.6 million football budget, Woody Hayes pronounces it all worthwhile. "Football," he says, "is the most wholesome activity on our campus."

It is also the most profitable. Unlike Texas, Tennessee, Michigan State and other major powers that have recently fallen on hard financial times, Ohio State's football program still operates solidly in the black, cranking out a surplus of as much as, and sometimes more than, $2 million a year.

The money flows in from a number of sources. Gate receipts, or "turnstyles," as Buckeye athletic officials like to call them, are far and away the biggest revenue producers. The Buckeyes grossed $3 million from ticket sales in 1972-73 along with $250,000 in ancillary income from program sales, concessions and parking fees. From television and radio another $250,000 went into athletic department coffers, and alumni gifts earmarked for scholarships added $100,000.

"I don't like to talk about our budget because the figures get used out of context," says O.S.U. Athletic Director J. Edward (Big Ed)

Weaver, a physically imposing man of 6' 4" and 230 pounds who played for the Buckeyes in the '30s. "I will say this, though. We make a small profit from basketball, but I'd say 98% of our income comes from football. We are totally self-sustaining and I'm proud of the fact that we never take a dime from the university, even though costs are rising all the time. We haven't had the apathy that you have at a lot of other schools. I think you'll find football interest here higher than anywhere else in the country — I don't care if you're talking about Lincoln, Neb., South Bend, Ind. or Tuscaloosa, Ala."

What happens to the football profits? Much of it goes back into the football program to assure its lopsided superiority. Out of what is left the athletic department has enough to finance 17 other intercollegiate varsity sports, pay the $135,000-a-year debt service on its sports arena and field house and add to its $2 million investment fund. But not a penny goes to the intramural or club sports programs that are available to most of Ohio State's 46,000 students. Some of those students are upset about it.

"It's a rip-off," says David Litt, a journalism graduate who covered sports for a year on *The Ohio State Lantern.* "They always have plenty of money for football. But when it comes to a student participating in athletics, that has to come out of the university's general funds and there's never enough money around. Only this year after a big lobbying campaign did the athletic department break down and finally give some money to women's varsity sports. But they still have to be forced to care about students participating in athletics. Why shouldn't they do something for the student? Business is good."

And getting better. It's no accident. The Machine's vast resources have made it nearly impossible in recent years for Big Ten opponents — except Michigan, which also has a financially successful football program — to present anything more than quivering resistance on the gridiron. Week after week Hayes makes his fans happy, keeps his team motivated and shows his muscle for the national rankings by rolling up landslide victories over adversaries who cannot afford to recruit, train or equip the way his Machine can. The undermanned, underfinanced opponents are lucky to score even one touchdown against him, just as they are lucky, in certain cases, to field a team at all, since they don't fill their stadiums, don't play on TV and don't get much in the way of donations from grateful alumni. It's a classic rich-getting-richer cycle.

"We smaller schools in the Big Ten just don't have the wherewithal and, a result, there's no balance anymore," says Francis Graham, the athletic department business manager at the University of Iowa. "Ohio State has the highest athletic budget in the country — $4.3 million. Michigan has a $4 million budget. Our budget is $1.5 million for all sports and we're just breaking even. We really can't afford to bring kids all the way across the country to visit our campus. Either we drastically cut back on scholarships and de-emphasize winning or all you'll have left is the Ohio States. And I personally don't think college football should boil down to the survival of the fittest."

Graham, like many athletic officials in similar straits, believes the only answer may lie in sweeping N.C.A.A. reforms imposing spending ceilings; limiting or even eliminating recruiting; reducing the size of football squads; returning perhaps to one-platoon football.

With calls for change getting louder, the widely respected Carnegie Foundation for the Advancement of Teaching, along with the Ford Foundation, has decided to support a proposed study of college athletics. The result is expected to be even more scathing than the first Carnegie Report — the most thorough and scholarly on the subject to date — which found many abuses in collegiate sports, especially football, stemming from what it called "the growth of professionalism" and "excessive organizational discipline." The Carnegie Report was published in 1929.

Woody Hayes, in countless speeches lambastes the criticism, any and all, past and present, as "a plot to undermine football" and concedes nothing. "I say again, and I am proud of it, football is the most wholesome activity we have on this campus. . . the only place a youngster learns teamwork, mental discipline and the value of hard work. . . where the men who teach the youngsters aren't openly encouraging permissiveness and protest. . . . And I can't think of an activity that's more valuable. The whole student body benefits from what we do, not just the athletic department. . . . University fund raisers tell me every time we win and fill the stadium and unify the students and alumni, it makes raising money much easier. . . . We provide wonderful publicity for the university. I don't think anybody will deny that."

Hayes knows that most people around him say he is right. He does not have to find excuses for any part of the powerful conglomerate of money, high-pressure recruiting, tutoring and special treatment out of which emerge his winning football teams. The distant rumblings of discontent with big-time, big-business college football are beginning to be felt across the country by students, faculty, administrators, alumni, players and even some coaches. But not by Woody Hayes.

"I don't think many people around here are against a big-time program," he has said. "We have more than 85,000 seats in our stadium and every one of them is filled every game. . . people from all over the state, no matter what their politics or religion or color. . . they love and rally round the Buckeyes."

It was almost 45 years after the Carnegie Report was issued that Hayes got up to speak before a downtown Columbus Rotary Club meeting that began with prayers for Richard Nixon and an undefeated season. Amid loud applause, grim but full of confidence, Woody said: "Somebody asked me the other day what I thought these so-called critics wanted and I said, 'I know what they want. They want to destroy college football.' Well, dammit all, they're *not* going to destroy a very wonderful American institution."

15

Woody Hayes Makes War

October 1974

By ROBERT VARE
Esquire

"Will he have time to talk to me today?"

The voice on the other end of the phone belonged to Woody Hayes' secretary. It was tentative, ill at ease.

"I don't see too much here on the schedule this afternoon," she said. "He's got the Dayton lawyers tonight and. . . let's see. . . nothing for tomorrow except the Portsmouth Rotarians. . . . I haven't seen him yet today, though. . . . Would you like me to have him call you and maybe make an appointment?"

I had been forewarned about seeking a formal audience with the legendary Ohio State football coach, about the unrelieved misery other writers and reporters had encountered. Reports almost unanimously described Hayes as abrasive, single-minded, petulant and bitterly antipress; not long ago he had attacked a *Los Angeles Times* photographer before the Rose Bowl game.

"He's an unpredictable sonofabitch," said a friend who, while on assignment for *Look* magazine, suffered a humiliating ejection after having scheduled an interview two months in advance. "The best thing to do is just drop in unannounced. He'll probably throw you out. But there's a chance that he'll feel like haranguing you for an hour or two."

Another writer familiar with the manners and mores of Woody Hayes urged that I get a haircut, shave my beard, wear a jacket and tie, give a firm handshake and proclaim my love for Hayes' hero, General George Patton.

"This is a pretty light week," the secretary said. "Spring practice ended last Saturday, and he probably won't be bothered by many people today. He doesn't usually tell me where he is but I guess he's over at the North Facility."

When it was built in 1970, the North Facility was officially named the Ernie Briggs Athletic Training Facility, after a trainer who had ministered to Ohio State athletes for thirty years. The building is located in the agricultural section of campus, well removed from prying eyes. It's an austere, cinder-block-and-aluminum fortress with a surrounding five-foot-high Cyclone fence, crossbar gates, heavy doors, metal burglar-alarm tape on the windows and other grim reminders that strangers are not welcome. The stark military bearing is at odds with the grazing cows and frolicking ponies nearby. It's as if a giant Quonset hut had been set down in the middle of a Grandma Moses painting.

It was close to noon when I jerked open the front door and walked down a long, grey-tiled corridor, passing several rooms with Universal gyms, whirlpool baths and assorted technology of football. Near the end of the hall, at Room 147, my knock produced no answer and, hearing nothing within, I turned to leave. Ten steps down the corridor I heard the sound of the door being thrown open. There, standing in the doorway, was a hulking man, his large arms folded above a stomach that protruded like a great boulder. He was wearing a scarlet windbreaker and baggy grey pants, the colors of an Ohio State loyalist. He had neatly trimmed, ash white hair combed straight back, and a neck thick enough to support a Rodin head. The small, hazel eyes flashed cold fire; the thin lips curled in a bellicose scowl. There was no doubt that I was in the uniquely disquieting presence of Wayne Woodrow Hayes, the terrible-tempered dragon of the gridiron, molder of great football teams, smiter of players and press, student of history, military strategist, brooder, brawler, high priest of the Midwest.

"How did you find me?" he asked softly.

"Your secretary told me that from the looks of your schedule you'd probably be over here."

He winced as he might if one of his offensive tackles had jumped off side; his lips were closed tight as a coffin.

"Nope," he said slowly, each word consuming a full beat, "I probably won't fire her for this. But I'll tell you this: I'm gonna give her *some kind of hell*. I'm gonna chew her butt out."

"But, she really isn't the one to blame —"

"Now goddamn it: She knows she's not supposed to give out my schedule, *particularly to fellas like you.* Now I'm gonna have to straighten her out. I've already decided I'm not gonna fire her, but she needs to be straightened out. That's all. I'll do it sometime when nobody's around because I don't want people to hear her crying. She's a crier."

Hayes leaned over and took a long drink from a water fountain. He wiped the corners of his mouth with the back of his enormous hand.

"Y'know," he snorted, "you fellas from the press are not exactly my favorite people."

"So I've been told," I said. "But I wouldn't want you to pigeonhole me as a typical member of the press any more than you would want me to regard you as a typical football coach."

"Aw shit! I know some people think I'm just a *big dumb football coach.* Maybe I'm *not* all that smart. But y'know, I have a saying: 'I may not be able to outsmart too many people, but I *can* outwork 'em.' Anyway, to get back to your little thing here. . . . I'm just gonna have to say I don't want to get involved. First of all I just don't have time. I'm much too busy to sit down and shoot the shit with a fella like you. Y'see, another thing is I've just been burned so goddamn many times. Every time I've talked to a writer I've regretted it, because you fellas end up *twisting* everything. Now take the 1973 Rose Bowl game. We go out there and lose to a fine U.S.C. team. So what do the goddamned people out there write about? They don't write about the wonderful football team which they had out there. They write about nothing but Woody Hayes beating up on a photographer. I get on the plane out there to go home and the reporters send me a message: 'Won't you come out and give us a statement?' I send 'em a message back that they don't need any help from me to tear down the game of football. They knew what they were gonna write without hearing what I had to say. So why even bother to talk to me? Y'see, this embitters a fella. I get so goddamn mad everytime I think about it I want to put my foot through a goddamned window."

Woody Hayes' office is a small windowless room with a tiny desk, a red couch on which he sleeps during the season, a couple of folding chairs and a telephone, the same telephone on which President Nixon called to ask Hayes to head the Peace Corps. There are dozens of books: *Profiles in Courage, Portraits of Power, The Study of the F.B.I., Six Crises, The Anatomy of Revolution, Jonathan Livingston Seagull*; biographies of generals — Patton, Rommel, Eisenhower, Sherman, MacArthur; anthologies — *Famous People of the World, Great Speeches of the World*; two shelves of *Time-Life* capsule books.

Woody Hayes motioned me to sit down in the corner. He put on a pair of silver-rimmed glasses. Then he picked up a worn, dog-eared paperback from the top of a stack of books and began flipping through its pages, some of which had been heavily underlined in black felt-tip pen. Hayes unzipped his windbreaker, took a seat on the other side of the office and stretched out his legs.

"All right now, listen to this man Emerson," Hayes said. "Now this is from his essay *Compensation*. Listen to this and maybe you'll learn something."

As he started to read, the voice was soft and loving, the cadence slow and even, like a minister rendering scripture at a Sunday service.

" '*For every strength there is a consequent weakness. Every excess causes a defect; every defect an excess. Every sweet hath its sour; every evil its good. For every thing you have missed, you have gained something else; and for every thing you gain, you lose something.*' "

Hayes looked up from his book. "Emerson's just right as hell on that," he said. "Now the greatest player I ever had playing for me was Hop Cassady, and Hop Cassady was also about the *smallest* who ever played for me. He was just a little guy. Only weighed about a hundred fifty-five pounds soaking wet. And he wasn't too fast either. But he *compensated*. He compensated for that lack of size and speed. First, he was just about the guttiest little guy I ever saw. Second, he was a goddamn *smart* football player. There was nobody could follow blockers better than old Hop."

The memory of his beloved charge brought a little moisture to the eyes of Woody Hayes. He turned a page, like someone leafing through an album of nostalgic snapshots, and found another passage.

"This'll really shake you up," he promised. " '*The President has paid dear for his White House. It has commonly cost him all his peace, and the best of his manly attributes. To preserve for a short time so conspicuous an appearance before the world, he is content to eat dust before the real masters who stand erect behind the throne.*' "

"Now the amazing thing about that," he said, "is that it was written more than a hundred years ago. Now just tell me one goddamned thing. Is that relevant to what's happening today with this Watergate thing or isn't it?"

But before anything could be offered in response, he was thumbing through pages again, stopping at still another heavily underlined passage.

" *'The wise man throws himself on the side of his assailants. It is more his interest than it is theirs to find his weak point. Blame is safer than praise. I hate to be defended in a newspaper. As long as all that is said is said against me, I feel a certain assurance of success. But as soon as honeyed words of praise are spoken for me I feel as one that lies unprotected before his enemies.'* "

Hayes closed the book and put it gently back on top of the stack. "Now that pretty well sums up my attitude towards the press," he said.

He sat in silence for a minute, staring at the bookshelves. His voice had become raspy and he coughed hard twice, trying to clear his throat. Then he started up again.

"Now this may sound corny to a fella like yourself," he proceeded, "but all my life I have been and always will be a *hero-worshiper*."

"Which means?"

"Well," he said, "when I get a great athlete — and I've had my share or you wouldn't be here talking to me now — I feel a little tingle inside because I'm a great respecter of the great athlete. I feel it's my duty to him as a coach to get the best out of them, and I get very bitter when they don't want to give us the best, because they *owe* it to us.

"Now," he went on, "you take my quarterback a few years back, a fella by the name of Rex Kern. You never saw anything like him. He was a great leader and he worked at football like a sonofabitch. Rex was also a pretty good student, not great, but good. All A's and B's. I remember one quarter in his junior year he made over fifty speeches for the Fellowship of Christian Athletes. He was truly a helluva great kid, and a coach ends up respecting those kinds of quality kids just all the way. So when somebody starts in with that bullshit about football players being dumb jocks and animals, I have just two words for them: Rex Kern. He's my idea of a football hero.

"Y'see, the football player has got to be a *better* human being than the other students on campus. He's got to have cleaner habits. He's got to work harder. He's got to schedule classes earlier to have time for practice. Now, I've done some research on this, and studies show twenty-five percent of the students need psychiatric counseling. But in all my years here I've sent only two of my players to a psychiatrist, and in both cases the problems had nothing at all to do with football. One kid was an exhibitionist. The other kid got all caught up in religion.

"Now they talk about football players being sadistic. I can only remember one kid here who really *was* sadistic, and I had to get rid of him even though he was a pretty darn good football player. He was a black kid and he used to ride up and down on the elevators of the dorm, turn the lights off, and when a couple of white kids would get in he'd just beat the hell out of 'em."

Woody Hayes repeated: "He just beat the goddamn hell out of 'em."

Hayes shifted the subject back to safer ground.

"Now by the way, Rex Kern is from a little town called Lancaster, Ohio, and do you know what other great leader came from there? Well now, it was General William Tecumseh Sherman. He's the man who ran an option play right through the South in the Civil War. If you study your history, you'll find that Billy Sherman's March to the Sea used the *alternative objective approach*, striking over a broad front. The defense never had a chance to dig in. Then a hundred years later comes a fella from the same little town, Rex Kern, and the way he ran that option play gave our Buckeye attack all the same offensive versatility Billy Sherman had. Y'see, history is full of such ironies."

All this was only preamble. For four more hours Woody Hayes kept reaching in and pulling out stories; throwing in opinions and polemics; quoting famous people; bolting out of his chair; declaiming against the press; predicting the fall of America; railing against permissiveness; clearing his throat; apotheosizing football. From time to time there would be a knock on the door and Hayes would go off and confer. Then he would come back and pick up the manic aria where he'd left off: recounting battles and military strategy; reciting his version of historical events; excoriating progressive ideas; relating football to anything and everything — all in a manner that constantly shuttled back and forth between hushed, fervid undertone and fist-slamming, Klaxon-horn rage. Meanwhile, there was nothing for me to do but sit and listen, a mute target for Hayes' cerebral Panzer divisions.

During one brief stretch Hayes managed to string together quotations from:

— General George Patton ("Wars may be fought with weapons but they are won by men").

— Abraham Lincoln ("Let us have faith that right makes might; and in that faith let us to the end dare do our duty as we understand it").

— Napoleon ("From the sublime to the ridiculous is but a step").

— Vince Lombardi ("You can't get along with sports writers").

— William Shakespeare ("The evil men do lives after them, the good is oft interred with their bones").

— George Santayana ("Those who cannot remember the past are condemned to repeat it").

— John Kennedy ("Victory has a hundred fathers and defeat is an orphan").

— Louis Pasteur ("Chance favor the prepared mind").

— Darrell Royal ("Luck is what happens when preparation meets opportunity").

— Sir Joshua Reynolds ("There is no expedient to which men will not resort to avoid the real labor of thinking").

— A Persian proverb ("Luck is infatuated with the efficient").

— U.S. Marine Corps motto ("Proper preparation prevents poor performance").

In Hayes' scheme of things, life imitates football. One minute he would be talking about the split T formation. Another minute he would be talking about Thucydides. Then Nathaniel Hawthorne. . . now homosexuality. . . then goal-line defenses. . . now Pearl Harbor. . . then the breakdown of respect for authority. . . now Metternich. . . then drugs. . . now George Halas. . . then the French Revolution. . . now the double-team block.

"Now the double-team block, of course, is the story of your First World War, very simple. Germany was caught in the double-team block, between the pressure from the Allies from the West — France and England — and then pressure from the Russians in the East. Now do you know what the Germans did to break the double-team block? They went to Switzerland and got a fella and sealed him up in a boxcar and sent him to Russia to foment a revolution just so as they could break that double-team block. He got there and he had an innate sense of timing. He realized it was too early to foment that revolution and he jumped into Finland. Do you know who I'm talking about? *Goddamn it*, of course, I'm talking about Lenin. But then

Lenin came in in the October Revolution of 1917 and therein started communism. And who had started it? The German general staff in order to get out of the double-team block.

"Okay now, take your history today. Today there's a great possibility of someone getting caught in the double-team block because there's three great powers in the world — a fourth perhaps emerging, but not ready yet. With three great powers in the world, someone is going to get caught in the double-team block. The trip that Dick Nixon made to China and Russia in 1972 had that in mind exactly. Because I think he studied the situation and he realized there is a great likelihood of war between China and Russia. Why? The Russians can take out that nuclear plant of the Chinese very easily. They can take it, and they're scared of it. Who wouldn't be scared of eight hundred million people — with nuclear power? There's a forty-five-hundred-mile common front between them. A lot of that is relatively flat terrain, in which a good tank division can travel mighty, mighty fast and get the job done, particularly against soldiers who will come up with small rifles and sticks. And so there's a great, great possibility of that thing happening. If you study your history at all, when you get large nations in modern warfare fighting it's always a question of double-team blocks.

"And I think you could say in a nutshell that Nixon's whole foreign policy is to keep us out of those double-team blocks. That's why I'm so bitter about Nixon not being able to call the signals anymore, because in football you learn when a coach calls play 'twenty-six' you run play 'twenty-six.' You don't say, 'Aw maybe he shouldn't have called that.' You're goddamned-dead if you do that."

He carried on without missing a beat. "To me football is a microcosmic reflection of the ideals, emotions, strategies, pitfalls, and problems of a society. Now go back to the Battle of Salamis, where the Greeks beat the tail off the Persians. Now doesn't that take in so many of the things you see in a football game? Fear, determination, backs to the wall, home-field advantage — all those things you see in a football game. And that Battle of Salamis wasn't for the national championship; it was for the *world* championship. If you study your history, the Battle of Salamis decided the fate of democracy, because if the Persians had won, the Greeks would have been sucked into the abyss of Oriental despotism.

"All right now, take your Battle of Midway. It was without a doubt the *greatest* battle we fought in World War Two. It was almost a *total victory*. The Japs lose every carrier they used at Pearl Harbor. We popped 'em all and sank 'em. And the way we did it was simple football strategy. Our Marines forced the Japs to overcommit their defense. We caught them with the planes down at the line of scrimmage."

Hayes flicked his tongue in and out like a garter snake seeking a grasshopper. Then he was on his feet again, puffing out his massive gut, making sweeping movements with his arms, and suddenly he was reciting Winston Churchill's famous address to the British Parliament after the evacuation of Dunkerque.

" *'We shall fight on the beaches, we shall fight on the landing grounds, we shall fight in the fields and in the streets, we shall fight in the hills; we shall never surrender, and even if, which I do not for a moment believe, this island or a large part of it were subjugated and starving, then our Empire beyond the seas, armed and guarded by the British fleet, would carry on the struggle, until, in God's good time, the New World, with all its power and might, steps forth to the rescue and liberation of the Old.'* "

When he was finished he slumped back in the chair. He was tired and out of breath but his brown eyes were shining triumphantly. "Did you ever hear a better locker-room speech?" he crowed.

There was a pause. "Y'know, people ask me so many times how I've maintained my drive, my enthusiasm. I think the only way a man can maintain his enthusiam for his job beyond a certain point is to be able to see his job in the larger context — the *sublime* context. This to me is an absolute necessity. I see my job as a part of American civilization and as a *damn important part*. I see football as being just so much above everything else."

It was late in the afternoon and we were sitting in Woody Hayes' meeting room when three football players came in. They were all black. Hayes, making the introductions, pointed to me and said, "This man here and I are getting along pretty good, but I don't think we will be after he goes home and twists around everything I told him."

The three players were Ted Powell, a sleepy-eyed tight end from Hampton, Va.; Neal Colzie, a tough and wiry defensive back from Miami, Fla.; and Lou Mathis, a baby-faced cornerback from Patterson, N.J. Woody Hayes was asking them questions, lots of questions. He asked them about workouts, weights, courses, grades, exams, women, summer plans and dorm life. He asked Powell, who was wearing a heavy cast on his right leg, about the foot he had sprained in a spring game. Told that it was improving, Hayes gloated that Powell had been the only player on the team to suffer a serious injury during spring practice. Which seemed of little consolation to the grim-faced Powell. Then Hayes turned to Colzie, the most flamboyant dresser of the group in a lime body shirt, open almost to the navel, and crotch-tight bell-bottoms.

"Tell me, what courses are you taking this quarter, Neal?" Hayes asked softly.

"Mmmm, let's see," came the slow, barely audible reply. "I got camp counseling."

"Umm-hm, umm-hm," Hayes nodded. "What else?"

"I got pharmacy."

"All right now, hold it right there," Hayes boomed. "Lemme ask you a question now. Do they tell you anything in that pharmacy course about marijuana?"

Colzie nodded vacantly.

"What do they say about it, Neal?"

"They say it bad."

"Umm-hm, umm-hm," said Hayes, his eyes widening. "Now do they talk much about the connection between marijuana and heroin?"

Colzie answered affirmatively again and adjusted a bell-bottom. There was a flushed look of exultation on Woody Hayes' face, as if he had just beaten Michigan by four touchdowns.

"Y'see," he cawed, gesturing in my direction, "these fellas from the press say there *isn't* any connection between marijuana and heroin. But I've done some research on it. I *know* there is. Every junkie that has ever been in the history of the world started out by smoking marijuana. And you know something, I can tell in a minute when a kid's been smoking just as soon as he walks out on that field. I don't even have to *ask* him."

Hayes looked over at Lou Mathis. "Now you know about marijuana, don't you, Lou?"

"Only from hearsay, coach," Mathis deadpanned. I smiled at Mathis and he winked. It was getting late, high time to depart, and as I got up to leave, Hayes picked himself up from his chair and bellied up to me. He extended that enormous hand, grabbed the tip of my tie and flipped it up in the air.

"Now the next time you come to see me," he chortled, quite warmly, "you better not wear that."

I looked down at the tie, puzzled. "What's wrong with it?"

"The colors!" Woody Hayes bellowed, pointing to the blue and yellow stripes. "Those are the goddamned colors of Michigan!"

16

Still Alive And Kicking

December 2, 1974

By RAY KENNEDY
Sports Illustrated

If there was ever any doubt about it, the preternatural goings on in Columbus, Ohio, last week proved once and for all that Woody Hayes is indeed a soothsayer in baggy pants. Invoking such household deities as Abraham Lincoln, Robert Redford, General Patton, Jonas Salk, Little Orphan Annie and Archie Griffin, the Olentangy Oracle prophesied that the clash between Ohio State and Michigan would be an athletic Armageddon, a holy war waged in behalf of God, country and well-groomed men everywhere.

"I feel sometimes that the man upstairs sort of likes us," Woody said on the eve of the big showdown. "Maybe we deserved the thing that happened to us — notice I didn't say 'defeat' — at Michigan State two weeks ago. Maybe He was testing us, saying, "Let's see what kind of people are at Ohio State. . . . Do they take defeat lightly? Can they come back from adversity?"

Well, no and yes. No, the Buckeyes' controversial 16-13 loss to the Spartans was not taken lightly, especially by a coach who still seems ready to backhand the first man who suggests that it was anything but "questionable." And yes, Ohio State can not only come back, but, as Michigan learned last week, do it with a vengeance. But throwing adversity for a loss, something of a Hayes specialty, did not in itself make this "the greatest thrill-packed game this country has to offer." What does qualify him for clairvoyant-of-the-year honors is the new and startling way his Buckeyes triumphed.

It was not easy considering the long and storied history of what Hayes calls "the greatest rivalry in any sport." All season long, in fact, the only real question has been what could Ohio State and Michigan possibly do for an encore?

Anything, it was hoped, but a repeat of the frustration of last year, when No. 1 Ohio State and No. 4 Michigan, both undefeated, struggled to a 10-10 tie that required a vote by the Big Ten athletic directors to determine who would go to the Rose Bowl. Indeed, the 6-4 decision in favor of Ohio State so outraged Michigan Coach Bo Schembechler that he was slapped with a two-year probation for accusing Big Ten Commissioner Wayne Duke of "engineering" the vote.

Hayes and his Buckeyes did their best to conjure up something different last week. Like winning, 12-10, while only once penetrating beyond the Michigan 25. Like bringing in an ailing defensive back from the hospital to make a critical interception before being carried from the field. And like setting a Buckeye record with four field goals by a walk-on Czech refugee who gets kicking tips from his younger sister.

But by winning, Ohio State forced another vote by the athletic directors and, because of the narrow margin of victory, it seemed possible that Michigan would go to Pasadena. The 10 directors met in Chicago on Sunday and their meeting was long and vocal, but when they emerged Ohio State was again told to start packing for California while for Michigan it was another chorus of "no place like home for the holidays."

Despite the postgame haggling, the weekend was one of those rare instances in which the event was worthy of the buildup. That is no small achievement considering all the drumbeating that Hayes was doing last week. "By comparison," he kept telling anyone who would listen, "the Super Bowl and the World Series don't even compare with our rivalry. U.S.C. versus U.C.L.A.? Ho hum." At other moments he would turn historian, "How did our great rivalry get started? Well, the real fight started back in 1836 when Andrew Jackson, that wily old cuss, took Toledo away from that state up north and gave it to us."

As for Schembechler, he was disinclined to rehash the events of a century ago — or even last year. "I don't want to talk about it," he said. "This is football, not politics. Nothing that happened last year matters this year."

Paul Warfield (42) led the Buckeyes in pass receiving in 1962 and '63.

Hayes addresses an O.S.U. pep rally during the early 1960s.

The Coach visits with his assistants Doyt Perry (*left*) and Esco Sarkkinen (*right*) on the sidelines prior to a game in 1954.

Buckeye assistant coach Bo Schembechler (*center*) clowns around with his prize linemen, Daryl Sanders (76) and Bob Vogel (73), prior to practice.

Hayes on the sidelines during two-T-shirt weather in 1967.

1965 captains, Greg Lashutka (*left*) and Dwight Kelley (*right*), pose with Woody at practice.

Hayes huddles with his squad prior to kickoff of the 1966 season.

Woody visited Vietnam several times in the 1960s. Here he listens intently to a Marine officer explain U.S. military strategy.

John Glenn, the former astronaut and a later U.S. Senator (D-Ohio), receives an autographed football from Hayes.

The O.S.U. student body boycotted classes following the O.S.U. Faculty Senate vote to ban the Buckeyes from playing in the 1962 Rose Bowl.

Woody blasts an official following a controversial call during the 1971 O.S.U. - Michigan game.

Bo apparently has not been frequenting the Michigan dorms lately. Linebacker Steve Strinko, for one, said before the game, "You're never going to see a team as high as Michigan in Columbus. It went to a vote last year and they shafted us. So we're not going to let them shaft us this time. The other day some of us were sitting around watching TV and one of the guys said, 'If you gave me an elbow pad before the Ohio State game I'd be ready to eat it.' " The Banks brothers, Harry and Larry, promised to be even more demonstrative. Larry, a defensive end, aware that Ohio State's Archie Griffin was going for his 22nd consecutive game of rushing for 100 or more yards, said, "The only way Griffin will get 100 yards is if I die." Harry, a defensive back, added, "If we lose, I hope to exhale my last breath on the field."

Dennis Franklin, Michigan's slick faking quarterback, who has been troubled with a sprained ankle, drew comparisons with another battle of titans. "When Ali fought Foreman he could have taken it easy because he'd already been champ. What did he have to win for? He had to win because he had so much pride to regain after all the inequities he had to go through. That's what it's like for us."

The Buckeyes were no less psyched up. "This is going to be college football at its very best," predicted defensive back Neal Colzie. "They say that pro ball is not like this. If that's true, I'll be very disappointed."

Colzie sounds like a chip off the old Woody. So did Schembechler when, like Hayes, he closed his practices last week. Slightly paranoid about intruders, he even sent a team of student assistants off to corner a U.P.I. photographer who was trying to get a shot from the roof of a house across the street from the practice field. Actually, Hayes and Schembechler, whose careers are so similar, also are so similar in method that their teams could exchange playbooks and it is doubtful if anyone in the stands would be any wiser.

Indeed, except for a surprise opening pass that came within a knuckle or two of being intercepted, the two teams were almost mirror images of one another last Saturday. Franklin threw more and Cornelius Greene, the Buckeye quarterback, did a lot of scrambling during the afternoon, but the primary tactics were the same: grind it out.

The first two quarters differed sharply. The Wolverines kicked off with the wind, pinned Ohio State inside its 15 and took over near midfield. On their fourth play, Franklin, his injured leg taped like a thoroughbred's, passed over the middle to Gil Chapman, who eluded one tackler and veered off to the corner of the end zone for a 42-yard score. On their second series, Gordon Bell, a bolter who runs at a forward angle that seems to defy gravity, crashed for 43 yards in seven plays to set up a field goal by Mike Lantry. With barely 10 minutes expired, the Wolverines were ahead, 10-0. It looked for a moment as if a high-scoring game, if not a rout, might be in the offing.

But only for a moment. With Griffin shifting into overdrive, Ohio State invaded Michigan territory at the end of the quarter. On the first play of the second period, with a 20-mile-an-hour wind behind him, Buckeye kicker Tom Klaban set up for what was to become a familiar sight. Though the snap was errant, Klaban got off a 47-yard sidewinder that hooked through the uprights.

Griffin kept pounding away to the increasing befuddlement of the Wolverine defense. At one point, when linebacker Strinko met the powering Griffin head on in a hugger-mugger clasp, Strinko went down and sat there for several long astonished moments watching Archie plow on for five more yards.

More discouraging was the sight of Klaban coming on to register another field goal, a 25-yarder, the second of the quarter. Then, with just seconds remaining in the first half, Greene connected with split end Dave Hazel for 26 yards to usher Klaban in once again. His third kick, a 45-yarder that cut the Michigan margin to 10-9.

Bell, who rushed for 93 yards in the first half, was held to a mere 16 yards after the break mainly because of the ferocious play of linebacker Bruce Elia and tackle Pete Cusick. With Greene finding his running legs, the Buckeyes penetrated far enough early in the third quarter to again bring in the omnipresent Klaban. His kick, a 45-yard boomer, put Ohio State into the lead for the first time, 12-10.

From there on it was all push and shove with Cusick & Co. getting in most of the hardest licks. During one series, the 250-pound Cusick singlehandedly stopped the Wolverines cold three times in succession.

The Ohio State defense, plus a pair of booming punts by Tom Skladany that traveled 63 and 55 yards, and that key interception by Colzie, who had been hospitalized with a throat infection, throttled the Wolverines.

True to the tradition of the rivalry, some last-ditch heroics were in order and Michigan tried to comply when Franklin passed to Jim Smith for 21 yards. Then, in what looked like a replay of last year's fading seconds, Lantry, a 26-year-old Vietnam veteran, came in for a 33-yard field goal attempt. The kick soared high and long enough but it was off to the left by about one foot — the same margin that denied Michigan a victory in 1973.

While Buckeye fans were dismantling the goal posts, Klaban, the man of the moment, was in the locker room addressing a new circle of admirers. Recalling the day when, as a Czech youth, he braved gunfire by border guards to escape with his family from behind the Iron Curtain, he said that he had "never even seen a football until a few years ago." He is still so unaccustomed to its idiosyncrasies, he said, that before the game he took some tips from his younger sister, because "she is the only one who understands my soccer style."

Later, a $1,000 scholarship was awarded to Ohio State in Klaban's name, honoring him for being the game's outstanding offensive player. Not to be outdone, Hayes, declaring that "this was the greatest kicking game I've ever seen," awarded Klaban the game ball — and a full scholarship. Klaban can use it.

"I've never had a scholarship before," he said. "I'm a walk-on, and at Ohio State walk-ons don't get a scholarship until they've proved themselves."

It seemed the least Woody could do.

17

O-High-O Buckeyes

December 1, 1975

By JOHN UNDERWOOD
Sports Illustrated

On the third play of the game, Rick Leach, the freshman quarter-back, threw a swing pass to Gordon Bell coming out of the Michigan backfield. As the play unfolded a voice in the press box, surely that of a veteran Ohio State-Michigan watcher, screamed, "He's passing!" The voice was thick with discovery and awe, the kind of sound one might make to announce that someone was stealing his wallet ("He's stealing my wallet!") or undressing at midfield ("He's undressing at midfield!"). The play gained only eight yards, hardly a blockbuster, but, ah, what a foretaste.

The game that probably won for Woody Hayes a fourth national championship to curl up with this winter as, say, he contemplates retirement at 62 — which he says he would not tell you if he were — was nothing if not a discovery. A discovery that Michigan-Ohio State *could* be one of those games you never dreamed about when you were watching them slog it out at 10-10. An exquisitely exciting, breathtakingly imperfect football game — that's what last week's showdown in Ann Arbor turned out to be. Just like nobody said it would.

So Ohio State wins, but the score is not two field goals to one, it is 21-14. Not since the start of the decade has the winner needed more than two touchdowns in this game. And if Ohio State-Michigan is always three yards and a spray of Astronap, what are they doing making 40-yard runs (well, underdog Michigan is making 40-yard runs; No. 1-ranked Ohio State is mostly recovering Michigan fumbles) and throwing long, arcing devil-may-care passes? And completing them. And if these are teams that button down all the flaps and always keep to the right on the freeway, what are they doing committing eight turnovers (they are also *intercepting* long, arcing devil-may-care passes) and pitching the ball around so hairily?

The question will arise — did the game get out of hand? Was it so good only because the two teams played out of character? Thirty-seven passes may not seem like much, but when it's Michigan-Ohio State it's much. By comparison, the 20 they threw last year made you feel as if the ball were flying around all afternoon. Alas, traditionalists, you will be surprised to learn that it was no accident at all, that it was all right there in the game plans just the way those two old sticklers-in-the-mud, Woody Hayes and Bo Schembechler, wrote them.

"We will pass," said Hayes to a friend in Columbus a day beforehand, "because that is where they are vulnerable." Hayes has been known to rip out the field phones when such strategy was proposed in the past. "I really wouldn't be surprised if it came down to passing," said Schembechler in his office on Friday. He said he knew he would necessarily be asking a great deal of freshman Leach, pitted against the experienced Ohio State secondary, but he had already crossed that bridge ("He may be a freshman, but he was born to compete"). Schembechler told Bud Wilkinson he would play it from the start "like we were behind in the fourth quarter."

In those frenetic countdown hours there had been no hint that the two old rivals (Bo coached under Woody for six years) were anything more than fashionably irascible for the big game. Getting closer to their collars, they made predictable news — Hayes locked practices, held one icy press conference that lasted 97 seconds (a reporter timed it) and was steadfast in not being willing to express the word "Michigan" in conversation. But a close friend said Woody was actually "breezing — I've never seen him so loose. Uh, relatively speaking." Schembechler, for his part, waged a two-day war with United Press International over a photographer he caught aiming a sequence camera at *his* secret practice from an apartment building across the street. Before that slapstick was over, Schembechler had led a charge — battalion strength, presumably — on the building, got the police to confiscate the undeveloped film and, to demonstrate his indignation, resigned from the U.P.I. ratings board. He also barred the U.P.I. from the next day's press conference and called the photographer's attempt to sneak a picture "a shabby trick." The photographer called the Michigan coaches "bullies."

Schembechler smiled on Friday, when he outlined the "secret formation" he was afraid the U.P.I. man had photographed — a short-yardage alignment (picked up from watching films of Indiana's near-upset of Ohio State) in which, a la Indiana, he shifted a 230-pound defensive tackle to blocking back and adorned him with a camouflaging (though legal) No. 30 jersey. As it developed, the one time he had a chance to use the play against Ohio State it lost a yard.

Ironically, the behind-in-the-fourth-quarter approach actually got Michigan *ahead* in the fourth quarter, and only then — after almost three quarters of practically perfect play — did the Wolverines go awry, unfastening in a blink what seemed a secured, and deserved, victory. This is not to say that Ohio State did not deserve to win, rather to give Schembechler credit for a gallant try to overcome what has become his and his team's singular failing: an inability to tick for 60 minutes against Ohio State. In the last 70 regular-season-games under Schembechler, the Wolverines have lost only four games — all to Ohio State.

Here, then, some familiar scenes and characters in Bo's recurring nightmare:

Archie Griffin. Heisman Trophy Archie. Hundred-yards-a-game Archie. Archie goes out for the pregame coin toss before 105,543 fans in Michigan Stadium (announced as a record crowd, though a contingent of freeloading Cub Scouts supposedly swelled the limit to 109,000 in an earlier game) on a bright, clear, cold day, with a national television audience witnessing, and gets *hugged* by archrival Gordie Bell. In front of all those hot-eyed partisans wearing "Ohio Is a Four-Letter Word" buttons, or singing "We don't give a damn about the whole state of Michigan." Is it a demonstration? (See, guys, here's how you put the clamps on Archie — right arm around his neck, left arm. . . .)

No matter. The rest of the afternoon Griffin is passed from hand to hand like a cheap artifact at a swap meet. Not since he was a freshman and a green apple in Woody Hayes' eye does Griffin have such a terrible time. Michigan's line plays straight-on when Ohio State expects it to slant; it slants when the Buckeyes do not expect it to at all; drops to a three-man front with filling linebackers; and swarms, swarms, swarms. Everywhere that Archie goes the blue shirts surely follow.

After a first-possession 63-yard touchdown drive which he sparks with a pass reception and a number of short, darting runs, Griffin is neutralized. Over a stretch of seven carries, he makes a net of three yards; his longest run is five. On a no-gainer sideline play he is submarined by Wolfman (Roverback) Don Dufek, an omnivorous defender, and in rapid order is struck by three flying Wolverines. Archie Griffin has gone 31 regular-season games without making fewer than 100 yards; in his last two against Michigan he has made 163 and 111. But on this day he gets 46 yards in 19 punishing (for him, not Michigan) carries. "It's not the 100 yards that matters, it's the average per carry," Schembechler had said. In this game Archie averages a meager 2.4 a carry.

So is Archie crying? No, Archie is rejoicing. "I'd give up all 31 of those 100-yard games for this one," he says afterward. Typical Griffin. "The greatest, the most unselfish player I've ever known. Archie Griffin could be the first black President," says Hayes, who is now unstoppable (no 97-second press conference this time). He calls the Buckeye comeback "the greatest in my 25 years of coaching."

What has Griffin's 46 yards to do with it? Heat, mainly. The heat he takes off the rest of the Ohio State offense. Eventually. But to set it up further.

In seven possessions, from their second play of the second quarter until only seven minutes remain in the fourth, the Buckeyes on offense are three plays and out. Not a first down in more than 30 minutes. Michigan dominates. During that stretch the Wolverines get six yards for every one they give up. Bell and fullback Rob Lytle rip into the Ohio State defense with startling success, and Leach refuses to accept the opportunity to choke. Only when he is confronted and confused, by a surprise seven-man line does he act his age, and even then, even after an errant pitchout stops one Michigan drive, and an interception another, and his own fumble a third, he is not discouraged.

He marshals Michigan 80 yards to a tying touchdown just before the half, Wolverines achieving it on an 11-yard pass from Bell to wingback Jim Smith, who makes as if to block cornerback Craig Cassady, then shields him away with his backside as he turns for a stretching fingertip catch just inside the flag at the goal. And after sparring fitfully through the third quarter, Leach takes Michigan 43 yards to a 14-7 lead, setting it up with two passes to Smith and getting the touchdown himself on a one-yard keep off the left side.

Now there is only 7:11 to play, and time to reintroduce Ohio State quarterback Cornelius Greene. You remember Corny from past episodes. He is also called "Flam," which is short for flamboyant. Flamboyant is the color of Corny Greene's wardrobe, but flamboyant is not what you would call his quarterbacking, through no fault of his own. His body might belong to his haberdasher, but Greene's arm belongs to Woody Hayes. Woody is sometimes called "Wood." His critics say that is just about the consistency of his thinking when it comes to passing the football. But with the ball on the Ohio State 20 after Michigan went ahead, Greene is sent in with orders to do exactly that.

Television is renewing itself with a commercial break so Greene summons the Buckeyes together "for a prayer." What does he pray for at a time like that? "Extra strength," he says. He seems to get it immediately. On the first play he winds up like Sandy Koufax and throws downfield, badly overshooting his receiver with what looks suspiciously like a desperation pass. On second down he is rushed into his end zone by blitzing Wolverines, somehow escapes and throws into a cluster of the wrong people. Two Michigan players get dibs at it and come up empty.

It must be recalled at this point that Corny Greene averages 8.7 passes a game. In two years he has not thrown as many as 16 passes, the number he is to throw in this game. On third and ten — *really* desperate now — he calls a play-action pass off a fake to Griffin. The Michigan linebacker on the side he want to throw draws in out of respect for Archie, and Greene throws to wingback Brian Baschnagel over the coverage for 17 yards — Ohio State's first first down since the second quarter.

And just like that it became Ohio State's game.

On the next four plays Greene got four more first downs — two passes to split end Len Willis, an 11-yard Griffin run (his longest of the day) and a 12-yard keeper to the Michigan 8. From there, Hayes reverted to what he calls his "button-shoes robust," a tight T with a full-house backfield. In four slugs fullback Pete Johnson scored the tying touchdown.

Alas, now freshman Leach gets his comeuppance. He is sacked for a nine-yard loss to his 11-yard line, throws an incomplete pass — and then hangs one dangerously high in the air over Jim Smith's head. Ray Griffin, Archie's younger brother, steps in front of Smith going full speed at the Michigan 32 and is down to the three before Leach blocks him out of bounds. On first down Johnson once more pounds into the end zone and Ohio State is ahead.

With an interception by Cassady to seal it, Hayes' "greatest comeback in 25 years" puts him in the Rose Bowl for the eighth time. It is clearly the easiest way to go for the national championship, considering the battered Pacific Eight opposition that awaits him there. By comparison, Bo gets to play Oklahoma in the Orange Bowl as a consolation prize.

Leave it to Woody to take care of his friend.

18

Ohio State's General Loses His Command

December 31, 1978

By TONY KORNHEISER
Special to The New York Times

He coached football and he studied military history. For Wayne Woodrow Hayes there was no conflict of interest. Football and war were a perfect fit, the apple pie and ice cream of his being. The offense was the strike force, the defense the repel force. Football was a game of territorial acquisition through controlled violence. The only difference in war was in the degree of control. And a good general had nothing if he didn't have control.

He was forever finding military parallels for football. To explain the design of a given play he would tell his players that Hannibal used the same maneuver to cross the Alps. He was a close friend of the former commandant of the Marine Corps, Lewis Walt, whom he met on a tour of Vietnam in 1965. He often quoted George Patton and Curtis LeMay. In fact, he once named a two-minute drill after them. "Patton" was off tackle, right and left; "LeMay" was the passing series.

He was ever so impressed with generals, and Patton was at the top of his list. One can almost imagine Hayes, standing on the sidelines during a game, surveying his troops as they battle and rage, quoting George C. Scott's famous Patton combat scene postscript, "God help me, I love it so."

As a student of military history, surely Hayes knows this about Patton — that once, in a fit of rage, he slapped one of his soldiers, and that he never escaped the stigma of that act. Surely Hayes knows that now, on the day following his dismissal as Ohio State's football coach, since it was a similar incident that caused his downfall. In the closing moments of Friday night's Gator Bowl game, before a national television audience, Hayes reacted this way to an interception that may have cost his team its victory:

The 65-year-old Hayes rushed Charlie Bauman, a college student who plays football for Clemson University, and apparently punched him. Bauman's crime was intercepting the Ohio State pass.

And that was the end for Woody Hayes.

Yesterday morning, Hugh Hindman, the athletic director at Ohio State, and himself a former player and assistant coach under Hayes, said, "Coach Hayes has been relieved of his duties as head football coach at Ohio State University. This decision has the full support of the president of the university." Later, Hindman said, "It was the toughest decision I will ever have to make."

To be relieved of his duties — a military term.

After 28 seasons of command, after piling up a won-lost-tied record of 205-61-10, more victories than all but three college coaches, Woody Hayes was relieved of his duties.

This was by no means the first time that Hayes had reacted in such a violent manner during adversity. Only the most recent time. In 1971, he was shown on national television breaking the sideline down markers in the final minute of the Michigan game, which Ohio State lost.

In 1973, he was accused of pushing a camera back into a photographer's eye prior to the start of the Rose Bowl, which Ohio State lost. In 1977, he was shown on national television punching Mike Friedman, an A.B.C. cameraman, during the Michigan game, which Ohio State lost.

Although Hayes was put on an essentially meaningless one-year probation by his home conference, the Big 10, and reprimanded by the National Collegiate Athletic Association for the incident, he steadfastly refused to apologize for his action. "You get doggone tired of cameras being pushed in your face," he said. "I'm fed up with it. I make no apologies."

There are reasons why Woody Hayes survived his temper long enough to complete 28 seasons at Ohio State. Not the least of them was his vast skill as a coach. Undeniably, he was one of the greats at his craft. His teams were consistently ranked in the top 10 of college football, and for that the people of Ohio State, Columbus and even the nation were always ready to forgive him his excess. College football is almost a religious experience in Columbus, and Hayes its patron saint.

Even yesterday, as reaction to his dismissal poured in from around the country, some people in Columbus were aghast at the move. John Bothe, who hosted a call-in show on W.B.N.S. radio in Columbus, said, "A lot of people said he was completely right in punching out that guy. But most are saying what he did was a disgrace to the university, that he should have retired a long time ago."

There was even ambivalence from some of his players, current and former. Tim Fox, now a safety for the New England Patriots, said he was "disappointed, but not surprised" at the dismissal. "He tended to embarrass me at times, but he did a lot for me in football and helped me mature in my college years." And from Tom Cousineau, the current all-America linebacker for the Buckeyes: "It's a disappointment to me that a great career, a coaching legend, has to end on a note like this. The only way was to fire him. He never would resign."

In recent years the subject of whether or not Woody Hayes would retire came up during each football season like chrysanthemums. In 1976, he made his most definitive comment on the subject — he usually tended to ignore the question when put to him by the media; he was rarely on speaking terms with reporters — when he said, "I have given the matter some thought, and I will make the proper decision at the proper time."

Yesterday, the decision was made for him.

Proper or not, he will have to live with it. Like a good soldier.

19

In Columbus, Tears and Relief

January 1, 1979

By ERIC LINCOLN
Special to The New York Times

The house at 1711 Cardiff Road in the Upper Arlington section of Columbus was locked and shuttered this morning. This has been Woody Hayes' home for the last 25 years, an old frame structure whose green and white paint is peeling in large pieces from the sides.

It was dark inside. Outside it was bleak — foggy and drizzling. At noon, as passers-by stopped and stared before driving on, a car pulled up to the curb, and a man got out and knocked at the door. He had tears in his eyes. "I've known Woody ever since he came to Columbus," the man said. "I just came here with my wife to find him. He needs help now. He needs all the friends he can get."

The man, who didn't want to be identified, put a hand to his face and paused. "I just didn't want to see him go out this way," he went on. "I have been watching him for years now, and I saw this all coming. I really think he's a sick man inside. Things are churning up inside him. All the frustrations are built up. In the end all he could think about was winning. And it started to boil over. That's what got him."

The man said he would spend the rest of the afternoon looking for Hayes. He said he would first drive to Ohio Stadium. "I'm going to keep looking," he said. "He needs friends."

When this quiet Middle American city awoke this morning (Sunday, December 31), for the first time in 28 years Wayne Woodrow Hayes was not the football coach at Ohio State University.

Hayes had been a fixture here, an institution, a legend. His face is plastered on billboards, posted in barbershops, autographed and framed behind oak bars in what seems like every saloon in town. When he suffered a heart attack in 1974, the town prayed for him. Woody came back.

He arrived here in 1951 and had since compiled a record of 205-61-10, taking his teams to three national championships and eight Rose Bowls. "He will not be forgotten here," said the Rev. Francis W. Park, the senior pastor of the Covenant Presbyterian Church, situated a few blocks from Hayes' home.

The man known to most people simply as Coach had been for the last few years an irascible, stubborn and often vindictive figure. Last year he attacked a television cameraman, an act for which he was placed on one year's probation by the Big Ten Conference. He tore up yard markers, charged at referees and attacked the local press. Some residents say he should have been dismissed long ago, but most supported anything Woody did — that is, until he did the absolutely wrong thing Friday night.

"Everyone in church today seemed resigned to the fact that it had to come sometime," said Mr. Park. "He has been having problems right along. He is 65, and he was perhaps ready to retire anyway. People seem just sorry that it had to come this way."

On Friday night, 950 miles away in Jacksonville, Fla., Hayes struck a Clemson University player who had made an interception that all but clinched Clemson's 17-15 victory with less than two minutes remaining in the nationally televised Gator Bowl. The incident was embarrassing. The president of the university, Dr. Harold Enarson, and the athletic director, Hugh Hindman, agreed right then to ask for the coach's resignation. Hayes refused. Later Hindman said: "There is not a university or athletic conference in this country which would permit a coach to physically assault a player. There was no difficulty in reaching the decision."

Mr. Park, the pastor, also had a decision to make.

"I thought about giving my sermon today on Woody," he said. "I thought about it a long time. But it just seemed tangential to other matters. You'll find that people will talk about it, and some will be sad, others will be joyous. Others won't care. But I just didn't think people really wanted to hear about it in church. Everyone knew it. Everyone expected it."

The Varsity Club on West Lane Avenue across from Ohio Stadium was jammed last night. Ohio State students who had not gone home for the holidays were sitting in the back, sipping beers and listening to the jukebox. At 11:30 a few people drifted down to the end of the bar to watch a televised retrospective of Woody Hayes' career. The juke continued blaring. The Gator Bowl incident was replayed at least a half-dozen times. The announcer looked grim, as if he were in mourning.

"It's really the older people who care deeply about Woody," said Darrell Baird, the bartender, an Ohio State alumnus. "I've already heard some kids say that it was 10 years too late. Football just isn't all that important to the students. They don't live and die on Woody anymore. It's the older alumni who supported him. I suppose that's the reason why it became so hard to get rid of him."

The telecast ended with a montage showing the highlights of Hayes' career. The background music was "Send In the Clowns."

"He was a great coach," said one student, a sophomore. "Wherever you lived in this country you had to know about Woody Hayes. But to mourn someone is kind of sappy. He is still alive, isn't he?

"He had been in trouble before. He had all those incidents. He seemed like an angry man to me. When I saw the incident at the Gator Bowl, I was embarrassed. I turned to my friend here and said, 'I really don't want to be a part of Ohio State right now.' I wanted to disown myself from the university."

Another student walked in through the back door. It was raining, and he was drenched. He had been outside listening to his car radio. "I was listening to the Ohio State basketball game in Madison Square Garden," he said. "That's the important thing now."

Margaret Griffin of Columbus sent three of her sons — Archie, Ray and Duncan — to play football for Ohio State. Archie Griffin won the Heisman Trophy twice, in 1974 and again in 1975. Mrs. Griffin remembers Hayes well.

"Oh, yes," she said. "He used to come into our kitchen and sit down just like regular folks. He was a good man. It makes you cry to think what happened. He shouldn't have gone out that way.

"I just wish there were some way he could have retired gracefully. Not this way. I felt so badly. I liked him, and all my sons liked him. I don't think there were too many players who didn't like Coach Hayes."

Tom Levenick, a freshman from Peoria, Ill., played in the Gator

Bowl. He returned to Columbus with the team early yesterday morning, and today he was picking up some clothes from the gymnasium. He was stunned, and tired.

A year ago Hayes sat in Levenick's home and persuaded him to come to Ohio State.

"At first my mother didn't even want Woody coming in my house," said Levenick. "She had heard so much about his reputation. She didn't think he was a very nice man."

Hayes felt the antipathy. So he boned up on the history of Peoria and went to the Levenick's house prepared to win the family over.

"He was incredible," said Levenick. "He was charming and seemed concerned about me as a student. This won over my mother. She was worried that he was just running a football factory here."

When the plane carrying the Ohio State team touched down at Port Columbus Airport yesterday, Hayes grabbed the intercom and spoke to the players. His eyes were hidden by sunglasses. He appeared tired, witnesses say. He told the players that they ought to go home and study, that a lot of them were failing.

"He said he didn't want to see any of us fail," Levenick said. "Then he simply put his head down and told us that, he wasn't going to be our coach next season. He got off the plane, and that's the last anyone has seen of him."

Levenick recalled the Gator Bowl incident with anguish. He was standing next to Hayes when it happened. According to Levenick, Charlie Bauman, the Clemson player, waved the ball at the Ohio State team after he had made his interception. The next thing Levenick knew, his coach was swinging at everyone.

"I have never felt so embarrassed for anyone in my life," said Levenick. "I was frozen for a second. I didn't believe it was happening. I turned and tried to shield Coach from the television camera. I just didn't want anyone to see what was going on. When the game ended we kind of knew it was the end. We felt it. The athletic director walked in and was tight-lipped and seemed angry. He never came into our locker room after a game. I knew something must have been really wrong."

The
Memorable
Games

20

Buckeyes Subdue Wisconsin

October 23, 1954

By THE UNITED PRESS
The New York Times

Unbeaten Ohio State scored four touchdowns in nine minutes today to rout previously unbeaten Wisconsin, 31-14. Howard (Hopalong) Cassady supplied the spark that stamped the Buckeyes as revised favorites to win the Big Ten title.

Cassady, a 168-pound halfback, rallied the Buckeyes when they trailed by 4 points late in the third period by intercepting quarterback Jim Miller's pass and running 88 yards for a touchdown. The Buckeyes then added three touchdowns, two as a result of Wisconsin fumbles and another after taking the ball on downs.

The victory before 82,636 homecoming fans was the fifth in a row for Coach Woody Hayes' team and the second in a row in which the Buckeyes had to rally. It was Wisconsin's first loss in five starts.

Ohio State jumped to an early lead, 3-0, on Tad Weed's 29-yard field goal, but trailed, 7-3, at the half. It appeared that Coach Ivy Williamson's team might finally break the jinx that has prevented Wisconsin from winning in Columbus since 1918.

The Badgers threatened twice in the third period. The crowd, the third largest to witness a game here, sat apprehensive that the Buckeyes were about to be toppled.

Wisconsin had driven to the Ohio State 20, with Miller hitting on passes regularly. He tossed one too many, however, for Cassady leaped high on the 12 to gather one in and was off for the goal line.

Ohio State went ahead, 10-7, on Cassady's gallop and then added the other markers behind vicious blocking and tackling.

Wisconsin's Bill Lowe returned a kickoff 41 yards, but Pat Levenhagen fumbled two plays later and Ohio State took over on the 31. Cassady skirted end for 39 yards and quarterback Dave Leggett hit Bobby Watkins with an 18-yard pass to put the ball on the 5, from where fullback Hubert Bobo crashed over for the score.

Ohio State needed only two plays for its next two touchdowns. Wisconsin got back to its own 34 on the kickoff, but Ohio State's Dean Dugger halted Miller three times on attempted passes and the Buckeyes took the ball on downs on the Wisconsin 27. Leggett broke away for a touchdown on the first play. Ohio State's Don Swartz pounced on the ball. Jerry Harkrader darted off tackle for 10 yards and a touchdown on the next play.

After Weed had made his field goal, Wisconsin's Miller intercepted quarterback John Borton's long pass and went 16 yards to the Ohio State 38. He ran for 4 more, then passed to Levenhagen, who went 20 yards for a touchdown. Glen Wilson converted and the score read 7-3 in favor of Wisconsin.

The Badgers' second touchdown was tallied in the waning minutes when quarterback Jim Haluska put together a nine-play attack, including four passes to take the ball to the 1, from where Bob Gingrass went over.

21

O.S.U. Overcomes U.S.C. And Weather In Rose Bowl

January 1, 1955

By THE UNITED PRESS
The New York Times

Ohio State's smooth-clicking Buckeyes, led by Dave Leggett at quarterback, plowed through the mud of the Rose Bowl in a rainstorm to a 20-to-7 victory today over Southern California before 89,191 fans.

Exploding for scores when they got the breaks, the Buckeyes demonstrated their championship caliber. The record individual performance, however, was on the side of U.S.C. as tailback Aramis Dandoy set a Rose Bowl punt-return mark of 86 yards for a touchdown.

But that brilliant broken-field run and two superlative near-record efforts by his substitute, Jon Arnett, were not enough to turn the tide of Buckeye might. Ohio State's all-America halfback, Howard Cassady, aided by Bobby Watkins and Jerry Harkrader, ran up big yardage to keep the lead throughout the game after their initial score.

The game was played under the worst conditions since the 1934 Rose Bowl contest between Stanford and Columbia. Rain fell throughout today's game. By the second period the numbers on the players' jerseys had been obliterated.

It was the eighth Big Ten victory in nine contests with Pacific Coast Conference representatives since their Rose Bowl pact began in 1947.

The power of the Buckeyes was displayed from the opening kickoff when they drove to the Trojans' 14, were penalized back to the U.S.C. 19 and Tad Weed missed a field goal attempt from the 27.

The Buckeyes' next took the ball on their 31 when guard Jim Parker recovered Jim Contratto's fumble. Cassady and Harkrader alternated in driving all the way, with Leggett scoring from the 3. The touchdown came at the start of the second period.

A fumble by a Southern California substitute, Frank Hall, set up the second Ohio State score. Leggett recovered and after Watkins made 14, Leggett threw a 21-yard scoring pass to Watkins.

The picture was grim at that point but Southern California came back with five minutes left in the period. Fullback Hubert Bobo went back from his 32 to kick. He received a bad pass from the center, but was able to get off a boot to Dandoy on the 14.

The Southern California tailback, after a key block by tackle George Belotti, ducked and weaved his way through the entire Ohio State team to score. His 86-yard punt runback to a touchdown shattered the mark of 62 yards set last year by Billy Wells of Michigan State in the game against U.C.L.A.

It was in the third period that Southern California's Arnett covered himself with individual glory, although his efforts were not enough to give the Trojans another score.

The brilliant 19-year-old sophomore got off a quick kick from his own 9 that was good for 70 yards to come within two yards of the bowl record. Later in the same period the young star broke loose for 70 yards from scrimmage to the Ohio State 26, where the Ohioans held on downs. The run came within a yard of the Rose Bowl record established by Frank Aschenbrenner of Northwestern against California in 1949.

But in holding the Buckeyes on the 4, Southern California had shot its bolt.

In the last period, the Buckeyes marched 77 yards in twelve plays, with Harkrader going the final 9 for the score.

Individual brilliant performances also were turned in for the Buckeyes by center Bob Thornton, guard Jim Parker, end Dean Dugger and tackle Dick Hilinski.

The difference in the teams was best illustrated by the first downs as unbeaten Ohio State made twenty-two to Southern California's six.

Despite that superiority, the Trojans fought savagely throughout; guard Orlando Ferrante was particularly brilliant in the line together with center Marvin Goux and end Leon Clarke.

The 13-point victory margin proved Ohio State had rated its role as as two-touchdown favorite. But it did not settle whether the Buckeyes were any better than The United Press poll champions, U.C.L.A., because of the poor playing conditions. U.C.L.A. beat Southern California, 34 to 0.

The Uclans were ineligible to play in the bowl because they represented the coast league there last year.

• • •

Coach Woody Hayes of the victorious Ohio State Buckeyes complained after today's Rose Bowl game that the contest took place under the "worst playing conditions" they had encountered in four years.

Pulling no punches, Hayes said he could pick at least four teams in the Big Ten that could have done to Southern California what his Buckeyes did today in their 20-7 victory. He said these teams were Michigan, Iowa, Wisconsin and Minnesota — in addition to the Buckeyes.

"You'll have to admit that our defense was tremendous," the jubilant Hayes told reporters after the game. "We held Pittsburgh to five first downs and Southern California to six."

"Our option play was our bread and butter play this afternoon. Quarterback (Dave) Leggett played a brilliant game. Before the game, we felt we were a better team than Southern California, so we chose to play a conservative role. We were not going to take too many chances," he said.

"We feared Southern Cal's kicking game which was superior to ours. They kick a crazy ball, out of bounds and deep. We changed quite a few of our plays at the line of scrimmage. Fortunately, they set their defense mainly as we anticipated — a deep six. When they went into a five the damage had been done."

Hayes said the Trojan tailback, John Arnett, lived up to his advance notice as a great back. He admitted he was "scared" of the sophomore star. He also said he was worried about the type of play which sprang Aramis Dandoy on his 86-yard punt return for a touchdown.

On a dry field, he said, "we would win by at least 13 points also," thus indirectly crediting Southern California with being able to stay within two touchdowns of the Buckeyes regardless of playing conditions.

"I definitely think we are still the No. 1 team in the country over U.C.L.A.," Hayes continued.

In the Trojan dressing room, Coach Jess Hill refused to make comparisons between his players and the Buckeyes.

"The spirit of our team was great going into the game," he said. "It was as good as it has been at any time this season."

When asked what Buckeye player hurt his team most, Hill replied: "They all seemed to take turns."

He also added: "They were as tough as we expected, but no tougher. Naturally, our kids feel bad. They do not like to lose."

Hill singled out Leon Clarke, an end, and Ed Fouch, a tackle, for praise on their efforts. He said the weather hurt his team, particularly at the guard position.

"We have light and very quick guards and the slippery footing diminished their effectiveness." K. L. (Tug) Wilson, the Big Ten commissioner, said these were the worst playing conditions he had seen all year, but "it was a great game."

22

Ohio State Rally Halts Iowa

November 16, 1957

By THE ASSOCIATED PRESS
The New York Times

A third-string fullback, Bob White, sparked Ohio State to the Big Ten football championship and a berth in the Rose Bowl today.

The 207-pound sophomore gained 157 yards on twenty-two rushes and scored the winning touchdown as the Buckeyes rallied twice to dethrone Iowa's Hawkeyes in a 17-13 thriller.

With Iowa leading, 13-10, late in the final period, White carried the ball on seven of eight plays for 65 yards in a 68-yard drive to the final touchdown. He scored the winning marker on a 5-yard smash over tackle.

Don Clark, Ohio State's ace ball carrier and top scorer, did not see action, but White more than took up the slack as he thrilled a crowd of 82,935, the largest ever to fill Buckeye Stadium, with his tremendous smashes up the middle.

The victory was Ohio State's sixth straight in Western Conference play and the defeat was Iowa's first against four league triumphs and a tie.

Regardless of the outcome of next week's Buckeye game with Michigan, Ohio State is certain of its third Conference championship in the last four years and its fourth trip to the Rose Bowl at Pasadena, Calif. In that post-season game, the Bucks have a 2-1 record.

Ohio State got off to a 3-0 lead in the first period on Don Sutherin's 15-yard field goal, which ended a 74-yard march, all on the ground.

After that, the teams traded touchdowns. Iowa went ahead, 6-3, in the first period on an 8-yard scoring pass from quarterback Randy Duncan to end Bob Prescott. The drive covered 66 yards in ten plays.

A sixteen-play, 79-yard ground march, with quarterback Frank Kremblas scoring from the 1, gave Ohio State a 10-6 lead early in the second period.

In the third, Iowa went 71 yards in eleven plays with Duncan plunging the last yard. Then came Ohio State's big fourth-period splurge to wrap it up.

Iowa fumbled away its chance to win. In the first quarter, the Hawkeyes fumbled and lost the ball on the Buckeye 15 and in the second period they fumbled the ball away on Ohio State's 5.

Pass interceptions also played a big part in checking the Hawkeye offensive. The Buckeyes picked off three Iowa aerials.

All three interceptions occurred in Ohio State territory. In the third period, a 15-yard pass bounced off Prescott's chest into the arms of Ohio State's Galen Cisco. In the fourth period, Dick LeBeau snared another Duncan pass on Ohio State's 40.

After the Buckeyes had gone out front and Duncan had hit Don Norton with a 16-yard pass and Jim Gibbons with a 17-yarder on consecutive plays, Bill Jobko, a guard, halted the threat with an interception deep in Ohio State territory.

The huge Iowa line, averaging 219 pounds per man, which had held its foes to an average of 103 yards rushing, was pounded for 295 yards by the Buckeye ground attack.

Ohio State threw eleven times, far more than its usual number of passes, but completed only two. Iowa completed nine of sixteen for 94 yards. Most of the incomplete tosses came in a last-minute flurry as the Hawks tried to turn the tables with a long one.

Collins Hagler, Iowa's right halfback, gained 49 yards in seven tries to lead the Hawkeyes, but White's 157 yards was 2 yards more than the entire Iowa team was able to amass by rushing.

The victory was Ohio State's twenty-third in its last twenty-five Conference games, and thousands swarmed onto the field to pull down the goal posts at the finish.

Ohio State's victory avenged a 6-0 loss to Iowa at Iowa City last year, in which the Hawkeyes ended a string of seventeen straight Conference victories by Coach Woody Hayes' team — the longest winning streak in the league's history.

23

Buckeye Field Goal
Beats Webfoots

January 1, 1958

By THE UNITED PRESS
The New York Times

Ohio State, outplayed most of the game by an inspired Oregon team, today eked out a 10-7 Rose Bowl victory on a fourth-period field goal by a substitute halfback, Don Sutherin.

Although the victory belonged to the Buckeyes, the honors went to Oregon's quarterback, Jack Crabtree, who led the Ducks close to an upset triumph after they had been listed as 21-point shortenders.

Joining Crabtree in a glowing performance by the Oregon backfield were Jim Shanley, Charley Tourville and Jack Morris. But they could not overcome the 34-yard field goal kicked by Sutherin after fifty-eight seconds of the last period.

Morris also had attempted a field goal from the 24, but he kicked the ball wide to the left of the uprights.

Crabtree was voted player of the game by the Helms Athletic Foundation. He passed, ran and pitched out brilliantly to his speedy backs and was an outstanding field general for the entire sixty minutes.

For the Buckeyes Don Clark occasionally showed his running fullback, frequently powered fullback, frequently powered through the Oregon line. But when the going got tough in the second half, Coach Woody Hayes put in Galen Cisco, who proved just as able at carrying the ball.

Crabtree completed ten of seventeen passes for 135 yards and Ron Stover snagged ten passes for 144 yards.

The Buckeyes' vaunted power was displayed for the capacity crowd of 100,000 from the opening kickoff. Ohio State drove 79 yards, with Frank Kremblas sneaking the final yard from quarterback to score. The drive featured a 27-yard spurt by Clark and a 37-yard pass from Kremblas to end Jim Houston, which gave a first down to Ohio State on the 2.

Oregon's effort to get a march rolling in the opening period was nullified when the Buckeyes' Joe Cannavino intercepted one of Crabtree's passes on Ohio State's 28.

Oregon opened up in the second period, starting on its own 20 and driving all the way in ten plays. Shanley, a halfback, skirted left end for the last 5 yards.

The "big four" of the Ducks had been responsible for the drive. Shanley got to near midfield with a 22-yard run on a pitchout. Crabtree kept it going with a 10-yard keep play. Then he threw an 11-yard pass to Tourville and Morris swept the wing for 13 yards.

With the score 7-7, Oregon showed its defensive strength by stopping the Buckeyes on the 12. The Ducks drove to the Ohio State 29, only to have Crabtree fumble and Dan Fronk recover on the Oregon 37.

The Webfoots dominated the third period and when they reached the Ohio State 18, Morris dropped back for his unsuccessful field goal effort.

With White charging the middle on eight of the next eleven plays, the Buckeyes got to the Oregon 17-yard line on a drive that carried into the fourth period. On fourth down, with 4 yards to go, Sutherin kicked his field goal. It carried from the 24-yard line over the crossbars 10 yards back in the end zone.

Then the Ducks drove to the Ohio State 24, reaching that point on a 23-yard pass from Crabtree to Stover. But Stover fumbled when hit hard and Cannavino recovered. In the wild final minutes, Ohio State got past midfield only to lose the ball on downs with fifty seconds remaining.

The lighter Webfoot team outplayed its heavy midwestern foes in the defense department, although its star lineman, Harry Mondale, went out of the game on the fifth play with a leg injury.

When the Buckeyes trooped off the field they looked as if they had taken a beating rather than picked up a victory.

Sutherlin's field goal was his fourth this season. One of them provided the winning margin over Wisconsin.

Sutherin said after the game: "I felt as soon as I got on the field that the kick would be good. I've kicked longer ones and this wasn't too tough. I booted against Michigan for 43 yards."

Sutherin had been out for a month with an injured back and didn't start practicing on his kicking until four days ago.

Hayes said that Oregon had the same chance and muffed it.

"They had a chance to go ahead with a field goal from the exact spot, angle and everything," said the Buckeye coach. "But our man came through. It proves again the best team always wins — no matter who has made the first downs." (Oregon had 21 first downs, Ohio State 19).

"Our kids are not happy with this victory," Hayes said. "But we met a fine team in Oregon."

"That Oregon team played terrific ball. Their secondary defensive unit was very good. And their ball-carrying backs were very fast."

"And you know something? That 24-yard field goal attempt by Morris looked awfully good to me. I was sure it went between the goal posts. It's lucky for us that the officials were calling it instead of me."

24

O.S.U. Outduels Iowa

November 15, 1958

By THE ASSOCIATED PRESS
The New York Times

Ohio State's Buckeyes, led by Bob White and Don Clark, carved a 38-28 scar on Iowa's Big Ten football crown today in a spectacular offensive duel.

Iowa, gunning for its first undefeated Big Ten season since 1922, matched Ohio State touchdown for touchdown through three quarters, but faded in the stretch under the pounding drives by White, a 210-pound fullback, and his mates.

The defeat was the first of the season for Iowa. A 13-13 tie with the Air Force Academy already had cast a slight blemish on an otherwise perfect record.

The deciding blows today were struck through a grudging Iowa line as a heavy mist covered the playing field midway in the fourth period.

Ohio State, the dethroned 1957 champion, punched 61 yards for the touchdown that sent the Buckeyes into a 34-28 lead.

White, who almost personally licked Iowa a year ago when Ohio State won, 17-13, carried the ball on eleven of fourteen plays for the decisive marker. He went over from the Iowa 1 with 8:15 left. Dave Kilgore kicked his fifth conversion.

Iowa, which had rallied after each of the previous Ohio State touchdowns, started out again, but Dick LeBeau intercepted a pass on the Buckeye 30 and returned the ball to midfield.

Ohio State then slashed toward another touchdown, but after reaching a fourth-down situation on the Iowa 2, Kilgore returned to the game and booted a field goal from the 8.

Whatever hopes the sellout crowd of 58,643 had for Iowa died as the ball sailed between the goal posts for a 38-28 score with only 2 minutes 12 seconds left.

White's last-period touchdown was his third of the day. He ran 71 yards after breaking through the Iowa line in the second period, and got another touchdown later in the period on a smash from the 1.

Clark, back at physical peak for the first time since early in the season, had touchdown runs of 25 and 37 yards.

Randy Duncan was Iowa's hero. The quarterback bettered his own school record by completing 23 of thirty-three passes for 249 yards, with one going for a touchdown to Willie Fleming.

Duncan's completion also smashed the conference single-game mark of twenty-two, set by Tommy O'Connell of Illinois in 1952 against Iowa.

White was only 7 yards short of the Conference single-game rushing record of 216 yards, set by Bill Daley of Michigan against Northwestern in 1943. White cracked the Iowa line for 209 yards on thirty-three carries. Daley made his record on twenty-six rushes.

Fleming scored twice in the second period, once on a pass form Duncan from the 3 after he had raced 57 yards to the Ohio State 5. The other came on a plunge from the 1.

Duncan tallied from the 1, and John Nocera raced 21 yards for Iowa's other touchdowns.

The game was fast and furious from the start. Ray Jauch returned the Ohio State kickoff to the Iowa 37, then fumbled on the first scrimmage play. Dan Fronk recovered for the Buckeyes on the 33.

On Ohio's second play, Clark dashed 25 yards for the first touchdown. Iowa bounced back for a touchdown, and duplicated each of Ohio State's scores until the final period.

It was Iowa's first loss in six Conference games and Ohio State's third victory in six. The Buckeyes have lost one Big Ten game and tied two.

25

Buckeyes Romp Over Michigan

November 25, 1961

By THE ASSOCIATED PRESS
The New York Times

Ohio State, aided by the power of Bob Ferguson and the electrifying running of Paul Warfield, completed a perfect Big Ten season today by beating its arch-rival, Michigan, 50-20.

The Buckeyes exploded for 29 points in the last quarter. They gained the Big Ten title outright when Minnesota was upset by Wisconsin. A possible Rose Bowl invitation is in the offing for Ohio State.

The Buckeyes, who have won or tied for twelve Western Conference titles, played an opening game tie with Texas Christian and then won their remaining eight games — six in the Big Ten.

Ferguson, an all-American fullback last year and a leading candidate to repeat, paced Ohio State's predominantly ground attack. He scored four touchdowns as a crowd of 80,444 and a regional television audience watched.

The 214-pounder rammed through the heavy Wolverine line for 152 yards in thirty carries. Ferguson scored the first two Buckeye touchdowns on 19- and 1-yard runs. Then, after Michigan pulled within 9 points midway in the third period, Ferguson led a march that put the game out of Michigan's reach.

He capped the 80-yard drive by scoring from the 1.

Ohio State used passes infrequently, but an 80-yard pass play from Joe Sparma to Bob Klein produced the Buckeyes' fifth touchdown. Ferguson added an insurance tally on another 1-yard burst in the final five minutes. State scored a second on a Sparma-to-Tom Tidmore pass for 10 yards.

The Wolverines made it a contest only briefly, scoring for the first time on Dave Raimey's 90-yard kickoff return after Ferguson's second touchdown. But Warfield, a sophomore back, quickly nullified that run with a 69-yard scoring jaunt less than two minutes later and O.S.U. was in command, 21-6, at halftime.

Michigan used more than half the third quarter in punching out its second touchdown, on a 78-yard drive that took fourteen plays. Bill Tunnicliff did the bulk of the work and Bruce McLenna went over from the 1.

Michigan scored again in the final minute on Paul Ward's 1-yard plunge.

This was the Buckeyes' nineteenth victory in a traditional and often heated fifty-eight-game series.

Crippled Michigan was forced to play without Bennie McCrae, its best runner, and was able to use Raimey only sparingly.

26

Buckeyes Overthrow Purdue

October 12, 1968

By LINCOLN A. WERDEN
Special to The New York Times

Ohio State upset Purdue's top-ranked football team, 13-0, today and gave the pollsters and a record crowd of 84,834 something to think about.

The Boilermakers had come to Ohio Stadium on this mild afternoon with a No. 1 ranking from both coaches and newsmen in pregame polls. But a surprising band of Buckeyes, which included a crop of talented sophomores on both offense and defense, contributed much to the unexpected victory.

Not since 1965 had Purdue been shut out, when Illinois did the trick by 31-0.

Yesterday afternoon, Coach Woody Hayes broke tradition by holding a final practice session that was closed to all visiting and local observers. But this afternoon it was no secret as Ohio State, primed for this Big Ten confrontation and with Rose Bowl ambitions, revealed it had both the versatility and the manpower.

After a scoreless first half, in which Ohio State failed on three field-goal attempts and Purdue on two, the scoring was crammed into the third period. A 35-yard runback on a pass interception by Ted Provost, a defensive back, brought the home squad its first score.

Ohio State has had big crowds jam its stadium in past years, but today's exceeded one five years ago by more than a hundred persons. When the roar that went up as the red-jerseyed Provost streaked through Boilermaker defenders, it sounded like one giant's yell. Although a subsequent kick for the extra point by Dick Merryman failed, Ohio State now had an edge that it stubbornly protected.

Before the period was over the hard-pressing Buckeyes spiked Mike Phipps and his aerial attempts. And Jim Stillwagon, a sophomore, intercepted to give Ohio State the ball on the enemy 25. Five plays later, Bill Long, who replaced the Buckeyes' brilliant quarterback, Rex Kern, when the latter was injured, dashed 14 yards as he saw potential receivers covered and scored.

Leroy Keyes, Purdue's Heisman Trophy candidate and the 1967 national scoring leader, was limited to 19 yards on seven carries and he caught four passes for 44 yards. But Phipps was overthrowing to Keyes who was used as a flanker.

Keyes was wearing rib pads as protective armor and was reported to have been slightly injured during a recent practice. Phipps, who was repeatedly thrown for losses in his efforts to complete a "bomb" or get the Purdue attack under way, received a "rap on the head" during the third period, according to Coach Jack Mollenkopf, and was taken out;

Mollenkopf added that the Ohio State defense did a "magnificent job," and added: "They had to have their best day. I hope they are not that good all the time."

With three victories to their credit, including a 37-22 verdict over Notre Dame, together with a 41-6 victory over the Buckeyes last year, Purdue was considered a 13-point favorite as the big crowd settled down.

After taking the opening kickoff, Ohio State lost little time indicating this would be a contest for the home rooters to applaud. With pitchouts, right and left, to John Brockington, one of five sophomores in the starting offense, Kern brought the team to the opponent's 15 in five plays.

Although a holding penalty momentarily checked the Buckeye advance, a 21-yard run by the fast-moving Kern moved the ball to the 8. Kern accounted for 45 yards rushing and completed 8 of 16 passes for 78 yards before it was over. But after the team reached the 4, Kern failed to connect and Jim Merryman attempted a 21-yard field goal that was wide to the right.

Ohio State came back to threaten again with Jim Otis, a fullback, smashing the line. But when Merryman tried another 40-yard field goal, he missed.

Purdue gained momentum in the final minutes and then carried to the State 14 as the second quarter got under way. On the third play, Jeff Jones tried a field goal from the 22, but the kick was off to the left.

Jones tried again as Purdue began to click, moving from their own 27 to the Buckeyes' 14. Keyes took a pass and reached the rival 33 after pass interference was charged against Ohio State. Phipps raced 17 yards, but the Buckeye defense, with Jack Tatum knocking down aerials, forced the field-goal attempt. Once more Jones kicked from the 22, and once more he missed.

Ohio State subsequently went from its own 12 in an 81-yard march that included a 15-yard personal-foul penalty against Purdue. Merryman attempted a 25-yard field goal in the closing seconds of the period, but Billy McCoy raced in and blocked the effort.

The second half was less than two minutes old when Phipps completed a toss to Keyes for nine yards. Tatum knocked down a pass, but Provost raced in and grabbed the next pass the Purdue quarterback fired and dashed unmolested 35 yards for the touchdown. The placement kick failed and Purdue was stalled on its overhead game again.

Ohio State, with Otis the principal ground gainer, and whose total performance accounted for 144 yards in 29 carries, moved the team to the visitor's 33. Purdue stopped this march and then had the ball on its own 19 after a kick.

This time another Boilermaker pass misfired and Stillwagon intercepted to give his side the ball on the Purdue 25. Kern was hurt and retired after O.S.U. reached the 8. He was forced out of bounds on the 14, for a six-yard loss. Then Long took over and when he failed to spot an open receiver he went for the touchdown. Jim Roman's kick for the extra point was good.

Later Coach Hayes said the team had been ready to settle for a field goal, but he credited Long with some quick thinking.

A fumble by the Buckeyes gave Purdue a fourth-period opportunity. The Boilermakers took over on their opponents' 34 and, with Don Kiefert as the injured Phipps' replacement, reached the 7. But that proved the end of the advance as Kiefert failed to connect on three aerials, the fourth-down effort being knocked down by Dough Adams, another sophomore.

Kern returned to the lineup and Ohio State was grinding out yardage along the ground in the closing minutes. There was no need now to pass and Otis led the way as the team completed its 333 yards rushing.

Besides Otis, Brockington rushed for 69 yards and Dave Brungard, a junior, for 41. Purdue was held to 57 yards rushing.

After all, as Coach Hayes said in a tribute to the whole squad, "those kids played a heck of a game. That's the greatest defensive effort I have ever seen."

27

Michigan Routed
By Buckeyes

November 23, 1968

By GEORGE VECSEY
Special to The New York Times

An undefeated season, a trip to the Rose Bowl and the Big Ten championship all came to Ohio State today. The Buckeyes defeated Michigan, 50-14, in perhaps the most significant meeting between the old rivals.

Ohio State and Michigan had met 64 times before today, in sunshine and in blizzards, with titles or Rose Bowl trips at stake for one or the other but everything was at stake today. The winner would be undefeated in the Big Ten and would play Southern California in the Rose Bowl on Jan. 1. Only a loss to California in its nonleague opener had marred Michigan's record.

But Ohio State, with hard running inside and outside, and a defense that forced fumbles and interceptions broke a 14-14 tie with 36 seconds left in the first half, increased the lead to 27-14 after three quarters and then scored three more touchdowns and a field goal in the final period to completely overwhelm the losers.

Jim Otis, a junior fullback, gained 143 yards in 34 carries and scored four touchdowns to further the bond between his father, a doctor in Celina, Ohio, and the Ohio State coach, Woodrow Wilson (Woody) Hayes. Otis's father and the coach were roommates at Denison College.

But Otis was hardly the only star for the Buckeyes before a record crowd of 85,371. Rex Kern, a 180-pound quarterback, ran with the ball and handed it off, the way quarterbacks are supposed to do at Ohio State, and Larry Zelina supplied the powerful outside running threat.

Kern gained 96 yards and Zelina gained 92, often behind the blocking of 245-pound Rufus Mayes, who alternated between right and left tackle.

The defense was just as good. Jack Tatum, a sophomore cornerback from Passaic, N.J., produced one fumble with a hard tackle, intercepted a pass that bounced away from Gill Harris of Michigan, and chased the Michigan ball carriers all day. He caught Ron Johnson, the Michigan ace, from behind once, and he wrestled Johnson from running out of bounds at a moment when time was still important.

Johnson, who had set a Big Ten record by gaining 347 yards and scoring five touchdowns against Wisconsin last week, scored the two touchdowns for the Wolverines today. The Michigan captain gained 91 yards in 21 carries.

Johnson's best run was a 39-yard romp in the first quarter, when the game was still scoreless. Tatum caught Johnson on this run, but four plays later Johnson burst off left tackle from the 1 and Michigan held a brief 7-0 lead.

Ohio State tied the score by rushing with the ball on fourth down with inches to go on Michigan's 4 1/2-yard line. Otis was hardly touched as he plunged through left tackle and the score was tied.

The Buckeyes then went ahead on Kern's 5-yard keeper up the middle early in the second quarter. Michigan tied the score at 14-14 after Mike Polaski of Ohio State had fumbled a punt on his own 28. Eight plays later, Johnson dove for the last yard.

But Ohio State regained the lead with 36 seconds left in the first half at the end of an 86-yard drive. Otis bounced off right tackle for 2 yards to score.

The third quarter produced only one touchdown, a 6-yard end run by Zelina, but State's defense was not letting the Wolverines move. Michigan had to play into the wind in the fourth period, and it soon fell further behind.

Jim Roman's 32-yard field goal at 2:35 gave State a 16-point lead and there was noticeable relief among the red-clad Ohio State players. After that, the deluge: An interception by Doug Adams set up Kern's 3-yard keeper at 4:46. A 50-yard jaunt by Ray Gillian set up the 2-yard dive by Otis at 11:23 and an interception by Art Burton set up the last 2-yard drive by Otis, who had gone back into the game after his substitute, Paul Huff, had lost a yard.

There was some jostling near the Michigan bench in the final minute. The bad feelings had started in the fourth period when Michigan's outstanding defensive end, Tom Stincic, had tackled Kern at the sideline perhaps even a foot outside the sideline.

Kern ran the next play at Stincic. Later, the Buckeyes seemed to be directing their energies at Stincic — with the outcome already decided — and one personal foul and some shoving was the result, although Stincic concentrated on making eight solo tackles and 15 assists, the most in the game.

When the game ended, the record crowd for Ohio Field poured onto the field and even managed to tear down the steel goal posts.

28

Buckeyes Rally To Beat Trojans In Rose Bowl

January 1, 1969

By BILL BECKER
Special to The New York Times

Ohio State's hard-bitten Buckeyes battled back from a 10-0 deficit today to defeat the Southern California Trojans, 27-16, in the 55th Rose Bowl game. The Bucks left no doubt they are the national collegiate champions for this season.

Under sunny skies, a crowd of 102,063, including President-elect Richard M. Nixon, watched the No. 1-rated Ohioans overpower and outfinesse the second-ranked Trojans for the final 40 minutes.

Southern Cal's electrifying Heisman Trophy winner, O.J. Simpson, ran 80 yards for a second-period touchdown that put the Buckeyes down, 10-0. But from there on, Simpson did little and Rex Kern, the cool Buckeye sophomore quarterback, took control.

He guided the Bucks on two marches that tied the score, 10-10, by halftime, and then threw two fourth-quarter touchdown passes to clinch the victory and the national title. The scoring tosses traveled 4 yards to Leophus Hayden, a sophomore halfback, and 16 yards to Ray Gillian, a junior flanker.

The Big Ten champions thus finished their season undefeated in 10 games. Southern California, the Pacific 8 champions, ended with nine victories, one loss and a tie with Notre Dame.

The sophomore-dominated Buckeyes — there are 13 of them on the starting units — showed remarkable poise in their comeback effort. But the coolest hand was Kern, who completed nine of 15 passes for 101 yards, ran for 35 yards and was selected the game's outstanding player.

Simpson, the record-setting collegiate rushing champion for a single season, gained 171 yards in 28 carries. However, O.J. was forced into costly fumbles by the hard-hitting Bucks. His last one was recovered by Mike Polaski on the Trojan 16-yard line to set up Kern's scoring strike to Gillian.

Steve Sogge, the U.S.C. quarterback, also felt the Bucks' defensive might. He was jarred by Bill Urbanik's tackle and his fumble was recovered by Vic Stottlemyer, middle guard, on the U.S.C. 21 late in the third period.

Kern raced 14 yards on a keeper and then, in the first minute of the final period, lobbed a 4-yard pass in the right flat to Hayden behind the Trojan defenders for the touchdown.

For the final half, the fishnet-clad Ohioans were hotter than the 75-degree temperature on the field. The Bucks wore white fishnet, short-sleeved jerseys to give them maximum ventilation on this balmy New Year's Day.

Both teams warmed slowly to their work and the first quarter was scoreless. On the first play of the second period Larry Zelina, Buckeye sophomore halfback, missed a 27-yard field-goal try.

Southern Cal scored after Sogge passed to Simpson for 16 yards. Simpson was knocked out of bounds by Jack Tatum, the Buckeye rover, on the Ohio 3 to avert a touchdown. On fourth down, Ron Ayala kicked a 21-yard field goal to put Troy ahead, 3-0.

Midway in the period, Simpson started off left tackle, cut back over the middle, broke two tackles and raced down the right sideline to complete an 80-yard touchdown run. It was the second largest scrimmage run in Rose Bowl annals. Mel Anthony of Michigan ran 84 yards in 1965. Ayala's conversion made it 10-0.

Then Kern & Co. went to work. Mixing up runs by Jim Otis, the junior fullback, Hayden and himself, the 19-year-old quarterback moved the Bucks 69 yards in 13 plays. Otis dived over guard for the final yard and Jim Roman converted.

Roman's 26-yard field goal three seconds before the half ended made the score 10-all. This followed a march in which Kern passed 17 yards to Jan White and 19 to Gillian.

Late in the third quarter, the Ohioans marched 54 yards to the Trojan 8. When U.S.C. stiffened, Roman, a sub center, went in and kicked his second field goal, from 25 yards out, to put the Bucks ahead for the first time, 13-10.

From then on, Ohio State increased the pressure and the Trojans wilted. The miscues-turned-into-touchdowns put the Bucks ahead, 27-10, in the first 10 minutes of the final period.

Sogge kept pitching and finally hit Sam Dickerson, the split end, with a 19-yard pass in the end zone for the last Trojan touchdown with 45 seconds left the Trojans 8. On the play, Dickerson and Polaski both caught the ball, but the officials ruled the offensive player has possession on a simultaneous catch.

A 2-point-pass conversion attempt failed when Jimmy Lawrence, Trojan flanker, dropped the ball.

This was Ohio State's fourth triumph against one defeat in the Rose Bowl. It was Coach Woody Hayes' third victory without a loss here. Southern Cal lost its fifth game in 16 Rose Bowl appearances.

Ohio State's ball-control game prevailed, although the statistics were closer than the final score. The Bucks had a 21-19 edge in first downs, but U.S.C. gained 366 yards to 361 for Ohio State.

"Southern Cal was a good team," Hayes conceded, but he declined to rate the Trojans above "Purdue and Michigan in our league." Ohio State beat Purdue, 13-0, and Michigan, 50-14.

Coach John McKay of U.S.C. said: "We should have protected our passer better. They have a good defensive team."

He also praised Simpson and for once O.J. admitted: "Yes, I'm tired. It's been a long season."

Besides leading all rushers, Simpson caught eight passes for 85 yards. For Ohio State, Otis gained 101 yards in 30 tries and Hayden 90 in 15 carries. Gillian caught four passes for 69 yards.

Sogge, who, like Simpson, was playing his final collegiate game, completed 19 of 30 passes for 189 yards. But his fumble and one costly interception sounded the end of the reign of the 1967 national champions.

29

Buckeyes Get Revenge On Michigan

November 21, 1970

By NEIL AMDUR
Special to The New York Times

The long agony of defeat became instant ecstasy for Ohio State today as the unbeaten Buckeyes powered past Michigan, 20-9, en route to a berth in the Rose Bowl on New Year's Day.

Spurred by a howling record crowd of 87,331 in Ohio Stadium, the Buckeyes reversed the lone blemish on their football record in the last 31 games. They did it convincingly in the awesome, aggressive style that has become the trademark of Ohio State football teams for two decades.

At times Ohio State appeared almost "superpsyched." Four times in the first 12 minutes the Buckeyes lined up with only 10 men on the field. On one series Coach Woody Hayes, ebullient and anxious, in a white, short-sleeve shirt and his familiar black baseball cap, lost track of the action and sent in his punting team on second down.

But the Buckeyes did what had to be done to redeem the torment of last year's stunning 24-12 setback by Michigan at Ann Arbor, a defeat that ended their 22-game winning streak and chances for a second successive national championship.

On offense today they slammed at the strength of a Wolverine interior ranked fifth nationally in rushing defense. Hayes called 12 pass plays to 65 rushing attempts, but one was a 26-yard touchdown toss from Rex Kern to Bruce Jankowski. It was Jankowski's first scoring reception of the season.

Attacking the Michigan defense with two tight ends instead of one, Ohio State amassed 242 yards rushing. By contrast the superb Buckeye defense continued its consistently magnificent play and limited the Michigan running attack to 37. In nine earlier victories the Wolverine ground game had averaged 274.

Ohio State scored first with Fred Schram's 28-yard field goal after having recovered a Michigan fumble on the opening kickoff. The Wolverines matched that 3-pointer with a 31-yard placement by Dana Coin on the first play of the second quarter.

But after Kern hit Jankowski behind Bruce Eliott in the end zone late in the first half, the Buckeyes were in front to stay. Michigan moved to within a point, 10-9, midway through the third quarter on a 13-yard scoring pass from Don Moorhead to Paul Staroba.

But Tim Anderson took a running start and crashed through to block Coin's extra-point kick — it was only his second miss in 17 attempts — and the Buckeyes tacked on another Schram field goal, from 27 yards, and a 4-yard scoring run by Leo Hayden in the final quarter.

The ultimate display of State's superiority and muscle came in the final 4 minutes 58 seconds, after the Buckeye defense had stopped a Michigan drive at the Ohio 24. Hayes called 11 straight rushing plays, and the offensive line produced the punishing format that has characterized recent State teams. Hayes calls it "grinding meat."

The Buckeyes ground out the remaining time with two first downs. As students and fans poured onto the field after the game, Hayes symbolically found his way to the game ball, grabbed it, clutched it tightly in his right arm like a fullback and ran off the field with a police escort providing interference.

Michigan appeared loose in workouts yesterday in contrast to the intensity within the Ohio State walls. But the Wolverines fumbled three times today and completed only 12 of 26 passes for 118 yards. An interception by Stan White led to Ohio State's final touchdown with 8:14 left.

The Wolverines also were penalized six times, including a 15-yarder for grabbing a face mask that nullified a wind-aided 73-yard punt by Staroba in the second quarter that would have pushed the Buckeyes back to their 18.

Instead Michigan had to punt again. Ohio State gained 36 yards on the exchange and took control on the Michigan 46. Kern's crucial 4-yard run on a fourth-and-3 situation from the Michigan 29 maintained the momentum; the pitch to Jankowski was the only pass in the drive.

Michigan's last chance typified the Wolverines' frustration during the 40-degree afternoon. After recovering a fumbled punt, which Hayes insisted his player did not touch, Michigan moved to the State 26.

Three plays gained 2 yards. On fourth down Moorhead threw perfectly to Glenn Doughty at the State 12. In another stadium on another day, perhaps at Ann Arbor, Doughty might have caught the ball, for it plopped squarely in his stomach. But he dropped it, and so went Michigan's slim hopes for a national title and conference crown.

Ohio State's Rose Bowl opponent will be Stanford, and another national championship again appears within the Buckeye grasp. Ohio State won the mythical title in 1968 with many of the same fine players (Kern, Jack Tatum, Jim Stillwagon, Jan White, Mike Sensibaugh) who were in their final regular-season game today.

Kern's leadership on offense was evident throughout. His slick faking and ball-handling continually kept the Michigan defense from keying too heavily on one back. His perfect option pitch to Hayden produced the last Buckeye score.

• • •

Some people may have given up on Rex Kern, but his Ohio State teammates kept the faith in their quarterback.

"I've never seen our squad so high," said the 184-pound senior who played the entire game today in the Buckeyes' 20-9 victory over Michigan. "The mass media was down on me and so were some of the fans, but my teammates had faith in me."

There had been pregame speculation that Ohio State might dramatically switch Kern from quarterback to running back for this game and utilize Ron Maciejowski's passing arm. But no super formations emerged in State's game plan.

At the finish it was Kern faking and handing off to John Brockington and Leo Hayden on punishing power plays. Hayden gained 118 yards in 28 rushing attempts and scored one of the two Buckeye touchdowns.

"We had good success with the delayed play with Hayden carrying the call," Coach Woody Hayes said. "We borrowed that play from Michigan. It is in our book and they must have borrowed it and refined it, so we borrowed it back."

Hayes praised Kern's performance. "He did a great job," said the 57-year-old coach who had made Kern his starting quarterback as a sophomore and watched him lead Ohio State to 22 consecutive victories until last year's Michigan defeat.

"We did not play Maciejowski because of the way Rex was going. You don't change horses in the middle of the stream."

Bo Schembechler, the Michigan coach who had master-minded the upset against the Buckeyes in his first season (1969) cited the Wolverines' inability to "move on the ground" as a major factor in their first defeat in 10 games.

"We felt their defense would have to crack somewhere if we were going to win," said Schembechler, who played for Hayes as a collegian and later served as an assistant at Ohio State. "But it didn't. They just played tough all day."

Both coaches said the tension had affected their players. Before the kickoff Hayes held his players in the tunnel leading to the field until the Michigan team had appeared. Then, in what seemed a psychological attempt to disrupt the Wolverines as they rushed across the field, he sent his players out. They broke through the line of Wolverines, exchanged a bump or two, then grouped in a mass huddle around midfield.

"Ninety-nine and two-thirds percent of the calls come from the bench," said Kern, meaning Hayes.

Did the game provide a measure of vindication for Kern?

"It was my last game here," he said. "I'm not trying to sound egocentric, but I thought I would start. It's very satisfying for me, since things haven't been going so great."

Coach Hayes said that President Nixon had phoned him and "was congratulatory and greatly impressed" with the game, which appeared on national television.

"He thought it was a great game," the coach added.

Had Hayes offered the President tickets to the soldout game?

"I told him he could sit on the bench," he said.

30

Stanford Upsets Ohio State

January 1, 1971

By BILL BECKER
Special to The New York Times

The Stanford Indians, propelled by Jim Plunkett's professional caliber passing rallied for two touchdowns in the final period today and upset favored Ohio State, 27-17, in the Rose Bowl. The victory quashed the Buckeyes' national championship dreams.

A roaring crowd of 103,839 watched this 57th Rose Bowl game which was one of the more surprising contests.

The thrice-beaten Indians, registering their first Rose Bowl success in 30 years, rode with Plunkett's fine arm in marching 80 yards and then 25 for their decisive scores.

Hitherto — Ohio State carried a 17-13 lead into the fourth quarter. The Buckeyes' numerous rooters, and Coach Woody Hayes, had high hopes of earning the national collegiate title after Texas had been upset by Notre Dame in the Cotton Bowl.

The winner instead was John Ralston of Stanford, coaching in the Rose Bowl for the first time. This was Hayes' first defeat here in four games.

But this was also the first time Woody and his Bucks had run up against the likes of Plunkett. The Heisman Trophy winner from San Jose, Calif., completed 20 of 30 passes for 265 yards including a perfect 10-yard touchdown throw to Randy Vataha, a flanker.

Plunkett had tremendous aides in Bob Moore, a big tight end, who made a tough catch of Plunkett's 35-yard pass to keep the

The Buckeyes' field general on the sidelines.

Rex Kern huddles with Hayes on the sidelines of the 1969 Rose Bowl game against U.S.C.

This sign says it all.

Woody is carried off the field in a post-game victory ride after his Buckeye squad defeated U.S.C. in the 1974 Rose Bowl.

Archie Griffin rejoices in the end zone. This was a frequent sight during his 4-year career at O.S.U.

Hayes and two-time Heisman Memorial Trophy winner Archie Griffin meet the press in New York in 1975.

Hayes and Bear Bryant swap recipes on winning football games at a dinner prior to the 1978 Sugar Bowl.

Hayes and Joe Paterno share a few laughs before the Buckeyes' game against Penn State in 1975.

Woody receives an award from former President (and Michigan football star) Gerald Ford during a roast in 1978.

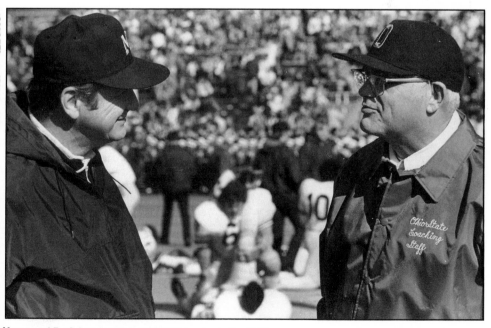

Hayes and Bo Schembechler of Michigan prior to the 1976 game.

Hayes visits with another Ohio legend, Bob Hope, prior to the 1978 Iowa game.

clinching drive alive, and Jackie Brown, a swift halfback who scored twice on right end sweeps of 4 and 1 yards.

Moore, Vataha and Demea Washington ran routes that befuddled the touted Buckeye secondary, and only one of Plunkett's passes was intercepted. On his touchdown catch, Vataha streaked away from Jack Tatum, an all-America cornerback.

The Stanford coach, who has been accused of being lax on defense, said in the dressing room, "our emotional surge in the second half helped us in fourth-down situations." The Indians several times held Ohio State for downs in the final period — once at Stanford's 20-yard line.

There the tide turned. Plunkett moved his team 80 yards in 13 plays, with the 35-yard pitch to Moore setting up the score at the Buckeye 2-yard line. Moore made a great catch with Mike Sensibaugh, an Ohio safety, all over him. On third down, Brown circled end from the 1-yard line, and the Indians were never behind again.

Rex Kern, the Buckeye quarterback who was the star of the first half, became the goat on Ohio State's very next series. His pass on third down into the flat was intercepted by Jack Schultz, a safety on the Ohio State 25.

On the fourth play, Plunkett connected with Vataha for the coup de grace. With Steve Horowitz's third conversion, the score mounted to 27-17.

Horowitz also contributed two field goals, including a Rose Bowl record kick of 48 yards in the third quarter. This surpassed George Fleming's 44-yarder for Washington in 1961. Horowitz kicked one of 37 yards that gave Stanford a 10-0 lead in the first period.

Then Hayes' Buckeye ball-control machine swung into high gear. With Kern executing all types of legerdemain, and running well himself, the Bucks rolled 65 yards in six plays and later 55 yards in nine plays and held a 14-10 halftime lead.

John Brockington, the Brooklyn bulldozer, scored the touchdowns from a yard out each time. Fred Schram converted twice and added a third-quarter field goal of 32 yards. Schram had a 20-yard field goal try blocked by Ben Barnes, a Stanford defensive back.

Plunkett engineered two other drives deep into Buckeye territory but they were foiled by fumbles. One, by Moore, was recovered by the Bucks on their 14. The other, by Plunkett, was lost on the 17-yard line.

Brockington wound up with 101 yards rushing, Kern with an amazing 129, as he found gaping holes in Stanford's left side. But the Indians tightened in the clutch and kept the screws on the final minutes, when Kern and his alternate, Ron Macjewski, proved they couldn't match Plunkett's accuracy. The Buckeye passers completed seven of 20 attempts.

This was Stanford's fourth victory in 10 Rose Bowl games, the last coming in 1941 when Frankie Albert led the Indians to a 21-13 conquest of Nebraska. Stanford's last appearance here produced a 40-7 drubbing by Illinois in 1952.

For Ohio State, it was the second loss in six trips to Pasadena. The Bucks hadn't lost here since California beat them, 28-0, in 1921.

31

U.S.C. Trounces Ohio State

January 1, 1973

By BILL BECKER
Special to The New York Times

The Southern California Trojans sewed up the 1972 national college football championship with a smashing 42-17 victory over the Ohio State Buckeyes before 106,869 spectators today in the 59th Rose Bowl game.

Stung by a 7-7 tie at halftime, the powerful, versatile Trojans romped to three touchdowns in the third quarter and added two more in the fourth.

Thus the Trojans wound up with a 12-0 won-lost record and assured themselves of the top spot in the last Associated Press poll.

Sam Cunningham, Southern Cal's 230-pound senior fullback, scored four touchdowns on short dives to set a Rose Bowl record. He was voted player of the game.

But Cunningham had to share hero honors with the sharp-shooting quarterback, Mike Rae, who riddled the Ohio State secondary, once on a 10-yard touchdown pass to Swann, and Anthony Davis, the sophomore hop-skip artist, who ran for 157 yards on 23 carries, including a 20-yard touchdown scamper.

This was the worst defeat administered to Ohio State here and the most one-sided against the Big Ten since Washington swamped Wisconsin, 44-8, in 1960.

While the Bucks shackled Davis and Cunningham for a half, they were unable to cope with Rae's expert passing. The Trojan passer completed 18 of 25 for 229 yards. It was the Bucks' secondary weakness which finally betrayed them.

The crowd also set a record for this enlarged stadium. The game was played in ideal sunny weather after first-half winds subsided. The Trojans blew up a gale of their own after that.

The Trojans came out aroused and immediately drove 57 yards to a touchdown at the start of the third quarter. Rae passed twice to Swann, for 12 and 23 yards, and to J.K. McKay for 14. That set the stage for a 2-yard touchdown dive by Cunningham. With Rae's conversion, the Trojans took a 14-7 lead and never looked back.

Ohio State narrowed it to 14-10 on Blair Conway's 21-yard field goal, following a 22-yard pass from Greg Hare to Tim Holycross.

But Southern Cal quickly responded. Rae passed 24 yards to Swann and then Davis burst 20 yards over guard, slipping four tackles, for a touchdown midway in the third quarter.

Before the period ended, U.S.C. led, 28-10. Charlie Phillips's 48-yard run with an interception set the stage for a quick 30-yard push. Cunningham dived 1 yard for the score.

Cunningham did another 1-yard dive for his third touchdown, culminating a 67-yard Trojan drive early in the fourth quarter. Rae's fifth conversion made it 35-10.

Rae's understudy, Pat Haden, engineered another scoring drive in the final period. He passed 15 yards to Manny Moore, Rod McNeill ran 11, and Cunningham dived the final yard again to run the score to 42-10.

Cunningham's four touchdowns eclipsed the previous record of three, shared by several players, the most recent being Mel Anthony of Michigan in 1965.

The Buckeyes carried the first-half fight to Southern Cal. Early they drove 46 yards before being held for downs at the U.S.C. 20. Archie Griffin and Randy Keith found gaping holes on the Trojan right side during the march.

Southern Cal then responded with a 55-yard push which died on the Buckeye 25.

However, after Phillips recovered Griffin's fumble on the Ohio State 38, the Trojans quickly bounced in for a touchdown. Rae passed to Charles Young for 12 and Davis rambled 19 yards around right end to the Buckeye 7.

After Davis was dropped for a 3-yard loss, Rae passed 10 yards to Swann for the score. Rae's conversion gave U.S.C. a 7-0 lead late in the first quarter.

Brian Baschnagel's 39-yard return of the ensuing kickoff ignited the Bucks. Eight plays later, Keith, a fullback, plunged across from the 1-yard line. Conway's conversion tied it, 7-7, where the count remained for the rest of the half.

32

O.S.U. Routs U.S.C. In Rose Bowl

January 1, 1974

By LEONARD KOPPETT
Special to The New York Times

Vindication on three levels — competitive, political, and tactical — was enjoyed to the fullest today by Ohio State and its supporters as its football team overpowered the University of Southern California, 42-21, in the 60th Rose Bowl game.

The competitive vindication was simple and direct. Exactly a year ago, in this same beautiful bowl (which held 105,267 spectators today), U.S.C. had routed the Buckeyes, 42-17, after a 7-7 first half. Today, in cool but dry weather, Ohio State went from a 14-14 first half to increasing dominance in the second, producing 28 points in the last 20 minutes after falling behind, 21-14.

The political situation had to do with the storm that arose when Big Ten officials chose Ohio State for the Rose Bowl after its 10-10 tie with Michigan in the final regular-season game between the two unbeaten teams. Whatever the merits of Michigan's claim (based on Ohio State's trip last year), this victory certified Ohio State's credentials and completed the eighth undefeated season in its 84-year football history.

And tactically, the way of Woody Hayes, the Ohio State coach whose approach to football is entirely infantry-minded, prevailed over the more contemporary pass-run mixtures Coach John McKay concocts so successfully.

Ohio State made 323 yards rushing and threw only eight passes

— but completed six for 129 yards. The Trojans threw the ball 40 times and completed 22 for 239 yards, but even with their fine runners gained only half as much — 167 yards — along the ground.

"This is the greatest victory I have ever had, and the greatest we have ever had," declared Hayes. "We worked hard on our passing these 15 days, because we thought that was the thing to do against U.S.C."

Having averaged 7.9 pass attempts a game during the preceding 10 games, Hayes went wild and called 8.0 in this one; but the six completions more than doubled Ohio's normal rate of 2.9.

The most noticeable heroes were the three principal backs, Corny Greene, Archie Griffin and Pete Johnson, and a defensive back, Neal Colzie; but naturally, it was the over-all offensive blocking and defensive hitting that made the game swing gradually in Ohio State's direction.

Johnson, a freshman from Long Beach, L.I., scored the first three touchdowns at close range and wound up with 94 yards in 21 carries.

Griffin, the sophomore who already has all-America recognition, gained 149 yards on 22 carries, and finally scored himself on a 47-yard run for the final touchdown. Most of his earlier work brought Johnson within range.

Greene, also a sophomore, was the quarterback who polished his passing to go along with his other talents. His first attempt of the game was intercepted, and his third missed, but the others connected, four times with Fred Pagac, a senior tight end. And when the go-ahead touchdown was needed on fourth down from the 1, Greene scored it himself.

Colzie, a junior, set up that score by returning a punt 56 yards to the U.S.C. 9 when the Trojans led, 21-20, late in the third period. The 27-21 lead supplied by that score became 35-21 when Greene ran in for a 2-point conversion after a touchdown set up by Griffin's 25-yard run early in the fourth quarter.

For U.S.C., ranked No. 1 a year ago, the season wasn't exactly a disgrace, either. The Trojans lost to Notre Dame, 23-14, and tied Oklahoma, 7-7. McKay declined to make comparisons.

Pat Haden, the junior quarterback, passed well and scrambled for gains. Anthony Davis, obviously a target of the Ohio State defense, did make 74 yards running. But Ohio State did seem to have a physical superiority that told as the game wore on.

This was most noticeable after the momentum shifted in the third quarter. Ohio State was moving toward a tie-breaking touchdown from the second-half kickoff when Griffin fumbled on the 16. The Trojans drove 84 yards from there, making third-down conversions with a 17-yard pass from their own 18 and on a 5-yard run to the Ohio 28. Davis ran 19 yards on the next play and eventually scored from the 1.

But Ohio State was unstoppable now, going 67 yards from the kickoff in only five plays, including a 39-yard pass play to the 4. But the extra-point try was blocked, so the Buckeyes still trailed by a point.

Not for long, however. They promptly forced a punt, and Colzie took it back almost all the way. Once ahead, after an exchange of punts, they struck from near midfield and made it 35-21 with 10 minutes to go.

U.S.C. made one last sustained drive, and reached third-and-6 on the Ohio 25. But Haden was sacked for a 15-yard loss on the next play, and a desperate fourth-down pass was almost caught by Lynn Swann on the 15, but wasn't. Moments later Griffin broke through and wrapped it up.

33

Buckeyes Boot Michigan

November 23, 1974

By GORDON S. WHITE Jr.
Special to The New York Times

Ohio State acted just like a member of the National Football League today as it failed to score a touchdown but won the biggest game of the season when Tom Klaban kicked four field goals to beat Michigan, 12-10.

This left Ohio State and Michigan, which suffered its first loss of the season, in a tie for the Big Ten title. But the result of this regular-season finale before 88,243 persons filling Ohio Stadium left unanswered for 24 hours the question of who will represent the Big Ten in the Rose Bowl game on January 1

Because Coach Woody Hayes's Buckeyes won, the 10 conference athletic directors will meet tomorrow near Chicago's O'Hare Airport to vote on whether Ohio State or Michigan will go to the Rose Bowl. The fact that the victory was by only two points and the fact that the Buckeyes never crossed the Michigan goal line may play an important part in Michigan's favor in the vote.

When Michigan's place-kicking specialist, Mike Lantry, missed a 33-yard field goal attempt with 18 seconds remaining in the game, the Ohio State players and fans jumped with glee and surely felt they deserved the trip to Pasadena, Calif. But strange things have happened in previous voting, such as last year when these powers finished in a 10-10 tie and co-champions of the conference. The Buckeyes were voted to the Rose Bowl then, even though they had gone just the year before.

This year's big game resembled one of those professional struggles the N.F.L. has so often. After Michigan scored a touchdown on its opening drive, the two college powers slugged it out and let their placekickers settle the issue. What it amounted to was that Klaban, a junior born in Czechoslovakia and raised in Cincinnati, proved to be a better field-goal kicker today than Lantry, a senior from Oxford, Mich.

Lantry booted a 37-yarder with five minutes to go in the first quarter, giving the Wolverines a 10-0 lead. But the left-footed, orthodox kicker missed three other field-goal attempts — of 51 and 58 yards as well as the final 33 yarder.

Klaban, meantime, kicked field goals in the second quarter of 47, 25 and 43 yards, tying a Buckeye record of three field goals in a half. Then the right-footed, soccer-style kicker hit the winner — a 45-yarder at 4:51 of the third quarter.

Michigan, one of four remaining major college teams to be undefeated and untied before today, finished the regular season with a 10-1 won-lost mark and the all-important loss in the Big Ten Conference. Ohio State, which was upset by Michigan State in conference play two weeks ago, finished with a similar mark of 10-1.

Today's game, which was nationally televised, never produced the spectacular ground thrusts characteristic of both teams. This may have been largely because the two defenses took control, particularly in the second half.

Archie Griffin, Ohio State's star tailback, picked up 111 yards in 25 carries, increasing his N.C.A.A. record to 22 straight games in which he has picked up over 100 yards. But Michigan's little tailback, Gordon Bell, just about matched Griffin in effort by carrying 25 times and picking up 108 yards.

These two junior runners epitomized the equal strengths of the two offenses. The teams finished in a dead heat for team rushing yardage at 195 each and were on a par in passing, with Ohio State gaining 58 yards in the air and Michigan 96. But the most notable similarity of their passing games was that neither was effective when it counted most.

Griffin's biggest single gain was an 18-yard burst early in the first period. The fact that he and other good Ohio State runners never scored attested to the fine defense up front for the Wolverines.

Two of the real standouts of the contest were Ohio State's Pete Cusick, a huge but quick defensive tackle, and Michigan's Jeff Perlinger, an equally huge and mobile defensive tackle. Perlinger was obviously assigned to Griffin all game long. He stuck to Coach Bo Schembechler's orders and rode down the running star many a time at the line of scrimmage, sometimes even catching Griffin from behind.

Cusick destroyed some of the best-laid plans of the Wolverines at key moments, such as third-down plays when Dennis Franklin, the Michigan quarterback, had to pass. Perlinger hit Ohio State's quarterback, Cornelius Greene, so hard that Greene lost the ball on a running play and Michigan's Tim Davis recovered at the Wolverines' 26.

From that point, Franklin directed the best sustained drive of the day for Michigan. He sent Bell on sweeps right and left in which he pitched way out to the scampering tailback for good gains. This got the visitors to the Ohio State 21 in just 10 plays. After Franklin failed on two consecutive passes into the end zone, Lantry booted his only successful field goal.

Shortly before Lantry's field goal, Franklin had his big moment of the day. On a first down at Ohio State's 42, he hit Gill Chapman, the wingback, at the Buckeyes' 22. Chapman kept right on running and turned the pass play into a 42-yard touchdown for the only successful move into either end zone all day.

Lantry kicked the extra point and Michigan had its 7-0 lead.

After that sudden move and the long drive for the field goal, Michigan could not get within an easy strike of a touchdown the rest of the way. But Ohio State never really threatened either. The closest the Buckeyes got was to the Michigan 7-yard line for a third-down-and-6 play.

This came about when a Franklin pass early in the second period was intercepted by Bruce Elia, a sparkling linebacker today. Elia ran the ball 11 yards to the Wolverines' 44.

Griffin then ran on seven of Ohio State's next nine plays to get the ball inside the 10-yard line. But on the third down from the 7, there was big Jeff Perlinger again to help Rick Kolschalk, the middle guard, throw Greene for a short loss. This forced Ohio State to go to Klaban's second field goal.

Klaban kicked his first field goal (47 yards) on the first play of the second period to conclude a drive that Ohio State began on its own 20 following Michigan's field goal. Michigan turned this moving offense into a field goal settlement when Dan Jilek, a Wolverine defensive end, sacked Greene for a 7-yard loss to the Michigan 35.

After a gain of 5 yards by Greene on the next play was not good enough for a first down, Ohio State went to a fourth-down field goal and trailed, 10-3.

Then came Elia's interception and the ensuing field goal. This was followed by a 26-yard pass from Greene to Dave Hazel that got Ohio State to the Michigan 26. But Perlinger was there again to nail Griffin on the next play for no gain, and with just six seconds remaining in the first half. Hayes ordered Klaban to kick his third field goal.

Thus Michigan took a 10-9 lead into the locker room at halftime.

What turned out to be the winning field goal came in the third period after a 20-yard drive by Ohio State from the Michigan 48 to the 28. Forced to a fourth-and-5, Ohio State once again asked for Klaban to produce, and he did with a 45-yard kick that may get the Buckeyes into the Rose Bowl.

Michigan's final chance came with 57 seconds to go as the Wolverines took an Ohio State punt at the Michigan 46. Franklin immediately hit Jim Smith for a 23-yard pass and a first down at the Buckeyes' 31. Now there were 52 seconds to go, and Franklin tossed high and out of bounds to stop the clock.

Then Bell's replacement, Rob Lytle, ran a draw for 10 yards and a first down with 25 seconds remaining. Another run by Lytle and the ball was at the Ohio State 16 with 18 seconds to go.

34

U.S.C. Rallies To Beat Ohio State

January 1, 1975

By WILLIAM N. WALLACE
Special to The New York Times

Pat Haden has thrown hundreds of passes to John McKay, his high school and college classmate, in scores of practices and dozens of games. Their last one, which came today toward the end of the frenetic Rose Bowl game between Southern California and Ohio State, was the best of all.

It was good for a 38-yard touchdown that brought the Trojans up to the edge of a dramatic upset of the Buckeyes, an upset completed on the following successful 2-point conversion pass, from Haden to Shelton Diggs. Those 8 points gave Southern Cal an 18-17 victory before the startled eyes of 106,721 spectators and a national television audience.

Haden, the quarterback who will soon begin a Rhodes scholarship tour in Britain, wound up the No. 1 hero. He was the chief architect of the 8 big points that won the game with such suddenness.

McKay, the slim receiver who is an unlikely candidate for future football, shared with his father, the winning coach, the other parts of the heroics in his final game for U.S.C.

Young McKay caught five big passes from Haden for 104 yards in a contest of rapidly shifting fortunes and eight turnovers. As for the 51-year-old coach, he didn't hesitate to try for the 2-point conversion play following the final touchdown, the difficult play that would bring victory or defeat rather than the easier 1-point kick that, if good, would have brought about a deflating 17-17 tie.

"We always go for the 2 points in a situation like that," said Coach McKay later. "We didn't come to play for a tie. We were a fortunate team to win. They were unfortunate to lose." McKay knew about misfortune. A 2-point conversion play by a Southern California team of his had failed in the 1967 Rose Bowl game won as a consequence by Purdue, 14-13.

Woody Hayes, the Ohio State coach, who in the past has been volatile following defeat, was mild. "We got beaten by a better team," he said. "One point better."

On the Haden-McKay big play, the passer had plenty of time to wait for his buddy, known for his craft rather than his speed, to reach the enemy end zone.

"He knew I'd be there," said young McKay later. "It's our favorite place. He knows I've been there before." The pass was perfect and it was caught in the back of the end zone, with McKay's slamming into a wire fence a few steps beyond where fans hugged his maroon helmet.

Did Haden see the catch? "I sure did. I had no doubt he'd get it." The play's designation was 96X Corner and that is where McKay was, in the corner of the end zone.

But Haden had to complete another aerial to win the game. He was less sure that the diving Diggs had held on to the conversion 2-point pass. "Then I saw the official's arms go up," Haden said of the signal for a score. "I was never so happy in my life."

Ohio State had two minutes left in which to try to score again and the dangerous Cornelius Greene, the Buckeye quarterback, gave it a good try. He got his team up to midfield and on the last play Tom Skladnay's 62-yard field-goal attempt fell short.

It was Greene, more than the acclaimed Archie Griffin, whom the Trojans feared the most because he had been the architect of Ohio State's victory over Southern Cal here a year ago. The fears were justified. Greene ran for 68 yards and one touchdown and he completed 8 of 14 pass attempts, a lot for Ohio State, for 93 yards.

Griffin was less in evidence. The Heisman trophy winner had gained 100 yards or more in Ohio State's last 22 games. That streak came to an end as Griffin made 76 against a superb Maroon defense. Worse yet he fumbled twice, at the Trojan 5- and 7-yard lines. Ouch!

Anthony Davis, Griffin's counterpart for Southern California, was hurt and left the game in the second period, never to reappear. He had injured ribs but had gained 71 yards in the early going. His replacement, Allen Carter, did very well and led the Trojan ground attack on the victor's two long second-half scoring drives.

Four lost fumbles, one key one by Davis that set up Ohio State's initial touchdown by Champ Henson, contributed to the bizarre game. For example, Coach McKay "returned" 3 points after Chris Limahelu had kicked a 39-yard field goal late in the second quarter.

McKay preferred to accept a 5-yard penalty against Ohio State on the play, which gave U.S.C. a first down and a chance to keep going. Four plays later Limahelu tried a 24-yard field goal, which was no good. That left the Buckeyes with a 7-3 halftime lead and the Trojans in pain.

Haden completed 12 of 22 passes for 181 yards and two touchdowns, the first to the fine tight end, Jim Obradovich. Neal Colzie intercepted two of Haden's passes and he was so elated on the second one that he spiked the ball, meaning he bounced it hard on the turf.

That cost his team a 15-yard unsportsmanlike conduct penalty, from the U.S.C. 9 to its 24 and from there Danny Reece then intercepted a pass by Greene. The Colzie spike was one more way the Buckeyes found to lose the game.

They missed a score on an early 15-yard field-goal attempt. They made nothing out of a blocked Southern Cal punt deep in Trojan territory. And they could not handle Davis' substitute, the unheralded Carter. The victors were hardly guiltless with six errors, two fumbles, two interceptions, the blocked punt and the give-back field goal.

But, as Coach Hayes put it, "Pat Haden made the big play which won the game."

But the elder McKay had the last word. He said, "There were 106,000 people in the stands and no one knew who would win right up until the end. I thought it was a great game between two great teams and in the end we had 18 points and they had 17."

35

Buckeyes Triumph On Late Touchdowns

November 22, 1975

By MURRAY CHASS
Special to The New York Times

Just as everyone figured, a lad named Griffin was the difference in today's annual Big Ten championship war between Ohio State and Michigan, both unbeaten and both bowl-bound.

But, surprise it wasn't Archie, the prolific ball-carrying machine, who sparked Ohio State to a 21-14 victory and a record, fourth consecutive Rose Bowl appearance. Not at all. An alert, swarming Michigan defense saw to that, limiting Archie to 46 yards in 19 carries and snapping his collegiate-record string of 31 straight games in which he had rushed for more than 100 yards.

The difference in this battle waged before a record 105,543 fans at Michigan Stadium was Archie's younger brother, Ray, a sophomore safety whose pass interception late in the fourth quarter set up the touchdown that capped the Buckeyes' comeback victory. Ray also made a game-high 10 unassisted tackles, helped on 4 others and broke up 2 other passes.

Pete Johnson's touchdown burst from 3 yards out with 2 minutes 19 seconds left, stunned the scrappy Wolverines who only a minute before, had led, 14-7, and were certain they finally had broken Ohio State's domination of the Big Ten spot in the Rose Bowl.

However, after holding top-ranked Ohio State to no first downs and a net of only 28 yards in a span of 36 minutes 50 seconds — from State's first play in the second quarter until 7 minutes remained in the game the Wolverines crumpled and wound up with the consolation prize — a $700,000 trip to the Orange Bowl.

Ohio State will go to Pasadena, Calif., where it will earn $1.4 million, to be allocated among all Big Ten teams, as the icing to a season of 11 victories and no defeats. Michigan concluded its regular season efforts with 8 victories, 1 loss and 2 ties, but its 41-game unbeaten streak at home, dating to 1969, also was ended.

This was an unusual game involving these two teams because they generally play the type of football that cavemen played in another era. Together, the teams had averaged 17 passes a game this season. In this contest, though, they passed a total of 37 times.

In the end, it was three passes by Cornelius Greene and one by Rick Leach, Michigan's freshman quarterback, that decided the game.

Stifled by the Michigan defense, the Buckeyes finally awoke midway through the fourth quarter and ripped off first downs in five straight plays. Greene, their quarterback, hit on three consecutive passes to Brian Baschnagel (17 yards) and Lenny Willis (14 and 18). Then Archie Griffin ran for 11 yards and Greene kept the ball for another 12.

That placed the ball at Michigan's 8-yard line and Ohio State, ignoring Griffin, the elder, as if he had the plague, scored the tying touchdown on the last of Johnson's four straight runs, a 1-yard smash.

Only 3:18 remained and the Wolverines, ranked fourth and fifth in the various polls, tried desperately to pull out the game because a tie still would have sent Ohio State and its better over-all record to the Rose Bowl.

"When the score is 14-14, you've got two choices to make," Bo Schembechler, the Michigan coach, said. "You either play conservatively or you play to win. We decided before the game not to play for a tie so we had to gamble late in the game and you all know what happened when we had to go to the air."

On third and 19 from the Michigan 11, Leach fired a pass over Jim Smith's head and Ray Griffin intercepted it at the 33.

Leach bumped the 19-year-old converted safety (he was a running back like Archie) out of bounds at the 3-yard line, but Johnson scored on the first play, sending all those Michigan fans into shock.

Archie Griffin suffered a huge shock himself from such aggressive Michigan tacklers as Dave Devich, Don Dufek, Dwight Hicks and Calvin O'Neal.

Hayes credited Michigan with having played the best defense ever against Griffin, who wound up his four-year regular season career with a record total of 5,177 yards. He hadn't gained so few yards in one game since the ninth contest of his freshman year. His 31-game, 100-yard streak started in the first game of his sophomore season.

Overlooked in the outcome was a fine performance by Gordon Bell, Michigan's 5-foot-9-inch tailback. Bell ran for 101 yards in the first half, ended with 124 and tossed an 11-yard touchdown pass to Smith in the second quarter that tied the game, 7-7. The pass was a play put in especially for this game and it was the first pass Bell had thrown in his four-year collegiate career.

Michigan went ahead, 14-7, in the fourth quarter when Leach bulled across from the 1. An offside penalty against Aaron Brown, the Ohio State linebacker, on an errant third-down pass, kept the Michigan 43-yard drive alive.

Earlier, in the second quarter, the Wolverines squandered four scoring chances. They lost the ball twice on fumbles and once on an interception, all in Ohio State's half of the field. Then, after Archie Griffin fumbled the kickoff at his 21 following the tying touchdown, Michigan could not get a first down and Bob Wood's 37-yard field goal attempt was slightly wide to the left.

Another missed opportunity hurt Michigan on Ohio State's 11-play, 80-yard tying drive in the fourth quarter. On second and 10 from his 20, Greene escaped a frenzied chase by Tim Davis, the middle guard, in the end zone and let fly with a desperation pass. Four Wolverines touched the ball, but none could hold it. And from then on, Michigan couldn't hold the lead.

36

U.C.L.A. Stuns Ohio State

January 1, 1976

By LEONARD KOPPETT
Special to The New York Times

John Sciarra, the all-America quarterback known more for running than passing in the U.C.L.A. option offense, displayed his aerial ability in the second half today and led his team to a stunning 23-10 victory over Ohio State in the 62nd Rose Bowl Game before a crowd of 105,464.

Badly outplayed but trailing by only 3-0 at half-time, the Bruins scored one of football season's major upsets and destroyed Ohio State's hope of a perfect season and clear title to No. 1 national ranking. Ohio State had not lost a game in exactly a year, since its 18-17 loss to the University of Southern California here last New Year's day.

Included in Ohio State's 11-0 won-lost record during the regular season was a 41-20 rout of U.C.L.A., in Los Angeles, in October. And through most of the first half today, it seemed there would be a similar result. The Buckeyes had the ball for 21 of the first 30 minutes, out-gained U.C.L.A. 174 yards to 48, and failed to convert long drives into points only because of penalties, a fumble and a slip.

But from the second-half kickoff, it was an entirely different story. Sciarra, with a chance to open his team's offense, moved it 66 yards on some pitchouts to Wendell Tyler and a pass to Norm Andersen. When the drive stalled on the Ohio State 14, Brett White tied the game with a 33-yard field goal, matching Tom Klaban's earlier 42-yarder for the Buckeyes.

And from there, it was all U.C.L.A. It stopped Ohio State cold, and went 61 yards for the go-ahead touchdown, scored on a 16-yard pass to Wally Henry. Two possessions later, another pass to Henry, which he caught at midfield, became a 67-yard scoring play, and it was 16-3.

Ohio State did strike back, marching to its only touchdown on the first sequence of the fourth quarter. But the next two times, U.C.L.A. intercepted passes by Corny Greene and, with 3:42 to play, Tyler wrapped up the game with a 54-yard run from scrimmage.

Dick Vermeil, U.C.L.A.'s youthful coach, had quite a bit to say about his team's victory.

"It was a great, great feeling. After the game, Coach Woody Hayes (of Ohio State) congratulated me and, as I recall, about the only other thing he had to say was something to the effect that they had screwed up."

"We didn't have any pep talks at halftime. We knew that we were fortunate to be trailing only 3-0 after our weak offensive performance in the first half. We spent the whole intermission period making technical adjustments. In the first half, Ohio State used a lot of man-to-man coverage, and we were too greedy in trying to complete long passes. We changed up at halftime and settled for a lot more of the shorter patterns."

"As for national rankings, now that the season is finally over, I think that probably Ohio State is the best team in the nation over a 12-game schedule, and I would put us somewhere in the top five."

Hayes at first wouldn't talk to anybody, but later issued the following statement: "U.C.L.A. simply played a great game. They just beat us."

Sciarra, voted the outstanding player of the game, finished with 13 completions in 19 attempts for 212 yards. During the regular season (in which U.C.L.A. won 8 games, lost 2 and tied 1), he had completed only 48 percent of his attempts, and had averaged only 11.5 attempts (and 5.5 completions) a game. On the other hand, he had gained a net of 806 yards rushing, including all the yards he lost attempting to pass, ranking second as a runner only to Tyler.

Today, however, Tyler ran for 172 yards on 21 carries, while Sciarra actually ran the ball only twice. Counting his scrambles and sacks, he had 11 carries for a net loss of 19 yards, but almost all his option plays ended in pitchouts rather than keeps.

For Ohio State, there were statistical crumbs that did not lessen the disappointment. Archie Griffin, after getting 70 yards in the first half, could add only 23 in the second. Still, playing in his fourth straight Rose Bowl game, he is all by himself with 412 yards gained, and 79 carries, in this most hallowed of bowl games.

Griffin, it was learned after the game, suffered a fractured bone in his left hand and will miss the Hula Bowl in Honolulu on January 10.

Pete Johnson, the Ohio State fullback, scored his team's only touchdown on a 3-yard plunge, giving him four Rose Bowl touchdowns, equalling the feat of Sam Cunningham, who played for Southern California.

Hayes, in his eighth Rose Bowl appearance, suffered his fourth defeat, three of them in the last four years. It was the second year in a row that his No 1-ranking hopes evaporated here. Nevertheless, the only coaches who have won more Rose Bowl games were Howard Jones and John McKay of U.S.C., who had more chances with "home" teams.

For Vermeil, the triumph was a striking accomplishment. This was only his second season at the helm, and in 1974 he missed by one game bringing his first team to the Rose Bowl, where no U.C.L.A. team had played since 1966.

37

O.S.U. Turns Back Colorado In Orange Bowl

January 1, 1977

By NEIL AMDUR
Special to The New York Times

Ohio State provided a preview of coming attractions for next season with a convincing 27-10 victory over Colorado tonight in the 43rd Orange Bowl game.

It was a game that will be remembered more for its clear 68-degree weather than for any memorable moment. And with no national title at stake, more than 10,000 fans among the 76,732 who bought tickets chose to bypass the event or watch it on television.

But when all the chips are counted in 1977, tonight may be remembered as the place where Coach Woody Hayes began putting the pieces together for another serious run at a national title.

Not only did the Buckeyes rebound from a 10-0 first-quarter deficit, but also as many as 15 of tonight's 22 regulars will return for another crack at Michigan, a Rose Bowl berth and a final fling at national honors for the 63-year-old Hayes.

Eight defensive starters, who limited Colorado to 117 total yards in the second half, will be back. Hayes also set up his 1977 backfield by teaming Rod Gerald, Jeff Logan and Ron Springs.

Springs, a 196-pound sophomore tailback, was used in place of Pete Johnson, the senior fullback, who saw only spot duty on short-yardage and goal-line situations. Springs rushed for 99 yards in 23 attempts (he carried only 49 times during the regular season).

Logan, a junior and the Buckeyes' leading rusher, who frequently lined up at fullback, scored Ohio State's first touchdown on a 36-yard burst and gained 80 yards in 14 carries.

It was Gerald, however, a wiry sophomore, who appeared to ignite the offense after replacing Jim Pacenta, a senior, at quarterback. Gerald directed a 99-yard scoring drive late in the second quarter that gave the Buckeyes a 17-10 halftime lead, scored the final touchdown, on a 4-yard run, and gained 81 yards on 14 keepers.

"The turning point came when Gerald did well on his very first play," Hayes said, referring to a 17-yard keeper preceding Logan's touchdown run that narrowed the Colorado lead.

It was a disheartening defeat for Bill Mallory, the Colorado coach, who was an assistant for three years under Hayes. The Buffaloes finished the season with an 8-4 won-lost record and Ohio State, 9-2-1.

"We didn't play as well as we can," Mallory said. "I take nothing away from Ohio State. They seemed to show much more quickness than they showed against Michigan. And Gerald's quickness gave us some problems."

Colorado scored on its first two series on a 26-yard field goal by Mark Zettering and an 11-yard pass from Jeff Knapple to Emery Moorehead.

The first half could have ended in a 10-10 deadlock but a 15-yard piling-on penalty allowed Ohio State to retain possession deep in its territory. The Buckeyes then completed their 99-yard, 16-play drive with Johnson's 3-yard scoring run 24 seconds before the half.

"It was a shame on the piling-on penalty," Mallory said. "We had them in the hold."

Ohio State's defense and Tom Skladany's punting kept the Buffs in a hold in the second half. Colorado went five successive series without a first down and Skladany's second field goal, a 20-yarder, increased State's margin to 20-10.

"Our defense did a fabulous job," Hayes said.

Hayes acknowledged that "I feel a lot better today than I did a year ago." Ohio State has lost Rose Bowl games the last two years and four of its last five.

Gerald started the first seven games for the Buckeyes but suffered a back injury and missed the remaining four. In the last two regular-season games, Ohio State scored only 9 points.

A veteran backfield will not be the only bright spot for the Buckeyes next season. Four of the six regulars on the offensive line return to block.

38

Sooners Beat O.S.U. On Last-Minute Kick

September 24, 1977

By GORDON S. WHITE Jr.
Special to The New York Times

Uwe von Schamann, an unflappable native of West Berlin who now lives in Fort Worth, Tex., settled a big football game that a bunch of fast, husky native Americans could not resolve when he kicked a 41-yard field goal in the last three seconds to give Oklahoma a thrilling 29-28 triumph over Ohio State today.

Just moments before his third and winning field goal, von Schamann had given the Sooners their last chance by dribbling a short, right-to-left onside kickoff. The ball was recovered by Mike Babb, a native Oklahoman, on the 50-yard line, and from there the Sooners moved to the Ohio State 23 in four plays before the field goal ended one of the most unusual and thrilling games ever staged by either of these two powers.

This was the first meeting between Oklahoma and Ohio State, a first that will long be remembered by the 88,119 people packed into Ohio Stadium and a large regional television audience.

At first it appeared Oklahoma would run away to the biggest victory ever gained against an Ohio State team coached by Woody Hayes. The Sooners scored each of the first four times they got the ball and led by 20-0 early in the second period.

Then things changed so abruptly that it appeared the Buckeyes would win easily while much of Oklahoma's offensive power was sidelined with injuries.

Then it became anybody's game at the end, and Oklahoma came up with a victory that its coach, Barry Switzer, said was "certainly one of the biggest in Oklahoma history right there up on top."

Hayes, in his 27th season as Ohio State's head coach, acknowledged the excitement and emotion of this game, in which the Buckeyes were dealt their first defeat in three contests this season, but said, "I would rather have it dull and win."

There just was not a dull moment throughout, as Oklahoma struck with as fast a wishbone attack as college football has produced. The Sooners even turned their own fumbles into successes in the early stages.

But by the time they had taken the 20-lead, the Sooners' starting quarterback, Tom Lott, was out with a leg injury, and their best running back of the game, Billy Sims, was limping and also out. Only one of Oklahoma's starting offensive backs, Elvis Peacock, remained uninjured to the end.

Once Ohio State took control, Rod Gerald guided the team to what became a 28-20 lead. But Ohio State also lost manpower, as Gerald, the quarterback, was put out with a head injury. The Buckeyes also lost their all-America linebacker, Tom Cousineau, to a shoulder separation.

Oklahoma was lucky that Peacock remained healthy. It was this speedy back who scored the last touchdown of the game, on a 2-yard right-pitchout sweep that got the Sooners back to a 28-26 deficit with 89 seconds to go.

Oklahoma attempted the same play for a 2-point conversion that would have tied the game. But this time Mike Guess, Paul Ross and Tom Blinco swarmed all over Peacock and stopped him short of the goal line.

Then came the short kickoff by von Schamann. The ball bounced off a huge Buckeye lineman, and Oklahoma's Babb fell on it.

When in control, each team struck with spellbinding suddenness that turned the big partisan crowd from total despondency to total enthusiasm within seconds.

On the Sooners' sixth offensive play Lott fumbled in a drive through center. But the ball was kicked up into the hands of Peacock, who never missed a step and ran 33 yards into the end zone.

Ohio State fumbled the ball on its next play, and Oklahoma's George Cumby, a linebacker, fell on it. Sims burst over left tackle two plays later for a 14-yard touchdown run just 54 seconds after Peacock's score. Von Schamann converted after both tallies.

The next time Oklahoma got the ball, the Big Eight power drove close enough for von Schamann to kick a 23-yard field goal, and the next time the Sooners set up von Schamann again, for a 33-yarder.

So Oklahoma had that 20-0 lead at 2 minutes 2 seconds of the second quarter, and Ohio State did not even have a first down yet.

Rarely does a team, even a power such as Ohio State, gain dominance of a game from an opponent that wa once in complete control. But that is just what Ohio State did after that second von Schamann field goal.

First it was Ron Springs, the fleet Virginian in the Buckeye backfield, who went 30 yards for the first Ohio State touchdown. Then the Buckeyes, like Oklahoma, struck again quickly, scoring 46 seconds after Springs' tally. This time Gerald went 19 yards on a keeper for the 6 points.

Ohio State had taken advantage of one of Oklahoma's fumbles to set up Gerald. Oklahoma, which has been having considerable trouble this season with fumble turnovers, lost four of its seven fumbles to the Buckeyes and also lost the ball on two pass interceptions. These all helped the home team, as Ohio State continued control and scored two touchdowns in the third period for its 28-20 lead.

39

Alabama Conquers O.S.U.

January 2, 1978

By DAVE ANDERSON
Special to The New York Times

On the sideline across from each other in the Sugar Bowl game today, they resembled two old generals, Grant and Lee perhaps. But this time, Lee won. Paul (Bear) Bryant, the 64-year-old Alabama coach, wearing a Confederate gray suede sports jacket, enjoyed a 35-6 rout of Ohio State, coached by 64-year-old Woody Hayes.

Coupled with Notre Dame's 38-10 upset of top-ranked Texas in the Cotton Bowl, the 'Bama rooters in the Superdome were shouting, "Bama No. 1," but their coach didn't claim the national championship.

"I have only one vote," Bryant said, alluding to the United Press International panel of coaches, "and unless I see something to change my mind, I'll vote for us. I might see something, but I don't think so."

"I don't have a vote (in the coaches' poll)," Hayes said, "but on the basis of what I saw today, I'd vote for Alabama."

Jeff Rutledge, a 6' 2" junior quarterback who was voted the most valuable player in the game, threw two touchdown passes for Alabama while completing eight of 11 passes for 109 yards. He collaborated with Bruce Bolton on a 27-yard play and with Rick Neal for 3 yards as Alabama took a commanding 20-0 lead early in the second half. Tony Nathan scored the first touchdown on a 1-yard dash.

Ohio State's touchdown occurred on a 38-yard pass play from

Rod Gerald, the junior quarterback, to James Harrell in the fourth quarter.

Alabama's clinching touchdowns were scored by Major Ogilvie on a 1-yard smash and by Johnny Davis on a 5-yard run.

"They had half as much material as we did." Hayes commented later, "but we had one-fourth as much coaching."

That was typical of the two old coaches' respect for each other in their first meeting after more than 30 years of being two of the nation's most dominant college football personalities. Bryant is the leading active coach with a career won-lost-tied record of 273-76-16, including a 182-35-8 mark at Alabama. Hayes is next with a 231-67-9 record, including a 198-57-9 mark at Ohio State.

The late Amos Alonzo Stagg, with 314, holds the career record for victories. The late Glenn (Pop) Warner has 313.

Bryant recently announced that he planned to coach "four more years" in an effort to surpass Stagg's total. With its third consecutive bowl triumph, Alabama had a 11-1 record in this campaign, while Ohio State, the Big Ten runner-up, finished at 9-3.

"But winning or losing this game," Bryant said in the Superdome interview area, "doesn't have anything to do with how good I am or how bad he (Hayes) is. He's a great coach and always will be." He paused, smiled and added, "and I ain't bad."

Bryant was surprised when told that Alabama had 10 fumbles, only two of which they lost.

"They must've had string on the ball. It bounced right back to them," said Hayes, whose team absorbed its worse beating since a 41-6 defeat by Purdue in 1967.

Hayes, who is on probation in the Big Ten after punching a TV cameraman during the loss to Michigan earlier this season, was on his best behavior on the sideline. His most emotional moment occurred when Ozzie Newsome, Alabama's swift wide receiver, caught a Rutledge pass for a 29-yard gain that positioned the Crimson Tide's first touchdown.

Hayes, who was wearing a scarlet windbreaker, took it off and slammed it to the artificial turf with a left-handed flourish.

Trotting off the field at halftime, Hayes had another bad moment. With his head down, he jogged into the padded goal post. Startled by the collision, he threw a left hook at the brown padding as nearby spectators in the crowd of 76,811 jeered. The old coach then hurried out the runway, waving angrily at his hecklers.

"I shook hands with Woody after the game," Bryant said later. "I tried to say something to him, but there was so much noise, we couldn't communicate."

Any that's the way it was at college football's Appomattox, in reverse.

40

Gator Bowl Melee
Ends Woody's Reign

December 30, 1978

By PAUL WINFIELD
Special to The New York Times

Woody Hayes was dismissed as Ohio State's football coach the morning after he punched a Clemson player in Friday night's Gator Bowl.

His dismissal was announced by Hugh Hindman, the Ohio State athletic director, in a news conference at 8:30 o'clock yesterday in Jacksonville, Fla., where the game had been played.

"Coach Hayes has been relieved on his duties as head football coach," Hindman said. "This decision has the full support of the president of the university."

Hindman met with the president, Dr. Harold Enarson, after the game. "I told him (Hayes) this morning at the hotel about the decision," Hindman said.

The athletic director, when asked if the dismissal had resulted from the Gator Bowl incident, replied, "Yes."

Enarson said last night: "There is not a university or athletic conference in this country that would permit a coach to physically assault a college athlete."

Hindman said he had asked Hayes if he would resign and Hayes said he would not. But a half-hour after their discussion, at about 8:10 a.m., Hayes telephoned a reporter at *The Columbus Dispatch* and said he had resigned.

Reports persisted that the school had been looking for a reason to dismiss the 65-year-old Hayes, who has coached at Ohio State for 28 years. He had been on probation in the Big Ten Conference for previous incidents.

After the Florida news conference, the team returned by plane to Columbus, Ohio, landing at 11:50 a.m. Hayes, who has been unavailable since the incident, left the airport in a police car.

The incident occurred with 1 minute 58 seconds left in the Buckeyes' 17-15 loss to Clemson. Charlie Bauman, Clemson's linebacker, had intercepted an Ohio State pass and was knocked out of bounds on the Ohio State sideline.

Hayes went after Bauman, swinging. An Ohio State player, Ken Fritz, tried to restrain him and was punched in the face by the rampaging coach.

After the game, Bauman first said, "Yeah, he hit me." But when asked about the incident later in the dressing room, he said: "After I was tackled, I just walked away. There was so much excitement, I don't know if he hit me. If it happened, I'm not going to say anything about it."

Reached yesterday, Bauman said: "I think he might have hit me. I know he's fired, but I want to see the films before I say anything definite."

One report said Bauman had taunted Hayes by waving the ball in his face.

Hayes stormed off the field with a police escort after the game and asked George Hill, his defensive coordinator, to attend the postgame news conference. Hill said, "I was there, but still couldn't see what happened at the sideline."

But a national television audience did see, if briefly. A.B.C., which televised the game, showed only one replay of the melee, and from an angle that obscured Hayes' churning arms. However, replays on television yesterday clearly showed Hayes throwing a punch at Bauman.

Despite the shock of the sudden dismissal, Ohio State was planning for next season, as reports persisted that Lou Holtz of Arkansas would be named the Buckeye coach in a few days.

The reaction to Hayes' ouster ranged from shock to sympathy.

Ron Springs, an Ohio State running back, and the rest of the team learned of the dismissal on the plane after it had landed in Columbus. "He just got up on the microphone and told us he wasn't going to be head coach anymore," said Springs. "I hope that the next coach is just as good as he is."

Danny Ford, the Clemson coach, said he was sorry about the dismissal.

"He has been a great football coach," said Ford, who replaced Charlie Pell at Clemson after Pell resigned December 10 to become coach at the University of Florida. "I would have settled for an apology from Coach Hayes, the Ohio State administration and the Big Ten. I didn't expect this big an apology."

In Pasadena, Calif., Wayne Duke, commissioner of the Big Ten said he had been informed of the decision by Hindman. He expressed regret at "the termination of a great, great career."

In Columbus, callers deluged a radio station with mixed comments. John Bothe, a reporter for W.B.N.S. radio, said: "A lot of people said he was completely right in punching out that guy. But most are saying he was a disgrace to the university, that he should have retired a long time ago."

Chuck Jenkins, a 1965 Ohio State graduate, was among a group who went to the Columbus airport to say hello and goodbye to Hayes. "It's the end of an era," said Jenkins. "We just came out to show the kids that some people really care."

They had a lot of years to care about; Hayes came to Ohio State in 1951. He compiled a glittering 205-61-10 won-lost-tied record, winning national championships in 1954, 1957 and 1968. He was named the top college coach in the country in 1957 and again in 1975.

Hayes had only two losing seasons at Ohio State. His overall record in 33 years as a college coach was 238-72-10, including 19-6 at Denison (Ohio) University, his alma mater, over three years, and 14-5 in two years at Miami University of Ohio. Only Paul (Bear) Bryant, among active coaches, has more victories (283).

But controversy won Hayes more headlines than success.

In a 1971 loss to Michigan he broke two yard markers across his knee. Two years later, he reportedly shoved a camera into the face of a photographer during a practice session for the Rose Bowl.

He was reprimanded by the Big Ten in 1974 for repeated unsportsmanlike conduct in excoriating officials after a 16-13 loss to Michigan State. Hayes was furious at Michigan State and later admitted that he had turned in the school to the National Collegiate Athletic Association for purported recruiting violations. "Did I turn in the team that cheated in the league?" he said at the time. "You're damn right I did. And I'll do it again."

Last season, he was reprimanded again and placed on probation after he had hit a television cameraman during a loss to Michigan. That incident occurred after Ohio State had fumbled when in scoring position. The loss cost Hayes and the Buckeyes a trip to the Rose Bowl.

Hayes' regular-season successes were not matched by his teams' recent bowl appearances — four losses in five games.

This season Hayes abandoned his coaching philosophy of staying on the ground and let his freshman quarterback, Art Schlichter, throw passes. The season started with a loss to Penn State and ended with the frustrating defeat by Clemson and a fourth-place finish in the conference. The Buckeyes had previously won or tied for the conference title six straight times. Twice during the season, Hayes had verbally attacked sports reporters and broadcasters.

To critics who said he was too old and temperamental to continue as a coach, he made it clear after he turned 65 in February that he would not retire until he had reached the university's mandatory retirement age of 70.

The
Appendix

CHAMPIONSHIPS AND AWARDS

Listed below are the team championships and player awards at Ohio State during the head-coaching tenure of Woody Hayes.

NATIONAL CHAMPIONS 1954, 1957, 1968

BIG TEN CHAMPIONS 1954, 1955, 1957, 1961, 1968, 1970, 1975

BIG TEN CO-CHAMPIONS 1969, 1972, 1973, 1974, 1976, 1977

HEISMAN TROPHY WINNERS .... Howard Cassady, 1954
Archie Griffin, 1974, 1975

BIG TEN MOST VALUABLE PLAYER .... Howard Cassady, 1955
Archie Griffin, 1973, 1974
Cornelius Greene, 1975

OUTLAND TROPHY WINNERS .... Jim Parker, 1956
Jim Stillwagon, 1970
John Hicks, 1973

LOMBARDI AWARD WINNERS .... Jim Stillwagon, 1970
John Hicks, 1973

WOODY'S ASSISTANT COACHES

Listed below are the individuals who served as assistant football coaches at Ohio State during the head-coaching tenure of Woody Hayes.

David Adolph	1977-78	Lou Holtz	1968
Bill Arnsparger	1951-53	Rudy Hubbard	1968-73
Earle Bruce	1966-72	Mickey Jackson	1974-78
Joe Bugel	1974	Gordon Larson	1959-60
Larry Catuzzi	1965-77	Bill Mallory	1966-68
George Champ	1968-78	Glen Mason	1978
Lyal Clark	1954-65	David McClain	1969-70
Charles Clausen	1971-75	Lou McCullough	1963-70
Glenn Ellison	1963-68	John Mummey	1969-76
Frank Ellwood	1958, 62-64	Bill Myles	1977-78
Gene Fekete	1951-58	Bill O'Hara	1952-53
Edward Ferkany	1972-73	Doyt Perry	1951-54
Alan Fiers	1961	Clive Rush	1955-57, 59
Alex Gibbs	1975-78	Esco Sarkkinen	1951-77
Ernie Godfrey	1951-61	Glenn Schembechler	1958-62
Bill Gunlock	1961-62	Gene Slaughter	1960
James Herbstreit	1961-62	Ralph Staub	1970-76
William Hess	1951-57	Harry Strobel	1951-67
Jim Hietikko	1954	Gary Tranquill	1977-78
George Hill	1971-78	Max Urick	1963-65
Hugh Hindman	1963-69	Richard Walker	1969-76

ALL-AMERICA

Listed below are the players who were all-America at Ohio State during the head-coaching tenure of Woody Hayes.

YEAR	PLAYER	POSITION	YEAR	PLAYER	POSITION
1952	Mike Takacs	Guard	1970	Jack Tatum	Defensive Back
1954	Dean Dugger	End		Mike Sensibaugh	Defensive Back
	Howard Cassady	Running Back		Tim Anderson	Defensive Back
1955	Jim Parker	Guard	1971	Tom Deleone	Center
	Howard Cassady	Running Back	1972	John Hicks	Tackle
1956	Jim Parker	Guard		Randy Gradishar	Linebacker
1957	Aurelius Thomas	Guard	1973	Van DeCree	End
1958	Jim Houston	End		John Hicks	Tackle
	James Marshall	Tackle		Randy Gradishar	Linebacker
	Robert White	Running Back		Archie Griffin	Running Back
1959	Jim Houston	End	1974	Van DeCree	End
1960	Robert Ferguson	Running Back		Kurt Schumacher	Tackle
1961	Robert Ferguson	Running Back		Pete Cusick	Tackle
1964	James Davidson	Tackle		Steve Meyers	Center
	Dwight Kelley	Linebacker		Archie Griffin	Running Back
	Arnold Chonko	Defensive Back		Neal Colzie	Running Back
1965	Douglas Van Horn	Tackle		Tom Skladany	Punter
	Dwight Kelley	Linebacker	1975	Ted Smith	Guard
1966	Ray Pryor	Center		Archie Griffin	Running Back
1968	David Foley	Tackle		Tim Fox	Defensive Back
	Rufus Mayes	Tackle		Tom Skladany	Punter
1969	James Stillwagon	Guard	1976	Bob Brudzinski	End
	Rex Kern	Quarterback		Chris Ward	Tackle
	Jim Otis	Running Back		Tom Skladany	Punter
	Ted Provost	Defensive Back	1977	Chris Ward	Tackle
	Jack Tatum	Defensive Back		Aaron Brown	Guard
1970	Jan White	End		Tom Cousineau	Linebacker
	James Stillwagon	Guard		Ray Griffin	Defensive Back
	John Brockington	Running Back	1978	Tom Cousineau	Linebacker

THE WOODY HAYES RECORD
AT OHIO STATE UNIVERSITY

1951

(4-3-2)

Captain: Robert Heid

Sept. 29	W	S.M.U.	7-0	H	80,735
Oct. 6	L	Michigan State	20-24	H	82,640
Oct. 13	T	Wisconsin	6-6	A	51,000
Oct. 20	L	Indiana	10-32	H	74,265
Oct. 27	W	Iowa	47-21	H	67,551
Nov. 3	W	Northwestern	3-0	H	71,089
Nov. 10	W	Pittsburgh	16-14	A	34,747
Nov. 17	T	Illinois	0-0	H	79,457
Nov. 24	L	Michigan	0-7	A	95,000

1952

(6-3-0)

Captain: Bernie Skvarka

Sept. 27	W	Indiana	33-13	H	70,208
Oct. 4	L	Purdue	14-21	H	75,417
Oct. 11	W	Wisconsin	23-14	H	80,345
Oct. 18	W	Washington State	35-7	H	71,280
Oct. 25	L	Iowa	0-8	A	44,659
Nov. 1	W	Northwestern	24-21	A	35,000
Nov. 8	L	Pittsburgh	14-21	H	75,120
Nov. 15	W	Illinois	27-7	A	60,077
Nov. 22	W	Michigan	27-7	H	81,541

1953

(6-3-0)

Captains: Robert Joslin, George Jacoby

Sept. 26	W	Indiana	36-12	H	75,898
Oct. 3	W	California	33-19	A	47,000
Oct. 10	L	Illinois	20-41	H	81,745
Oct. 17	W	Pennsylvania	12-6	A	42,207
Oct. 24	W	Wisconsin	20-19	A	52,819
Oct. 31	W	Northwestern	27-13	H	80,562
Nov. 7	L	Michigan State	13-28	H	82,220
Nov. 14	W	Purdue	21-6	H	77,465
Nov. 21	L	Michigan	0-20	A	90,126

1954

(10-0-0)

NATIONAL CHAMPIONS
BIG TEN CHAMPIONS

Captains: Richard Brubaker, John Borton

Sept. 25	W	Indiana	28-0	H	72,703
Oct. 2	W	California	21-13	H	79,524
Oct. 9	W	Illinois	40-7	A	69,567
Oct. 16	W	Iowa	20-14	H	82,141
Oct. 23	W	Wisconsin	31-14	H	82,636
Oct. 30	W	Northwestern	14-7	A	41,650
Nov. 6	W	Pittsburgh	26-0	H	80,898
Nov. 13	W	Purdue	28-6	A	51,000
Nov. 20	W	Michigan	21-7	H	82,438

ROSE BOWL

Jan. 1	W	U.S.C.	20-7	N	89,191

N — at Pasadena, Calif.

1955

(7-2-0)

BIG TEN CHAMPIONS

Captains: Frank Machinsky, Ken Vargo

Sept. 24	W	Nebraska	28-20	H	80,171
Oct. 1	L	Stanford	0-6	A	28,000
Oct. 8	W	Illinois	27-12	H	82,407
Oct. 15	L	Duke	14-20	H	82,254
Oct. 22	W	Wisconsin	26-16	A	53,529
Oct. 29	W	Northwestern	49-0	H	82,214
Nov. 5	W	Indiana	20-13	H	80,730
Nov. 12	W	Iowa	20-10	H	82,701
Nov. 19	W	Michigan	17-0	A	97,369

1956

(6-3-0)

Captains: Franklin Ellwood, William Michael

Sept. 29	W	Nebraska	34-7	H	82,153
Oct. 6	W	Stanford	32-20	H	82,881
Oct. 13	W	Illinois	26-6	A	58,247
Oct. 20	L	Penn State	6-7	H	82,584
Oct. 27	W	Wisconsin	21-0	H	82,661
Nov. 3	W	Northwestern	6-2	A	41,000
Nov. 10	W	Indiana	35-14	H	82,073
Nov. 17	L	Iowa	0-6	A	57,732
Nov. 24	L	Michigan	0-19	H	82,223

1957

(9-1-0)

NATIONAL CHAMPIONS
BIG TEN CHAMPIONS

Captains: Galen Cisco, Leo Brown

Sept. 28	L	T.C.U.	14-18	H	81,784
Oct. 5	W	Washington	35-7	A	37,000
Oct. 12	W	Illinois	21-7	H	82,239
Oct. 19	W	Indiana	56-0	H	78,348
Oct. 26	W	Wisconsin	16-13	A	50,051
Nov. 2	W	Northwestern	47-6	H	79,635
Nov. 9	W	Purdue	20-7	H	79,177
Nov. 16	W	Iowa	17-13	H	82,935
Nov. 23	W	Michigan	20-14	A	101,001

ROSE BOWL

Jan. 1	W	Oregon	10-7	N	100,000

N — at Pasadena, Calif.

1958

(6-1-2)

Captains: Francis Kremblas, Richard Schafrath

Sept. 27	W	S.M.U.	23-20	H	83,113
Oct. 4	W	Washington	12-7	H	82,901
Oct. 11	W	Illinois	19-13	A	50,416
Oct. 18	W	Indiana	49-8	H	82,964
Oct. 25	T	Wisconsin	7-7	H	83,412
Nov. 1	L	Northwestern	0-21	A	51,102
Nov. 8	T	Purdue	14-14	H	83,481
Nov. 15	W	Iowa	38-28	A	58,643
Nov. 22	W	Michigan	20-14	H	83,248

1959

(3-5-1)

Captain: Jim Houston

Sept. 26	W	Duke	14-13	H	82,834
Oct. 2	L	U.S.C.	0-17	A	49,592
Oct. 10	L	Illinois	0-9	H	82,980
Oct. 17	W	Purdue	15-0	H	83,391
Oct. 24	L	Wisconsin	3-12	A	55,440
Oct. 31	W	Michigan State	30-24	H	82,130
Nov. 7	T	Indiana	0-0	H	82,075
Nov. 14	L	Iowa	7-16	H	82,146
Nov. 21	L	Michigan	14-23	A	90,093

1960

(7-2-0)

Captains: James Tyrer, James Herbstreit

Sept. 24	W	S.M.U.	24-0	H	82,496
Oct. 1	W	U.S.C.	20-0	H	83,204
Oct. 8	W	Illinois	34-7	A	71,119
Oct. 15	L	Purdue	21-24	A	46,284
Oct. 22	W	Wisconsin	34-7	H	83,246
Nov. 29	W	Michigan State	21-10	A	76,520
Nov. 5	W	Indiana	36-7	H	81,530
Nov. 12	L	Iowa	12-35	A	57,900
Nov. 19	W	Michigan	7-0	H	83,107

1961

(8-0-1)

BIG TEN CHAMPIONS

Captains: Thomas Purdue, Michael Ingram

Sept. 30	T	T.C.U.	7-7	H	82,878
Oct. 7	W	U.C.L.A.	13-3	H	82,992
Oct. 14	W	Illinois	44-0	H	82,974
Oct. 21	W	Northwestern	10-0	A	43,259
Oct. 28	W	Wisconsin	30-21	A	58,411
Nov. 4	W	Iowa	29-13	H	83,795
Nov. 11	W	Indiana	16-7	A	27,108
Nov. 18	W	Oregon	22-12	H	82,073
Nov. 25	W	Michigan	50-20	A	80,444

1962

(6-3-0)

Captains: Gary Moeller, Robert Vogel

Sept. 29	W	North Carolina	41-7	H	84,009
Oct. 6	L	U.C.L.A.	7-9	A	48,513
Oct. 13	W	Illinois	15-15	A	56,017
Oct. 20	L	Northwestern	14-18	H	84,376
Oct. 27	W	Wisconsin	14-7	H	82,540
Nov. 3	L	Iowa	14-28	A	58,400
Nov. 10	W	Indiana	10-7	H	75,378
Nov. 17	W	Oregon	26-7	H	72,828
Nov. 24	W	Michigan	28-0	H	82,349

1963

(5-3-1)

Captains: Ormonde Ricketts, Matt Snell

Sept. 28	W	Texas A&M	17-0	H	81,241
Oct. 5	W	Indiana	21-0	A	42,296
Oct. 12	T	Illinois	20-20	H	84,712
Oct. 19	L	U.S.C.	3-32	A	61,883
Oct. 26	W	Wisconsin	13-10	A	65,319
Nov. 2	W	Iowa	7-3	H	83,163
Nov. 9	L	Penn State	7-10	H	83,519
Nov. 16	L	Northwestern	8-17	H	83,988
Nov. 23	W	Michigan	14-10	A	36,424

1964

(7-2-0)

Captains: James Davidson, Warren Spahr, Thomas Kiehfuss

Sept. 26	W	S.M.U.	27-8	H	80,737
Oct. 3	W	Indiana	17-9	H	81,834
Oct. 10	W	Illinois	26-0	A	71,227
Oct. 17	W	U.S.C.	17-0	H	84,315
Oct. 24	W	Wisconsin	28-3	H	84,365
Oct. 31	W	Iowa	21-19	A	58,700
Nov. 7	L	Penn State	0-27	H	84,279
Nov. 14	W	Northwestern	10-0	H	83,525
Nov. 21	L	Michigan	0-10	H	84,685

1965

(7-2-0)

Captains: Dwight Kelley, Greg Lashutka

Sept. 25	L	North Carolina	3-14	H	80,182
Oct. 2	W	Washington	23-21	A	52,500
Oct. 9	W	Illinois	28-14	H	83,712
Oct. 16	L	Michigan State	7-32	A	75,288
Oct. 23	W	Wisconsin	20-10	A	65,269
Oct. 30	W	Minnesota	11-10	H	84,359
Nov. 6	W	Indiana	17-10	H	83,863
Nov. 13	W	Iowa	38-0	H	84,116
Nov. 20	W	Michigan	9-7	A	77,733

1966

(4-5-0)

Captains: John Fill, Mike Current, Ray Pryor

Sept. 24	W	T.C.U.	14-7	H	75,374
Oct. 1	L	Washington	22-38	H	80,241
Oct. 8	L	Illinois	9-10	A	51,069
Oct. 15	L	Michigan State	8-11	H	84,282
Oct. 22	W	Wisconsin	24-13	H	84,265
Oct. 29	L	Minnesota	7-17	A	49,489
Nov. 5	W	Indiana	7-0	H	80,834
Nov. 12	W	Iowa	14-10	A	44,677
Nov. 19	L	Michigan	3-17	H	83,403

1967

(6-3-0)

Captains: Billy Ray Anders, Samuel Elliott

Sept. 30	L	Arizona	7-14	H	77,468
Oct. 7	W	Oregon	30-0	A	25,000
Oct. 14	L	Purdue	6-41	H	84,069
Oct. 21	W	Northwestern	6-2	A	42,812
Oct. 28	L	Illinois	13-17	H	83,928
Nov. 4	W	Michigan State	21-17	A	76,235
Nov. 11	W	Wisconsin	17-15	H	65,470
Nov. 18	W	Iowa	21-10	H	72,567
Nov. 25	W	Michigan	24-14	A	64,144

1968

(10-0-0)

NATIONAL CHAMPIONS
BIG TEN CHAMPIONS

Captains: David Foley, Dirk Worden

Sept. 28	W	S.M.U.	35-14	H	73,855
Oct. 5	W	Oregon	21-6	H	70,191
Oct. 12	W	Purdue	13-0	H	84,834
Oct. 19	W	Northwestern	45-21	H	83,454
Oct. 26	W	Illinois	31-24	A	56,174
Nov. 2	W	Michigan State	25-20	H	84,859
Nov. 9	W	Wisconsin	43-8	A	40,972
Nov. 16	W	Iowa	33-27	A	44,131
Nov. 23	W	Michigan	50-14	H	85,371

ROSE BOWL

Jan. 1	W	U.S.C.	27-16	N	102,042

N — at Pasadena, Calif.

1969

(8-1-0)

BIG TEN CHAMPIONS

Captains: David Whitfield, Alan Jack

Sept. 27	W	T.C.U.	62-0	H	86,412
Oct. 4	W	Washington	44-14	A	58,800
Oct. 11	W	Michigan State	54-21	H	86,641
Oct. 18	W	Minnesota	34-7	A	53,016
Oct. 25	W	Illinois	41-0	H	86,576
Nov. 1	W	Northwestern	35-6	A	41,279
Nov. 8	W	Wisconsin	62-7	H	86,519
Nov. 15	W	Purdue	42-14	H	85,027
Nov. 22	L	Michigan	12-24	A	103,588

1970

(9-1-0)

BIG TEN CHAMPIONS

Captains: Rex Kern, Jan White, James Stillwagon, Douglas Adams

Sept. 26	W	Texas A&M	56-13	H	85,657
Oct. 3	W	Duke	34-10	H	86,123
Oct. 10	W	Michigan State	29-0	A	75,511
Oct. 17	W	Minnesota	28-8	H	86,667
Oct. 24	W	Illinois	48-29	A	46,208
Oct. 31	W	Northwestern	24-10	H	86,673
Nov. 7	W	Wisconsin	24-7	A	72,758
Nov. 14	W	Purdue	10-7	A	68,157
Nov. 21	W	Michigan	20-9	H	87,331

ROSE BOWL

Jan. 1	L	Stanford	17-27	N	103,839

N — at Pasadena, Calif.

1971

(6-4-0)

Captains: Harry Howard, Tom DeLeone

Sept. 11	W	Iowa	52-21	H	75,596
Sept. 25	L	Colorado	14-20	H	85,586
Oct. 2	W	California	35-3	H	86,280
Oct. 9	W	Illinois	24-10	A	53,555
Oct. 16	W	Indiana	27-7	A	50,812
Oct. 23	W	Wisconsin	31-6	H	86,559
Oct. 30	W	Minnesota	14-12	A	36,281
Nov. 6	L	Michigan State	10-17	H	86,616
Nov. 13	L	Northwestern	10-14	H	86,062
Nov. 20	L	Michigan	7-10	A	104,116

1972

(9-2-0)

BIG TEN CO-CHAMPIONS

Captains: Richard Galbos, George Hasenohrl

Sept. 16	W	Iowa	21-0	H	77,089
Sept. 30	W	North Carolina	29-14	H	86,180
Oct. 7	W	California	35-18	A	45,000
Oct. 14	W	Illinois	26-7	H	86,298
Oct. 21	W	Indiana	44-7	H	86,365
Oct. 28	W	Wisconsin	28-20	A	78,713
Nov. 4	W	Minnesota	27-19	H	86,439
Nov. 11	L	Michigan State	12-19	A	76,264
Nov. 18	W	Northwestern	27-14	A	34,475
Nov. 25	W	Michigan	14-11	H	87,040

ROSE BOWL

Jan. 1	L	U.S.C.	17-42	N	106,869

N — at Pasadena, Calif.

1973

(10-0-1)

BIG TEN CO-CHAMPIONS

Captains: Greg Hare, Richard Middleton

Sept. 15	W	Minnesota	56-7	H	86,005
Sept. 29	W	T.C.U.	37-3	H	87,439
Oct. 6	W	Washington State	27-3	H	87,425
Oct. 13	W	Wisconsin	24-0	A	77,413
Oct. 20	W	Indiana	37-7	A	53,183
Oct. 27	W	Northwestern	60-0	H	87,453
Nov. 3	W	Illinois	30-0	A	60,707
Nov. 10	W	Michigan State	35-0	H	87,600
Nov. 17	W	Iowa	55-13	H	87,447
Nov. 24	T	Michigan	10-10	A	105,223

ROSE BOWL

Jan. 1	W	U.S.C.	42-21	N	105,267

N — at Pasadena, Calif.

1974

(10-2-0)

BIG TEN CO-CHAMPIONS

Captains: Steve Myers, Archie Griffin, Arnold Jones,
Neal Cozie, Pete Cusick

Sept. 14	W	Minnesota	34-19	A	45,511
Sept. 21	W	Oregon State	51-10	H	86,383
Sept. 28	W	S.M.U.	28-9	H	87,487
Oct. 5	W	Washington State	42-7	A	50,000
Oct. 12	W	Wisconsin	52-7	H	87,717
Oct. 19	W	Indiana	49-9	H	87,617
Oct. 26	W	Northwestern	55-7	A	42,337
Nov. 2	W	Illinois	49-7	H	87,813
Nov. 9	L	Michigan State	13-16	A	78,533
Nov. 16	W	Iowa	35-10	A	48,700
Nov. 23	W	Michigan	12-10	H	88,243

ROSE BOWL

Jan. 1	L	U.S.C.	17-18	N	106,721

N — at Pasadena, Calif.

1975

(11-1-0)

BIG TEN CHAMPIONS

Captains: Archie Griffin, Brian Baschnagel, Tim Fox, Ken Kuhn

Sept. 13	W	Michigan State	21-0	A	80,383
Sept. 20	W	Penn State	17-9	H	88,093
Sept. 27	W	North Carolina	32-7	H	87,750
Oct. 4	W	U.C.L.A.	41-20	A	55,248
Oct. 11	W	Iowa	49-0	H	87,826
Oct. 18	W	Wisconsin	56-0	H	87,820
Oct. 25	W	Purdue	35-6	A	69,405
Nov. 1	W	Indiana	24-14	H	87,835
Nov. 8	W	Illinois	40-3	A	67,571
Nov. 15	W	Minnesota	38-6	H	87,817
Nov. 22	W	Michigan	21-14	A	105,543

ROSE BOWL

Jan. 1	L	U.C.L.A.	10-23	N	105,464

N — at Pasadena, Calif.

1976

(9-2-1)

Captains: Bill Lukens, Ed Thompson, Tom Skladany

Sept. 11	W	Michigan State	49-21	H	86,509
Sept. 18	W	Penn State	12-7	A	62,503
Sept. 25	L	Missouri	21-22	H	87,936
Oct. 2	T	U.C.L.A.	10-10	H	87,969
Oct. 9	W	Iowa	34-14	A	59,170
Oct. 16	W	Wisconsin	30-20	A	79,579
Oct. 23	W	Purdue	24-3	H	87,898
Oct. 30	W	Indiana	47-7	A	39,663
Nov. 6	W	Illinois	42-10	H	87,654
Nov. 13	W	Minnesota	9-3	A	53,190
Nov. 20	L	Michigan	0-22	H	88,250

ORANGE BOWL

Jan. 1	W	Colorado	27-10	N	65,537

N — at Miami, Fla.

1977

(9-3-0)

Captains: Chris Ward, Jeff Logan, Aaron Brown, Ray Griffin

Sept. 10	W	Miami (Fla.)	10-0	H	86,287
Sept. 17	W	Minnesota	38-7	H	87,779
Sept. 24	L	Oklahoma	28-29	H	88,119
Oct. 1	W	S.M.U.	35-7	A	51,970
Oct. 8	W	Purdue	46-0	H	87,707
Oct. 15	W	Iowa	27-6	A	60,070
Oct. 22	W	Northwestern	35-15	A	29,563
Oct. 29	W	Wisconsin	42-0	H	87,837
Nov. 5	W	Illinois	35-0	A	66,973
Nov. 12	W	Indiana	35-7	H	87,786
Nov. 19	L	Michigan	6-14	A	106,024

SUGAR BOWL

Jan. 2	L	Alabama	6-35	N	76,811

N — at New Orleans, La.

1978

(7-4-1)

Captains: Ron Springs, Tim Vogler Tom Cousineau, Bryon Cato

Sept. 16	L	Penn State	0-19	H	88,202
Sept. 23	W	Minnesota	27-10	A	55,200
Sept. 30	W	Baylor	34-28	H	87,998
Oct. 7	T	S.M.U.	35-35	H	87,721
Oct. 14	L	Purdue	16-27	A	69,465
Oct. 21	W	Iowa	31-7	H	87,586
Oct. 28	W	Northwestern	63-20	H	87,296
Nov. 4	W	Wisconsin	49-14	A	79,940
Nov. 11	W	Illinois	45-7	H	87,719
Nov. 18	W	Indiana	21-18	A	47,540
Nov. 25	L	Michigan	3-14	H	88,358

GATOR BOWL

Dec. 29	L	Clemson	15-17	N	72,011

N — at Jacksonville, Fla.

HAYES' MONOGRAM WINNERS

Listed below are the names of the Ohio State University monogram winners during the Woody Hayes era.

A

Douglas O. Adams	1968-70
Nelson W. Adderly	1965
David Adkins	1974-77
Casimir Adulewicz	1959
Joe Allegro	1975-77
George Amlin	1966
Billy Anders	1965-77
Kim Anderson	1964-66
Richard L. Anderson	1964-65
Richard Anderson	1952
Tom Anderson	1964
William Anderson	1968-70
Lawrence Andrews	1951
Ernest Andria	1975, 77-78
Theodore Andrick	1964-65
Richard Applegate	1974-75
Richard Arledge	1951
Billy Armstrong	1960-62
Ralph Armstrong	1951
Birtho Arnold	1957-59
Daniel Aston	1969
Robert Atha	1978
John Auer	1953
Jack Augenstein	1953
Ronald Ayers	1974-76

B

James Baas	1965-66
Terry Bach	1977-78
Tom Backhus	1967-69
Ralph Bailey	1958
Thomas Baldacci	1955-57
Paul Ballmer	1958

Douglas Bargerstock	1974
Orlando Barnett	1963-65
Thomas Barrington	1963-65
Thomas Bartley	1967-68
Mike Bartoszek	1972-74
Ronald Barwig	1977-78
Brian Baschnagel	1972-75
Thomas Battista	1971
Thomas Baxa	1972
William Beam	1959
Eddie Beamon	1974-77
Earl Bechtel	1952
Charles Beecroft	1971-72
Marts Beekley	1951-52
Raymond Beerman	1957
Earl Belgrave	1972
Farley Bell	1975-76
Todd Bell	1977-78
Cliff Belmer	1978
Edward Bender	1968
Michael Benis	1960
Wayne Betz	1961-62
John Bledsoe	1971-72
Thomas Blinco	1976-77
Hubert Bobo	1954
David Bodenbender	1964
Jaren Bombach	1967
Robert Bond	1952-55
Charles Bonica	1970-72
William Booth	1953-55
John Borton	1951-54
Russell Bowermaster	1956-58
Brian Bowers	1973-74
Gerald Bowsher	1959
Morris Bradshaw	1971-73
Edward Breehl	1957

John Brockington	1968-70	Ronald Cook	1955-57
Aaron Brown	1974-77	James Cope	1972-74
Jeff Brown	1972	Tom Cousineau	1975-78
Leo Brown	1955-57	Garth Cox	1974, 76-77
Timothy Brown	1978	Randy Cowman	1972
Carl Brubaker	1953-54	Steven Crapser	1969
Robert Brudzinski	1973-76	Albert Crawford	1956-58
Fred Bruney	1951-52	Thomas Crawford	1957
Robert Bruney	1962-63	John Cummings	1972
David Brungard	1967-68	William Cummings	1956
Charles Bryant	1959-61	Charles Cunningham	1971
Thomas Bugel	1963-65	Anthony Curcillo	1951-52
Nicholas Buonamici	1973-76	Michael Current	1965-66
Asbury Burgin	1965-66	Patrick Curto	1973-75
Timothy Burke	1978	Martin Cusick	1977
Scott Burris	1978	Peter Cusick	1972-74
Norman Burrows	1978	Dan Cutillo	1971-73
Roger Burrows	1970		
Arthur F. Burton	1967-69	**D**	
Robert Butts	1960-62		
		Michael Dale	1970
C		Scott Dannelley	1972-75
		Kelton Dansler	1975-78
Gary Cairns	1966-67	Michael Datish	1975
Thomas Campana	1969-71	James Davidson	1963-64
Paul Campbell	1976-78	Jeff Davis	1971-73
Joseph Cannavino	1955-57	Jerome Davis	1973-74
Richard Cappell	1969-71	Donald Dawdy	1953
Craig Cassady	1973-75	Mark Debevc	1968-70
Howard (Hop) Cassady	1952-55	Van DeCree	1972-74
Gregory Castignola	1977-78	Thomas DeLeone	1969-71
Byron Cato	1975-78	Irv Denker	1952
David Cheney	1968-70	Roger Detrick	1959-60
Arnie Chonko	1962-64	Thomas Dillman	1954-56
Galen Cisco	1955-57	Daniel Dillon	1966
Donald Clark	1956-58	Larry Disher	1957
Dennis Clotz	1961	Joe Dixon	1975-77
James Coburn	1970	Ken Dixon	1970-71
Terrence Cochran	1965	John Doll	1972
Robert Cole	1956	Douglas Donley	1977-78
William Collmar	1954-55	Brian Donovan	1968-70
Neal Colzie	1972-74	Richard Doyle	1951-52
William Conley	1970-71	Stephan Dreffer	1962-64
Daniel Connor	1961	Douglas Drenik	1962-64
James Conroy	1969	Dean Dugger	1952-54
Blair Conway	1972-73	Gary Dulin	1976-78

Donald Dwyer   1965-67

G

E

Mike Gaffney	1972
Ralph Gage	1958

William Eachus	1965-66
Elbert Ebinger	1955
Gerald Ehrsam	1966-68
Bruce Elia	1972-74
Samuel Elliott	1965-77
Ray Ellis	1977-78
Franklin Ellwood	1955-56
Robert Endres	1951
John Epitropoulos	1978
Terry Ervin	1966-67
Bennie Espy	1962-63
Billy Ezzo	1972-74

Richard Galbos	1971-72
Richard Gales	1971-72
Sherwin Gandee	1951
Jim Gentile	1968-70
Rod Gerald	1975-78
William German	1959-60
Jack Gibbs	1954
Lonnie Gillian	1967-69
Dan Givens	1971
Douglas Goodsell	1951-52
Les Gordon	1975
Randy Gradishar	1971-73
Lawrence Graf	1973
Cornelius Greene	1973-75
Horatius Greene	1969
Archie Griffin	1972-75
Duncan Griffin	1975-78
Ray Griffin	1974-77
Robert Grimes	1950-52
Michael Guess	1976-78
George Guthrie	1951-52
Richard Guy	1954-56
Frank Guzik	1953

F

Richard. Facchine	1955
Robert Fair	1963
John Farrell	1960
Tom Federle	1963-64
Paul Fender	1967
Keith Ferguson	1978
Robert Ferguson	1959-61
Richard Ferko	1970-71
Jeffrey Ferrelli	1975-76
Dwight Fertig	1967
Jerry Fields	1958-59
Alan Fiers	1959-60
John Fill	1964-66
Louis Fischer	1950-51
Thomas Fitz	1964
Kevin Fletcher	1970-72
David Foley	1966-68
Arnold Fontes	1965-66
Leonard Fontes	1958-59
Harrison Fortney	1963
Rodney Foster	1961-62
Tim Fox	1972-75
Doug France	1972-74
David Francis	1960-62
Kenneth Fritz	1976-78
Dan Fronk	1957-58
Robert Funk	1964-65

H

William Hackett	1967-69
Archie Haer	1967
Thomas Hague	1952-53
Ray Hamilton	1951
Stanley Hamlin	1965
Terence Hansley	1959
von Allen Hardman	1961
Gregory Hare	1971-73
Donald Harkins	1962-64
Jerry Harkrader	1953-55
Timothy Harman	1970
James Harrell	1975-77
Jimmie Harris	1969-71
Tyrone Harris	1974-75, 77
Randall Hart	1967-69
Gabriel Hartman	1958-60

George Hasenohrl	1970-72	Vlade Janakievski	1977-78
Oscar Hauer	1958-60	Bruce Jankowski	1968-70
Richard Haupt	1961	Victor Janowicz	1951
Leophus Hayden	1968-70	Joseph Jenkins	1967
David Hazel	1972-74	Thomas Jenkins	1961-63
Robert Heid	1951	Charles Jentes	1960
Harold Henson	1972-74	James Jesty	1970
Luther Henson	1977-78	William Jobko	1954-56
James Herbstreit	1958-60	Kenneth Johnson	1960-61
Harvey Herrmann	1959	Ricky Johnson	1977-78
William Hess	1960-62	Pete Johnson	1973-76
John Hicks	1970, 72-73	Robert Johnson	1965-66
Tyrone Hicks	1978	Ben Jones	1960
James Hietikko	1951	Arnold Jones	1972-74
Richard Hilinski	1953-54	Herbert Jones	1956-57
Richard Himes	1965-67	Herman Jones	1975-77
John Hlay	1951	Robert Joslin	1951-53
Ralph Holloway	1968-70		
Tim Holycross	1972-74	**K**	
Joe Hornik	1975-78		
Ronald Houk	1959-60	Lawrence Kain	1973-75
James Houston, Sr.	1957-59	Gerald Kasunic	1963-64
James Houston, Jr.	1978	David Katterhenrich	1960-62
Harry Howard	1969-71	Ronald Kaylor	1964
Carroll Howell	1952-54	Mike Keeton	1973
Rudy Hubbard	1965-67	Randal Keith	1971-72
Paul Hudson	1964-66	Dwight Kelley	1963-65
Paul Huff	1967-68	John Kelley	1966-67
John Hughes	1970, 72-73	Robert Kelly	1971
Charles Hunter	1977-78	Carl Kern	1972-73
John Hutchings	1978	Rex Kern	1968-70
Charles Hutchison	1967-69	Thomas Kiehfuss	1962-64
Bob Hyatt	1974-76	David Kilgore	1958-59
		Gerald King	1970
I		Marvin Kinsey	1971
		Roy Kirk	1963
Robert Ingram	1959-61	Tom Klaban	1974-75
Kenneth Ireland	1962	Robert Klein	1960-62
		Walter Klevay	1951
J		Vic Koegel	1971-73
		Robert Koepnick	1951-52
Alan Jack	1967-69	William Kohut	1964
Matthew Jackson	1976	James Kregel	1971-73
William Jaco	1976-77	Francis Kremblas	1956-58
George Jacoby	1951-53	Gerald Glenn Krisher	1951-54
Daniel James	1956-58	Frederick Kriss	1954-56

Raymond Krstolic	1961-62	John Manyak	1952
Kenneth Kuhn	1972-75	Thomas Marendt	1971-72
Richard Kuhn	1968-70	James Marsh	1970
Karl Kumler	1962	James Marshall	1957-58
Theordore Kurz	1968-69	Harold P. Martin	1952
		John Martin	1955-57
L		Paul Martin	1959
		Glen Mason	1970
Gary Lago	1970-72	Almond Mathis	1971-73
Howard Lambert	1961	Thomas Matte	1958-60
Donald Lamka	1969-71	James Matz	1958-60
Mark Lang	1974-77	John Maxwell	1962
Greg Lashutka	1963-65	Rufus Mayes	1966-68
Richard Laskoski	1961	John McCoy	1964-66
James Laughlin	1977-79	Timothy McGuire	1966
Charles LeBeau	1956-58	David McKee	1977
Ben Lee	1978	Laird McNeal	1967
William Leggett	1952-54	John Meade	1978
Donald Lewis	1955	Anthony Megaro	1977-78
James Lindner	1959-60	James Merrell	1951
William Lindsey	1964	Paul Michael	1954-56
Elmer Lippert	1971-73	Richard Michael	1958-59
Robert Lister	1961	Richard Middleton	1971-73
Brian Livingston	1965	Robert Middleton	1960-62
Jeff Logan	1974-77	Max Midlam	1974-76
Richard Logan	1951	Charles Miller	1953
David Long	1971	Gary Miller	1964-66
William Long	1966-68	Leonard Mills	1975-78
Robert Longer	1964	Chester Mirick	1961-63
John Lord	1958	Benjamin Mobley	1964
Raymond Luckay	1951	Gary Moeller	1960-62
Paul Ludwig	1952-54	Larry Molls	1976
Steven Luke	1972-74	Jimmy Moore	1975-78
William Lukens	1974-76	Tommy Joe Morgan	1956-57
Ken Luttner	1969-71	Steven Morrison	1972-74
Robert Lykes	1965	William Mott	1953
James Lyons	1963	Gregory Mountz	1971
		Bruce Moyer	1967
M		William Mrukowski	1960-62
		John Muhlback	1966-68
Frank Machinsky	1953-55	John Mummey	1960-62
Ronald Maciejowski	1968-70	Robert Murphy	1978
Richard W. Mack	1972-74	Calvin Murray	1977-78
Douglas Mackie	1976-77	Robert Myers	1952
Charles Mamula	1962-63	Steven Myers	1972-74
Richard Mangiamelle	1962		

N

Alex Nagy	1957
James Nein	1964, 66-67
William Nielson	1967-69
Dale Niez	1960
Thomas Nixon	1970-72
Richard Nosky	1953

O

James Oates	1965
Andrew Okulovich	1957
James Oppermann	1968-70
Edward Orazen	1962-64
Thomas Orosz	1977-78
Larry O'Rourke	1974
James Otis	1967-69

P

James Pacenta	1975-76
Fred Pagac	1971-73
William Painter	1968
John Palmer	1964-66
Albert Parker	1962
James Parker	1954-56
Richard Parsons	1972-74
Joel Payton	1977-78
Thomas Perdue	1959-61
Martin Peterson	1951
William Peterson	1952
Dale Pflaumer	1956
Louis Pietrini	1974-76
Fred Pisanelli	1971
Anthony Pitstick	1971
Doug Plank	1972-74
Don Polaski	1967-69
Harry Pollitt	1968-69
Daniel Porretta	1962-64
Douglas Porter	1974-77
Thomas Portsmouth	1965-67
Theodore Powell	1972-73
Russell Provenza	1957
Ted Provost	1967-69
Ray Von Pryor	1964-66
David Purdy	1972-74

R

Michael Radtke	1967-69
Thomas Rath	1951
Wayne Reese	1961
James Reichenbach	1951-54
Robert Rein	1964-66
Rocco Rich	1971-73
David Richards	1955
Richard Richley	1965
Ormonde Ricketts	1961-63
William Ridder	1963-65
Raymond Riticher	1952
Woodrow Roach	1973-75
Jack Roberts	1961
Robert Roberts	1952-53
Philip Robinson	1956-57
Joseph Robinson	1975-78
Tom Roche	1974-77
James Roman	1966-68
Nicholas Roman	1966-69
Thor Ronemus	1951
James Roseboro	1954-56
Paul Ross	1976-78
Richard Ross	1960
George Rosso	1951-53
Gary Roush	1968
James Rowland	1959
James Ruehl	1952
Bruce Ruhl	1973-76
Kevin Rusnak	1967-69
William Rutherford	1966
Stephen Ruzich	1951

S

Willard Sander	1963-65
Daryl Sanders	1960-62
Keith Saunders	1977
James Savoca	1974-76, 78
Tim Sawicki	1976
Michael Scannell	1971-72
Richard Schafrath	1956-58
Richard Schiller	1952
Art Schlichter	1978
Paul R. Schmidlin	1967-69

Michael Schneider	1977	Philip Strickland	1968-70
Fred Schram	1971	Terry Strong	1970
James Schumacher	1952-53	Mark Sullivan	1975-78
Kurt Schumacher	1972-74	Donald Sutherin	1955-57
Brian Schwartz	1976-78	Donald Swartz	1952-54
Gerald Schwartz	1952		
Dan Scott	1971-73	**T**	
Robert Scott	1962		
Rick Seifert	1970-72	Michael Takacs	1951-53
Kenneth Seilkop	1959	Jack Tatum	1968-70
Mike Sensibaugh	1968-70	Alvin Taylor	1978
Jan Shedd	1955	Willie Teague	1970-72
Richard Simon	1969-71	William Ternent	1952
Charles Simon	1974	Franklyn Theis	1955
Vincent Skillings	1977-78	Aurelius Thomas	1955-57
Thomas Skladany	1973-76	Richard Thomas	1951-52
Bernie Skvarka	1951	Will Thomas	1965-66
A. G. Smith	1951	Ed Thompson	1974-76
Bruce Smith	1970	Kenneth Thompson	1955
Carroll Smith	1951	Robert Thornton	1952-54
Huston Smith	1966-67	Samuel Tidmore	1960-61
Joseph Smith	1979-82	David Tingley	1959, 61
Larry Smith	1965	George Tolford	1959-61
Robert Smith	1967-69	Robert Trapuzzano	1969
Robert Smith	1968	Joseph Trivisonno	1955-57
Ted Smith	1973-75	Richard Troha	1969
John Smurda	1972-73	James Tyrer	1958-60
Matt Snell	1961-63		
John Sobolewski	1966-68	**U**	
Karl Sommer	1956		
William Spahr	1962-64	Edward Ulmer	1960-61
Joseph Sparma	1961-62	Donald Unverferth	1963-65
Thomas Spears	1953-55	William Urbanik	1967-69
Ron Springs	1976-78		
Ernest Spychalski	1956-58	**V**	
Bernie Stanley	1963		
Larry Stephens	1959-61	Douglas Van Horn	1963-65
Mark Stier	1966-68	Richard Van Raaphorst	1961-63
James Stillwagon	1968-70	Norman Vanscoy	1960
Robert Stock	1964	Kenneth Vargo	1953-55
Donald Stoeckel	1953-55	Thomas Vargo	1965
Greg Storer	1975-77	Thomas Varner	1960
Victor Stottlemyer	1966-68	Milan Vecanski	1970-71
John Stowe	1968	Donald Vicic	1954-56
Michael Strahine	1977	Robert Vogel	1960-62
Mark Straka	1973	Donald Vogelgesang	1960

Terry Vogler	1977-78
Tim Vogler	1975-78
Ricardo Volley	1977-78

W

Jack Wagner	1951
Richard Wakefield	1969-71
Robert Walden	1964-66
Jack Walker	1960
Stephen Walker	1971
Richard Walther	1951
Chris Ward	1974-77
Paul Warfield	1961-63
Duane Warner	1960
Alvin Washington	1977-78
James Wassmund	1956
Richard Wasson	1963
Jene Watkins	1959
Robert Watkins	1952-54
Otha Watson	1978
Charles Waugh	1970
Thomas Waugh	1976-78
David Weaver	1953-55
Edward Weaver	1970
Thurlow Weed	1952-54
William Wentz	1959-60
Timothy Wersel	1972
Robert Whetstone	1953-55
Jan White	1968-70
Loren White	1957-59
Stanley White	1969-71
David Whitfield	1967-69
Larry Wiggins	1972
Dwight Wilkins	1972
William Wilks	1951
Robert Willard	1973
David Williams	1953-54
Lee Williams	1955-58
Robert Williams	1968
Shad Williams	1970-72
Louis Willott	1974-75
Leonard Willis	1974-75
Julius Wittman	1951
Charles Wittmer	1959-61
Scott Wolery	1974

Dirk Worden	1966-68
Robert Wortman	1964
David Wright	1970
Ernest Wright	1958

Y

Nicholas Yonclas	1963-64
Donald Young	1958-60
Richard Young	1953-54

Z

Charles Zawacki	1955
Lawrence Zelina	1968-70
Randall Ziegler	1963
Albert Zima	1962

About the Editor

Mike Bynum is one of the South's most successful young authors. He is the author of ten previous books which are all based on football, including the highly successful *Bear Bryant's Boys of Autumn* and *Knute Rockne: His Life and Legend,* and served as consulting producer to the Mizlou TV special *Bear Bryant — Countdown to 315* which was aired on N.B.C.

Mr. Bynum is currently completing a series of biographies on football's greatest coaches.